Automation through Chef Opscode

A Hands-on Approach to Chef

Navin Sabharwal
Manak Wadhwa

Apress·

Publisher: Heinz Weinheimer
Lead Editor: Saswata Mishra
Technical Reviewers: Kalyan Kumar and Piyush Pandey
Editorial Board: Steve Anglin, Mark Beckner, Ewan Buckingham, Gary Cornell, Louise Corrigan,
    Jonathan Gennick, Jonathan Hassell, Robert Hutchinson, Michelle Lowman,
    James Markham, Matthew Moodie, Jeff Olson, Jeffrey Pepper, Saswata Mishra,
    Douglas Pundick, Ben Renow-Clarke, Dominic Shakeshaft, Gwenan Spearing, Matt Wade,
    Steve Weiss
Coordinating Editor: Mark Powers
Copy Editor: Lori Jacobs
Compositor: SPi Global
Indexer: SPi Global
Artist: SPi Global
Cover Designer: Anna Ishchenko

Distributed to the book trade worldwide by Springer Science+Business Media New York, 233 Spring Street, 6th Floor, New York, NY 10013. Phone 1-800-SPRINGER, fax (201) 348-4505, e-mail orders-ny@springer-sbm.com, or visit www.springeronline.com. Apress Media, LLC is a California LLC and the sole member (owner) is Springer Science + Business Media Finance Inc (SSBM Finance Inc). SSBM Finance Inc is a **Delaware** corporation.

For information on translations, please e-mail rights@apress.com, or visit www.apress.com.

Apress and friends of ED books may be purchased in bulk for academic, corporate, or promotional use. eBook versions and licenses are also available for most titles. For more information, reference our Special Bulk Sales–eBook Licensing web page at www.apress.com/bulk-sales.

Any source code or other supplementary material referenced by the author in this text is available to readers at www.apress.com/9781430262954. For detailed information about how to locate your book's source code, go to www.apress.com/source-code/.

Dedicated to the people I love and God whom I trust.
—Navin

Dedicated to all the people who have supported me in difficult times and have helped me grow into the individual who I am today, God, and the people I love.
—Manak

Contents at a Glance

Contents

About the Authors

Navin Sabharwal is an Innovator, Thought Leader, Author, and Consultant in the areas of cloud computing and lifecycle management, DevOps, automation, and configuration management tools such as chef, Puppet, BMC CLM, HP CDA, IBM Jazz, ITOps, runbook automation, and software product development.

Navin has been involved in the creation of IP Development & Service Delivery in the areas of cloud computing, AWS, Azure, data center automation, DevOps, and IT analytics.

Manak Wadhwa holds a master's degree in information technology from Indian Institute of Information Technology and has been working as DevOps engineer in HCL for the past two years. He has also worked with various data center automation tools such as chef, Puppet, and Ansible.

Manak has also been working on various public cloud platforms which include AWS and Azure.

About the Technical Reviewers

Kalyan Kumar is the Chief Technologist for HCL Technologies–ISD and leads all the Global Technology Practices.

In his current role Kalyan is responsible defining Architecture & Technology Strategy, New Solutions Development & Engineering across all Enterprise Infrastructure, Business Productivity, Unified Communication Collaboration & Enterprise Platform/DevOps Service Lines. Kalyan is also responsible for Business and Service Delivery for Cross Functional Services & SIAM for HCL across all service lines globally.

Kalyan is widely acknowledged as an expert and path-breaker on BSM/ITSM & IT Architecture and Cloud Platforms and has developed many IPs for the company in these domains. He is also credited with building HCL MTaaSTM Service from the scratch, which has a multi-million turnover today and a proprietary benchmark for Global IT Infrastructure Services Delivery. His team is also credited with developing the MyCloudSM platform for Cloud Service Management & MyDevOps, which is a pioneering breakthrough in the Utility Computing and Hybrid Agile Ops Model space. He has been presented with many internal and industry awards for his thought leadership in the IT Management space.

Kalyan also runs the HCL ISD IPDEV Incubator Group where he is responsible for incubating new services, platforms and IPs for the company. Additionally, he co-authored the Book Process Excellence for IT Operations: A practical guide to IT Service Management (http://tinyurl.com/k7u3wyf).

Kalyan has spoken at many prestigious industry platforms and is currently actively engaged in the Partner Advisory Board of CA Technologies, and IBM Cloud & Smarter Infrastructure BOA.

In his free time Kalyan likes to jam with his band Contraband as a drummer /percussionist and reviews Consumer Technology Gadgets and follows Cricket Games diligently. Kalyan lives in New Delhi, India with his family. He can be followed on Twitter @KKLIVE and at Linkedin (http://www.linkedin.com/in/kalyankumar).

Piyush Pandey is currently working as Track Lead at HCL Comnet, where he oversees the DevOps, Service Automation and Cloud Lifecycle Management Practice for HCL's UK office. He is responsible for designing automation solutions for enterprise IT infrastructure management. In the past four years, he has developed enterprise tools for the public cloud (AWS, Azure, Google Compute); Automation tools (BMC, HP CA, Microsoft, Puppet, Chef, and Cobbler); orchestration tools (BMC AO, Microsoft System Center Orchestrator, and VMWare orchestrator); and monitoring tools (Nagios, Zenoss, and SCOM).

He has worked to provide Automation Solutions for Fortune 500 clients such as AstraZeneca, News International, Cummins, Ingram Micro, SGX, GulfStream and Xerox. He holds a Bachelor's degree in computer engineering from NSIT Delhi.

Acknowledgments

Special thanks to Himanshu Tyagi, Bibin W, Piyush Pandey, and Rohit Sharma for all their help and support. Also, this book would not have been possible without Saswata Mishra, Mark Powers, and the rest of the team at Apress. It has been wonderful to work with the Apress team.

Thanks for the motivation and review by Kalyan Kumar, who has been instrumental in guiding us through the journey on automation.

Special thanks to Dheeraj Raghav and Rajendra Prasad who used their creativity to make the book images look beautiful.

Introduction

Automation through Opscode Chef provides an in-depth understanding of chef, which is written in Ruby and Erlang for configuration management, cloud infrastructure management, system administration, and network management.

Targeted at administrators, consultants, and architects, the book guides them through the advanced features of the tool that are necessary for infrastructure automation, DevOps automation, and reporting. The book presumes knowledge of Ruby and Erlang, which are used as reference languages for creating recipes and cookbooks and as a refresher to help the reader get on speed with the flow of book.

The book provides step-by-step instructions on the installation and configuration of chef, usage scenarios of chef, in infrastructure automation with common scenarios such as virtual machine provisioning, OS configuration for Windows, Linux, and Unix, and provisioning and configuration of web servers like Apache along with popular databases like MySQL.

It further elaborates on the creation of recipes and cookbooks, which help in the deployment of servers and applications to any physical, virtual, or cloud location, no matter the size of the infrastructure.

The book covers advanced features like LWRPs (lightweight resource providers) and knife and also contains several illustrative sample cookbooks on MySQL, Apache, and CouchDB deployment using a step-by-step approach.

CHAPTER 1

■ ■ ■

Introduction

In this chapter we briefly discuss the concept of infrastructure as code and DevOps. We also touch upon Chef and Ruby and cover some of the use cases of Opscode Chef and how it is being leveraged to solve technical problems faced by IT (information technology) departments.

Infrastructure as Code

The advent of public cloud computing has revolutionized the software development world. Small companies with a good idea can leverage the pay-per-use model provided by the public cloud computing companies and setup their infrastructure quickly and without any upfront costs.

For the traditional IT enterprises, the public cloud brings in cost advantages, flexibility, and the agility to setup their infrastructure environments very quickly without waiting for the ordering, procurement, and setup cycles involved in traditional datacenter setup.

Most of the public cloud providers deliverAPIs (application programming interfaces), which expose the features and functionality of the underlying cloud. Thus the infrastructure that typically used to be a setup and configuration activity in traditional datacenters has now become programmable through APIs.

The infrastructure components like *Network, Firewalls, Compute,* and *Storage* are exposed to programmers through APIs and can be consumed through command lines, REST APIcalls, and so on.

The large-scale infrastructure used by cloud providers and Internet scale companies like Google, Facebook, and Twitter needs a very different approach to setup, monitoring, and management from a typical enterprise with a few thousand servers.

Some of the provisioning and deployment models applicable for large-scale Internet infrastructure are very different from the typical enterprise use cases. The number of applications and servers are more homogeneous in an online business than the number of applications and diversity of infrastructure found in an enterprise.

Although AWS (Amazon Web Services) does not share details on its capacity or the addition of capacity, it states that it is adding capacity equivalent to what Amazon.com had in 2005 daily. This kind of massive capacity buildup and management of millions of virtual machines leveraging technologies, processes, and tools built for a smaller scale are not possible.

1

The public cloud is built on principles of scaled-out architecture. Thus, rather than adding computer resources to a virtual machine, applications quickly spin new machines when the demand increases and gracefully shut down machines when the demand decreases. This has become essential since cloud providers charge the customer on the basis of metered usage of services. Thus, if you are using a virtual machine in a cloud environment for a few hours, you will only be billed for the hours of usage.

The cloud providers provide integrations and APIs for making the up scaling and downscaling of resources simple and easy to do. Customers benefit by having capacity when needed and getting billed for what they use.

Today, a range of new technologies has emerged which makes the task of managing large-scale infrastructure and application landscape much easier.

Infrastructure as a code emerged in the last few years because of advancement in two technologies and the rise of consumer IT companies. Cloud computing and new web frameworks made it simpler and easier to develop out scale applications and created technologies that enabled infrastructure as a code.

The cloud and the new web frameworks have essentially democratized innovation and IT. No longer do you need expensive equipment and a datacenter setup to start your innovative company. The cloud provides seemingly limitless capacity to fulfill the needs of developers and startup with zero capital expenditure. You can be up and running on a prototype using your credit card. Thus smaller companies now can compete with their larger competitors, and the advantage that large organizations have by virtue of capital and infrastructure no longer remains a differentiator.

The idea of the cloud and the newer web development languages and frameworks was all about simplicity. The cloud made it simple for organizations to setup infrastructure, and the new web frameworks and languages like Ruby on Rails made it simpler, easier, and faster to develop applications.

Startup companies also have to operate within tight budgets; they do not have the luxury of spending money on operations and operations teams. Thus, the developers had to find a way to make operations as automated as possible, and the convergence of all the new technologies, along with the needs of developer communities and large-scale Internet companies, resulted in the fructification of the concepts of DevOps and infrastructure as code.

A lot of changes have led to this new breed of configuration management tools that help in automating your infrastructure. These tools help you in maintaining a blueprint of your infrastructure by breaking it down into components that interact with each other so that you can deploy it whenever you want.

It is important to understand that "infrastructure" does not mean infrastructure in the traditional IT definition, which is network devices, servers, firewalls, and so on. By infrastructure, we mean a collection of components that are used to deliver a service to the end user. The components can be virtual machines, network settings, configuration files, software packages, applications, processes, users, and so on.

Jesse Robins describes the goal of infrastructure as code:

"Enable the reconstruction of the business from nothing but a source code repository, an application data backup, and bare metal resources."

Thus, infrastructure as code tools like chef came into picture. Chef enables developers to assemble and consume infrastructure components similarly to the way software components are designed, assembled, and consumed.

Figure 1-1 shows the different types of components of infrastructure.

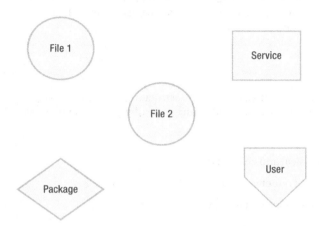

Figure 1-1. *Infrastructure components*

Infrastructure components are abstracted similarly to the way abstract classes and interfaces work in a software module.

Chef and other automation tools allow you to define objects and methods for an object; as an example, you may add and remove methods for installing packages.

The beauty of this approach is that the administrators of the end systems do not have to worry about the implementation details of how each component is deployed by the system and can focus on the exact task to be achieved.

Infrastructure is created as a blueprint in a software system which is executed by a provider on the end device. The provider provides the execution code based on the capabilities of the end device. Thus, the abstraction of the provider brings simplicity, and the developers can reuse the providers as per the needs of the application. The provider model encapsulates the execution aspects of the end system, and thus it greatly simplifies the work of the administrator.

Once the blueprint has been created, the same model can be applied multiple times to multiple similar endpoints.

The automation aspects of these tools also allows the endpoints to be audited to a specific baseline, and if the end points state is different than what it should be, systems like chef can automatically bring the end point back to the expected state of configuration.

The blueprint can be used to create various environments easily and quickly, and you can easily provision development, test, QA, and production environments using chef.

Without infrastructure as code and tools like chef, it would take days of effort from multiple teams to create these environments.

The additional benefit of this approach is that the complete environment becomes documented and modeled in a tool. Thus, using chef as a tool helps organizations to have a scalable and agile approach to configuration management and the deployment of infrastructure components. Automation using configuration automation tools like chef would save precious man-hours, which can be utilized for service improvement and the creation of new services. This also leads to significant cost savings as well as higher quality of service because of fewer human errors.

Overview

Chef is a framework that makes it easy to manage your infrastructure. Chef was initially written in Ruby, but the latest version is a mixture of Erlang and Ruby. A single chef server can handle upto 10,000 nodes.

With chef, we can

- Manage both our physical and cloud servers.

- Create perfect clones of our environments.

- Easily configure applications that require knowledge about your infrastructure via 'Search.'

Once we have automated our infrastructure with chef, we can replicate the whole infrastructure very easily. Chef can be mainly broken down into three components.

- Server: The chef server holds the configuration data for each and every node registered with it.

- Workstation: A workstation basically holds the local chef repository.

- A node is a client that is registered with the chef server. It has an agent known as chef client installed on it.

Cookbooks, covered in Chapter 7 also are a very important part of chef. Cookbooks are the basic building blocks of chef. They hold the type of configuration that needs to be done on a node. Each cookbook defines a complete scenario, like package installation and configuration.

Nodes

A node can be termed a "virtual" or a "physical" server that is managed by chef. A node can also be on the cloud. A node needs to have an agent, known as chef client, installed on it. The agent is used to interact with the chef server. Ohai is a built-in tool that comes with chef and is used to provide node attributes to the chef client so that a node can be configured. There are basically two types of nodes that chef can manage.

1. Cloud-based: It is basically a node that is hosted on any of the cloud providers (e.g., Amazon or Windows Azure). There is a chef CLI (command line interface) known as knife which can be used to create instances on the cloud. Once deployed, these nodes can be managed with the help of chef.

2. Physical: It can be hardware or a virtual machine that exists in our own environment.

There are mainly two important components of a node.

1. Chef client: An agent that runs on each node. The agent contacts the chef server and pulls the configuration that needs to be done on the node. Its main functions include

   a. Registering the node with the chef server.

   b. Downloading the required cookbook in the local cache.

   c. Compiling the required recipes.

   d. Configuring the node and bringing it to the expected state.

2. Ohai: Chef client requires some information about the node whenever it runs. Ohai is a built-in tool that comes with chef and is used to detect certain attributes of that particular node and then provide them to the chef client whenever required. Ohai can also be used as a stand-alone component for discovery purposes. Ohai can provide a variety of details from networking to platform information.

Workstation

A workstation is a system that is used to manage chef. There can be multiple workstations for a single chef server. A workstation has the following functionalities:

- Developing cookbooks and recipes.

- Managing nodes.

- Synchronizing the chef repository.

- Uploading cookbook and other items to the chef server.

There are mainly two important components of a workstation.

1. Knife: A command line tool used to interact with the chef server. The complete management of the chef server is done using knife. Some of the functions of knife include

       a.   Managing nodes

       b.   Uploading cook books and recipes

       c.   Managing roles and environments

2.   Local chef repository: Chef repository is a repository where everything related to the chef server/nodes is stored.

Server

There is a centrally located server which holds all the data related to the chef server; this data includes everything related to the server (i.e., cookbooks, the node object, and metadata for each and every node registered to the chef server).

The agent (chef client) runs on each and every node, and it gets the configuration data from the server and then applies the configuration to a particular node. This approach is quite helpful in distributing the effort throughout the organization rather than on a single server.

There are three different types of chef server.

- Enterprise chef
- Open source chef
- Chef solo

Enterprise Chef

Enterprise chef is the paid version of the chef server which comes with two types of installations: one is on-premise installation (i.e., in your datacenter behind your own firewall) and the other is the hosted version in which chef is offered as a service hosted and managed by Opscode.

The major difference between the enterprise version and the open source version is that the enterprise version comes with high-availability deployment support and has additional features on reporting and security.

Open Source Chef

The open source chef has most of the capabilities of the enterprise version. However, this version of chef server also has certain limitations. The open source version of chef can be installed only in stand-alone mode (i.e., it is not available in the hosted model). The open source chef components need to be installed on a single server, and it doesn't offer the levels of security available in the enterprise version. It also doesn't provide reporting capabilities like the enterprise version.

ChefSolo

Chefsolo comes with the chef client package and is used to manage a node without any access to the server. It runs locally on any node, and it requires the cookbook or any of its dependencies to be present on the node itself. This is generally used for testing purposes.

Cookbooks

A cookbook is a basic unit of configuration and policy definition in chef. A cookbook essentially defines a complete scenario. As an example, a cookbook for Apache or Tomcat would provide all details to install and configure a fully configured Apache or Tomcat server.

A cookbook contains all the components that are required to support the installation and configuration of an application or component, including

- Files that need to be distributed for that component.

- Attribute values that should be present on the nodes.

- Definitions so that we need not write the same code again and again.

- Libraries which can be used to extend the functionality of chef.

- Recipes that specify the resources and the order of execution of code.

- Templates for file configurations.

- Metadata which can be used specify any kind of dependency, version constraints, and so on.

Chef mainly uses Ruby as its reference language for writing cookbooks and recipes. For writing specific resources, we used extended DSL (Domain Specific Language).

Chef provides an extensive library of resources which are required to support various infrastructure automation scenarios. The DSL provided by chef can also be extended to support additional capabilities or requirements.

Figure 1-2 shows the basic chef components and how they are used in automation.

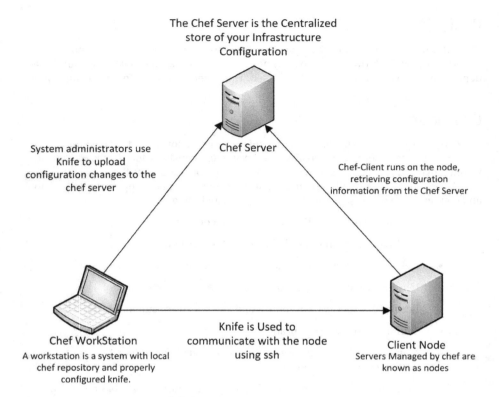

Figure 1-2. *Basic structure of chef*

Figure 1-3 shows the chef components in detail.

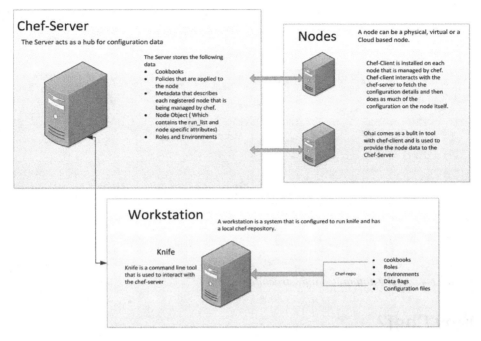

Figure 1-3. *Chef components in detail*

The Value of Chef

With chef, you can automate your whole infrastructure and rebuild the whole environment very easily. Chef can automate every task that we perform manually in our datacenter in our daily routine and can save lots of time. Figure 1-4 shows a typical environment. We can delete and launch any instance at a point in time, and we do this manually, but with chef we can automate the whole process.

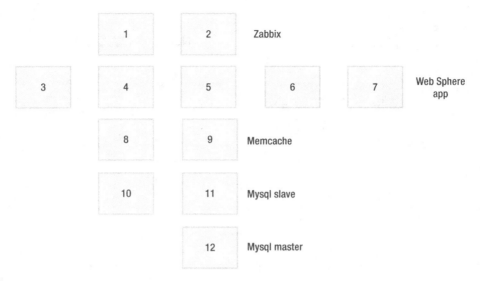

Figure 1-4. *A fully automated infrastructure*

Why Chef?

As explained previously, chef gives your infrastructure the flexibility, speed, and efficiency you have always wanted. Automation through chef can provide the speed and agility needed by business today to compete. Chef can be used to quickly provide IT solutions and repeatable configurations with minimal human intervention.

Automating your infrastructure with chef could help you to deploy features in minutes rather than days. Chef can manage any number of servers without much complexity, and thus it helps you in managing your infrastructure easily, at less cost, and while avoiding human errors.

Chef helps your enterprise in moving to public clouds and complements the public cloud model by providing integrations with major public cloud providers.

Core Principles of Chef

Chef is a highly configurable and extensible tool with immense power in the hands of administrators to automate their infrastructure. It provides flexibility, agility, and speed to administrators, and they can leverage the tool the way they best deem fit in their scenarios.

The main principles on which chef works are

- Idempotence
- Thick client, thin server
- Order of execution

Idempotence

Idempotence means that a chef recipe can run multiple times on the same system and the return will be identical. Chef ensures that the configuration changes to the end system (node) are done when the underlying configuration differs from the desired state and no changes are made to the system if they are not needed.

Thus, administrators can define the end configurations, and chef will ensure that the nodes have the desired configuration on them.

Thick Client, Thick Server

Chef uses an agent known as chef client to interact with the chef server.

The chef agent does the heavy lifting; it downloads the required files from the chef server onto a local cache. The chef client is responsible for compiling the client-side code, and then the code is executed by the agent on the node.

The thick client approach of chef makes it highly scalable, since the heavy lifting is done by the agent on each node and not on the server. This makes chef an ideal candidate for large-scale Internet application deployment and management.

Order of Execution

The compilation of recipes on the node is done in the exact order that is specified. The code execution of the agent is also done in the order that it is specified.

Thus, it is important to ensure that the correct order of execution is followed in the creation of recipes, so that the desired results are correct.

This approach makes sure that a prerequisite is met first so it becomes easier to manage.

Who Uses Chef?

Chef is being used very widely. One of chef's biggest customers is Facebook. Many Internet companies and enterprises use chef today to automate their infrastructure environments.

Key Technologies

In this section, we discuss some of the technologies that are used in chef—mainly, Ruby and Erlang.

Ruby

Ruby is a simple object-oriented programming language which has been developed and designed in such a way that it is easy to read and understand, and it behaves in a predictable fashion. Ruby was developed and designed by Yukihiro "Matz" Matsumoto of Japan in 1995 and is influenced by scripting languages like Python, Perl, Smalltalk, Eiffel,

Ada, and Lisp. Ruby borrows heavily from Perl, and the class library is an object-oriented reorganization of Perl's functionality. Ruby was launched for the general public in 1995, and since then it has drawn devoted coders worldwide. Ruby became famous in 2006 and has been widely used since then.

Chef mainly uses Ruby as its reference language for writing cookbooks and recipes, with an extended DSL. Here we discuss some of the basic concepts of Ruby that might be needed while using chef.

Variables

Variables are used to store any kind of value, which can be a string or an integer, which is then used reference purposes. We need to declare a variable and then assign a value to that variable, which can be done with the help of assignment operator (=). For example, if we need to assign a numeric value to a variable, X, we would do the following:

X=20

This would create a variable, X, and would assign a value of 20 to it.

Figure 1-5 shows assigning values to four different variables. It would create four variables (a, b, c, and d) with values of 10,20,30, and 40, respectively.

```
irb(main):001:0> a=10
=> 10
irb(main):002:0> b=20
=> 20
irb(main):003:0> c=30
=> 30
irb(main):004:0> d=40
=> 40
irb(main):005:0>
```

Figure 1-5. *Assigning values to variables*

Ruby also supports parallel assignment of variables. The same result can be achieved more quickly, using parallel assignment.

Figure 1-6 shows this operation.

```
irb(main):001:0> a,b,c,d=10,20,30,40
=> [10, 20, 30, 40]
irb(main):002:0>
```

Figure 1-6. *Assigning values to variables using parallel assignment*

Working with Strings

Ruby uses the string object to store strings. The string object can also be used to call a number of methods. These methods can be used to manipulate a string in many ways. To create a new empty string, we use the new method of the string object as shown in Figure 1-7.

```
irb(main):001:0> mystring = String.new
=> ""
irb(main):002:0>
```

Figure 1-7. *Creating an empty string*

If we want to create a new string with some value, we can pass an argument in the new method as shown in Figure 1-8.

```
irb(main):001:0> mystring= String.new("This is a new String")
=> "This is a new String"
irb(main):002:0>
```

Figure 1-8. *Creating a string with some value*

There is another way to create a string which uses the string method provided by kernel, as shown in Figure 1-9.

```
irb(main):001:0> mystring=String("This is also a new String")
=> "This is also a new String"
irb(main):002:0>
```

Figure 1-9. *Creating a string with some value (kernel method)*

The best thing about Ruby is that it takes care of many things. We can create a string by simply declaring it as shown in Figure 1-10.

```
irb(main):001:0> mystring= "This is a String"
=> "This is a String"
irb(main):002:0>
```

Figure 1-10. *Initializing a string with some value (direct declaration)*

We can use both single quotes (') and double quotes (") to delimit stings in Ruby. However, there is a difference in both. Double quotes are used when we want to interpret escaped characters like tabs or newlines while single quotes are used when we need to print the actual sequence.

Figure 1-11 depicts the difference between the two.

```
irb(main):001:0> mystring ="This is a new String \nwith double quotes"
=> "This is a new String \nwith double quotes"
irb(main):002:0> mystring1 ='This is another string \nwith single quotes'
=> "This is another string \\nwith single quotes"
irb(main):003:0> puts mystring
This is a new String
with double quotes
=> nil
irb(main):004:0> puts mystring1
This is another string \nwith single quotes
=> nil
irb(main):005:0>
```

Figure 1-11. *Working with single and double quotes*

Ruby can be easily embedded in a string. Figure 1-12 illustrates this process.

```
irb(main):001:0> x="Bob"
=> "Bob"
irb(main):002:0> puts "Hi #{x}"
Hi Bob
```

Figure 1-12. *Accessing a variable*

We need to use double quotes if we want to embed Ruby in a string. Single quotes won't work in this case.

Arrays

Like a string, a Ruby array is also an object which can contain a single item or more. These items can be a string, an integer, or a fixnum. We can create an array in Ruby using a number of mechanisms. We can create an uninitialized array in Ruby using the new method of array class shown in Figure 1-13.

```
irb(main):001:0> days_of_month = Array.new
=> []
irb(main):002:0>
```

Figure 1-13. *Initializing an empty array*

Figure 1-13 creates an array named days_of_month with nothing in it.

We can also create an array with a fixed number of elements in it by passing the size as an argument (see Figure 1-14).

```
irb(main):001:0> days_of_motn = Array.new(5)
=> [nil, nil, nil, nil, nil]
irb(main):002:0>
```

Figure 1-14. *Initializing an array with five elements*

Figure 1-14 will create an array of five elements with no value in it. If we need to add some data to the array, many options are available (see Figure 1-15). One of them would be to place the same data in each element during the array creation process

```
irb(main):001:0> days_of_month =Array.new(5, "Five")
=> ["Five", "Five", "Five", "Five", "Five"]
irb(main):002:0>
```

Figure 1-15. *Initializing an array with some value*

We can also create an array by using the [] method of the array class and specifying the elements one after one as shown in Figure 1-16.

```
irb(main):001:0> days_of_month = Array["One", "Two", "Three", "Four", "Five"]
=> ["One", "Two", "Three", "Four", "Five"]
irb(main):002:0>
```

Figure 1-16. *Populating different value in each element of an array*

We can access any element of a Ruby array by referencing the index of the element. For example, see Figure 1-17 if you want to access the second element of the array created in Figure 1-16.

```
irb(main):002:0> days_of_month[2]
=> "Three"
irb(main):003:0>
```

Figure 1-17. *Accessing an object in an array*

Operators

Ruby has a number of classified operators.

- Assignment operators

- Math operators

- Comparison operators

- Bitwise operators

In Ruby, as in other languages, a number of arithmetic operators can be used to perform a number of functions. Table 1-1 provides a list of these operators.

Table 1-1. *Arthimetic Operators*

Operator	Function
+	Used to add the variables on both sides of the operator.
-	Used to subtract the right side operand from the left side operand.
*	Used to multiply the values on both sides of the operator.
/	Used to divide the left hand operand by right hand operand.
%	Used to divide the left hand operand by right hand operand and return the remainder.
**	Used to perform exponential calculation on operators.

Figure 1-18 shows the use of the division operator; if we don't want the result to be truncated then we need to express at least one of the operands as a float.

```
irb(main):001:0> 10/7
=> 1
irb(main):002:0> 10.0/7
=> 1.4285714285714286
irb(main):003:0>
```

Figure 1-18. *Working with operators*

If we need to compare two variables then we need to use comparison operators. Table 1-2 shows a list of comparison operators available in Ruby.

Table 1-2. *Comparison Operators*

Operator	Function
==	It is used to check equality. The output would be a *true* or a *false*.
.eql?	It has the same functionality as == operator.
!=	It is used to check for inequality. The output would be false in case equality and true in case of equality.
<	Used to compare two operands. The output will be true if the first operand is less than the second one and false otherwise.
>	Used to compare two operands. The output will be true if the first operand is greater than the second one and false otherwise.
>=	Used to compare two operands. The output will be true if the first operand is greater than or equal to the second one and false otherwise.
<=	Used to compare two operands. The output will be true if the first operand is less than or equal to the second one and false otherwise.

Figure 1-19 shows the use of comparison operators.

```
irb(main):001:0> 5 ==5
=> true
irb(main):002:0> 5.eql? 6
=> false
irb(main):003:0> 8 <=9
=> true
irb(main):004:0> 9<=>9
=> 0
irb(main):005:0> 9 <=>1
=> 1
irb(main):006:0> 10 <=> 11
=> -1
irb(main):007:0>
```

Figure 1-19. *Working with operators*

Ruby bitwise operators allow operations to be performed on numbers at the bit level.

Methods

Methods in Ruby are used to organize your code in a proper way. Ruby also promotes the reuse of code so that we do not write the same code again and again.

Ruby helps in organizing your code into groups to call said code whenever required.

The following piece of code shows a typical method:

```
def name( arg1, arg2, arg3, ... )
   .. ruby code ..
   return value
end
```

Erlang

Overview

Erlang is a general-purpose concurrent programing language that is mainly used to build highly available and scalable real-time systems. Erlang is being widely used in many industries like telecom, e-commerce, and so on. It has a system that provides built-in support for concurrency, fault tolerance, and distribution.

Along with being a programming language, Erlang also focuses on high reliability and concurrency. Erlang can perform dozens of task at a time. It uses an actor model to achieve it (i.e., each actor is treated as a separate process in a virtual machine). For example, consider yourself to be an actor in Erlang's world: you would be a person sitting alone in a dark room waiting for a message, and as soon as you receive a message you provide a valid response.

With the help of this actor model, Erlang is able to perform tasks at a faster rate, which in turn makes it faster. We can treat this actor model as a world where everyone can perform a few distinct tasks and just wait to receive a proper message. It means everyone is dedicatedly working on a specific task and not concerned about what other people are upto. To achieve this, we write processes (actors) in Erlang, and these actors do not share any kind of information. Every communication that is taking place is traceable, safe, and explicit. The ability of Erlang to scale, recover, and organize code makes it more awesome.

The main reason Erlang is able to scale so easily is that the nature of the process is very light, and a large number of processes exist. Although it is not required to use all of them at a time, you have them as a backup and can use them if required.

Evolution and History

In 1984, CSLabs at Ericsson conducted on going research on various languages and methodology approaches that were best suited for the applications in telephony domains. A few techniques were rule-based programming, imperative programming, declarative programming, and object oriented programming.

There are some properties that telephony domains demand, such as

- **Grained concurrency**: Typical telecommunication involves large equipment, complex real-time systems, and various activities which should occur concurrently and are handled by processes or threads.

- **Asynchronous message passing:** This is a basic requirement of telephone systems. Asynchronous message passing gives ways to distribute processing.

The research done on varieties of languages finally confirmed that building a scalable and distributed telephony application cannot be done by using any of the languages or with any of the methodologies. There are some parts of an application which can be best programmed in one methodology and other parts in using some other methodology.

The primary aim of this research was to develop a style of programming which can lead to beautiful code, and which will also help programmers gain efficiency when writing bug-free code.

Erlang Creation

Joe Armstrong started another experiment with Prolog, and gave the name Erlang to this new experimental language after the Danish mathematician Agner Krarup Erlang, creator of the Erlang loss formula. Erlang can be defined as a concurrent functional programming language which mainly follows two traditions (see Figure 1-20).

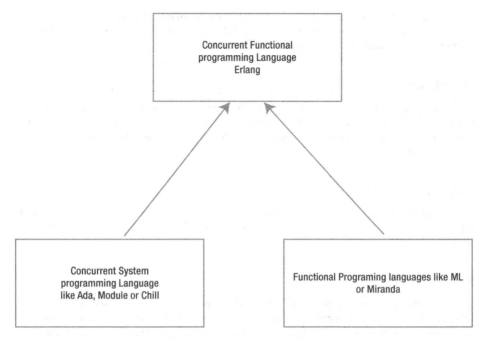

Figure 1-20. *How Erlang evolved*

- **Functional and logic programming languages**: Erlang inherits lists, pattern making, atoms, catch and throw, and so on, from these languages. Examples of these types of languages are Lisp, Miranda, Haskel, and ML.

- **Concurrent programming languages**: Erlang uses features like process communication modules and processes from these types of languages. Examples of these types of languages include Modula, Chill, and Ada.

Erlang was created while keeping in mind various designs that are ideal for telephony applications. It contains features like concurrency, OS independent, garbage collection, tail recursion, different data types and collections, support selective message receive statement, asynchronous message passing, and default error handling.

Erlang Features
Concurrency

Erlang implements concurrency independent of the operating system. Processes in Erlang have no shared memory. Different processes in Erlang communicate to each other by sending and receiving messages asynchronously. These processes are very lightweight; hence hundreds and thousands of process can run at a time, but their memory requirement varies dynamically. Erlang is useful for applications that require response time of order of milliseconds

Distributed

Erlang supports transparent distribution. An Erlang program can run on more than one machine which may each have different operating systems running. Erlang processes on one node and communicates a different process on another node using asynchronous message passing.

Sequential Erlang

The syntax of Erlang is quite similar to that of ML. It has data types like numbers, lists, and tuples and it uses pattern matching to select between alternatives. Recursion is used to construct loops.

Robust

When an Erlang process crashes it will only crash the process, not the entire system. Erlang processes can monitor each other so that if there is an error in one process, others can receive the error message. This also provides monitoring processes to take corrective actions like restart transactions, for example. In distributed systems, nodes can be configured to provide failover scenarios. Due to this feature of Erlang we are able to design soft-fail systems. For example, an error in the call of a telecommunication system will bring down that call only and not the entire system.

Software Upgrading in Running Systems

This function in Erlang can be performed without disturbing the current state of the system. We can directly change the code in the running system which means we can upgrade a system without disturbing the currently running operations.

The newly spawned process will use the new version of the module while the ongoing process will use the old one and remain undisturbed.

Portability

Erlang has been developed mainly in C, so it is available on most of the operating systems that can run C.

■ ■ ■

## CHAPTER 2

The Chef Server

This chapter covers Chef server and its components in detail. First we cover the different types of chef servers and then move on to discuss the components of the open source chef server.

The Chef Server

The chef server is the server component of the Opscode chef tool. The server is a centralized location where data related to chef is stored.

The data that is stored on the server includes cookbooks, node objects, and any policy that needs to be applied on any node. Each node registered with the chef server has an agent known as chef client installed on it. The agent contacts the chef servers and pulls the configuration that needs to be applied on the node. The chef client is responsible for execution of the actual code on the node. Chef is a thick client architecture tool that enables the client to do the heavy lifting. Due to this approach the effort is distributed throughout the infrastructure nodes and not on a single server.

Types of Chef Server

Chef servers can be classified into three types.

1. Hosted enterprise chef

2. Enterprise chef

3. Open source chef server

Hosted Enterprise Chef

This type of chef server is a paid version and is offered as a service. As the name suggests, it is a cloud-based, highly available, and scalable version of chef. It has all the capability of chef and one can just sign up to use it. It has to be accessed via the Internet. Thus, a hosted enterprise chef is a great way for enterprises to leverage a fully supported and hosted version, such as cloud computing, for their applications. The managed offering frees the enterprise to focus its efforts on its core applications rather than installing, configuring, and managing chef.

Enterprise Chef

This version of chef is the same as the hosted version. The only difference between them is that this one needs to be installed in the enterprise data centers and is not available as a hosted and managed offering.

In terms of technical capabilities, it is the same as the hosted version. It also has dedicated support directly from chef and features such as RBAC (Role-Based Access Control), built-in support for high availability, and so on.

Open Source Chef Server

This is a free version of the chef server which has many of the capabilities of the enterprise version but also some limitations. It does not include support directly from chef but has support from the chef community. The customer needs to manage the chef instances. High availability and scalability are not offered out of the box. Any data migration or patching also needs to be done by the user.

Extra Functionalities in Enterprise Chef

Enterprise chef has all the functionalities of the open source chef server along with the following features:

- *Improved RBAC*: Enterprise chef comes with built-in RBAC, which is used to configure fine-grained permissions for users. This is an important requirement for any automation tool from a security perspective.

- *Built-in support for high availability*: Enterprise chef comes with multiple installation options. The enterprise version of chef can be installed in a stand-alone mode and also in a high-availability mode. High availability can be a key requirement for some of the enterprises.

- *Push client jobs*: The server can push the configuration to a client node in enterprise chef. In open source chef server the chef client needs to pull the data.

- *Improved management console* for ease of administration.

- *Monitoring and reporting*: Reporting and monitoring features are enhanced in enterprise chef; while in open source we have minimal monitoring and reporting.

- *Support directly from chef*: It has support directly from chef.

Components of Open Source Chef Server

The previous versions of chef were written in Ruby. Chef 11 was released in early 2013. One of the major changes was that the API (application programming interface) server was written in Erlang.

Erlang is a functional programming language that has many good features, like fault tolerance, concurrency, and high scalability, and it can also work in distributed environments. Due to the massive scalable nature of Erlang, it is used in telecom software and other high-performance real-time systems.

Due to this change and leveraging the Erlang language, this version of chef is more scalable and provides higher performance.

Figure 2-1 shows the various components that are part of a chef server and how they are connected to one another.

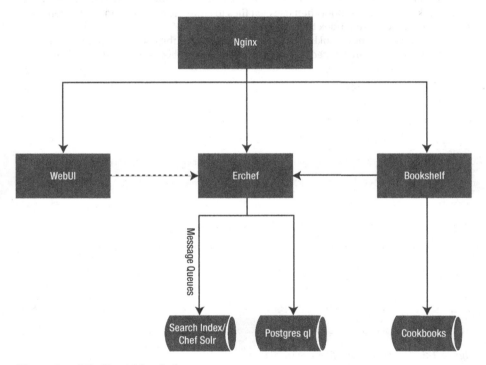

Figure 2-1. *Working of the chef server*

Nginx

Nginx is a popular open source http server and reverse proxy. Nginx is a high-performance http server which can handle heavy workload websites.

Nginx is leveraged by chef as the http server and every request that comes to the chef server is routed to Nginx. Then, Nginx forwards the request based on the type of request. If it's a cookbook-related-request then it is forwarded to Bookshelf. Bookshelf then forwards the request to Erchef, and it is handled accordingly. Any request coming is finally handled by Erchef.

Bookshelf

Bookshelf is a component of chef which holds the cookbooks in the chef server. All cookbooks that are uploaded to the chef server are stored in Bookshelf. The cookbook contains different types of files, from templates to recipes, and so on. Bookshelf also maintains different versions of the cookbooks.

The content in Bookshelf is stored using the checksum; the files are updated only if the checksum changes. Bookshelf uses flat files to store the content and the content is separate from the search index repositories.

Figure 2-2 shows how cookbooks are typically stored in the cookbook content. The path where these files are located is/var/opt/chef-server/bookshelf/data/bookshelf/.

```
[root@googler bookshelf]# ls
organization-00000000000000000000000000000000%2Fchecksum-014cfdb046a02077ab5f1a4
04590ae9f
organization-00000000000000000000000000000000%2Fchecksum-016026db2bdb79277775eab
ddea6ed0c
organization-00000000000000000000000000000000%2Fchecksum-018cbbdc7c5865390282ee8
b0036ce7f
organization-00000000000000000000000000000000%2Fchecksum-01f359bdb8882f81e0d4c28
976af5e35
organization-00000000000000000000000000000000%2Fchecksum-029c0ccdf3ecb70a053ace7
7e49ebd4a
organization-00000000000000000000000000000000%2Fchecksum-029cc725faed8adc8a74d37
54852b803
organization-00000000000000000000000000000000%2Fchecksum-03087d1952718259a4e3b25
61ad809bd
organization-00000000000000000000000000000000%2Fchecksum-0322645dca94e39148d47fa
6a0d134c2
organization-00000000000000000000000000000000%2Fchecksum-0337fd168c48f8b966e3b3f
a92e3a6f9
organization-00000000000000000000000000000000%2Fchecksum-06b81ee36fbc10d2c01c173
1c55dbeaa
organization-00000000000000000000000000000000%2Fchecksum-070c2d9eee81b2ba621c45d
1d3849f66
organization-00000000000000000000000000000000%2Fchecksum-07440811960eb25070bd5e4
```

Figure 2-2. *How cookbook files are stored*

WebUI

The web interface of the chef server is a Ruby on Rails 3.0 application.

Figure 2-3 shows the web interface of a chef server. This is the screen that appears when you open the web interface for the first time.

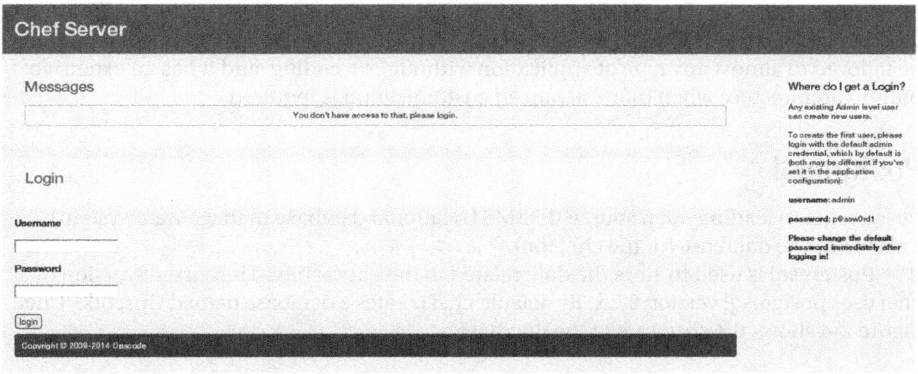

Figure 2-3. *Web interface of the chef server*

Web UI provides the graphical interface for the administrator and users to work with the chef tool.

Erchef

The core API of the chef server is written in Erlang and is known as Erchef. As it is written in Erlang it is much faster compared to its previous versions. The previous versions were written in Ruby. This version is also compatible with the previous version of the server. The cookbooks that were written for the previous versions will work in this version also.

The new version provides higher performance and scalability and it was one of the reasons for rewrite of the API server using Erlang.

Message Queue

Chef uses RabbitMQ for queueing the messages. RabbitMQ is one of the leading open source message queueing platforms. The messages that are received by the chef server are sent to the search index using the Message Queue.

All the messages are added to a queue; the chef expander pulls these messages from the RabbitMQ queue, changes them to the required format, and then sends them to the chef solr for indexing. Chef solr is a search engine which exposes its Rest API for indexing.

By using message queues, high workloads can be handled through the queue mechanism and then eventually indexed and made available through the index.

Chef Solr

Chef Solr is the search engine in chef. It wraps Apache solr and exposes its REST API for searching and indexing. Apache solr is an open source search platform that provides search capabilities with features like dynamic clustering and integrations with databases. It is fault tolerant and highly reliable. Solr is written in Java and runs as a stand-alone full-text search server within a servlet container such as Jetty. Solr uses the Lucene Java search library at its core for full-text indexing and search, and it has REST-like

HTTP/XML and JSON (JavaScript Object Notation) APIs that make it easy to use from virtually any programming language. Solr's powerful external configuration allows it to be tailored to almost any type of application without Java coding, and it has an extensive plug-in architecture when more advanced customization is required.

Postgresql

Postgresql is a leading open source RDBMS (relational database management system). This forms the database for the chef tool.

Postgresql is used to store the data related to the chef server. The current version of chef uses postgresql version 9.2.x. By default, chef creates a database named Opscode_Chef. Figure 2-4 shows the structure of the database.

```
-sh-4.1$ psql opscode_chef
psql (9.2.1)
Type "help" for help.

opscode_chef=# \l
                                    List of databases
    Name     |     Owner      | Encoding | Collate | Ctype |        Access privileges
-------------+----------------+----------+---------+-------+---------------------------------------
 opscode_chef | opscode-pgsql  | UTF8     | C       | C     | =Tc/"opscode-pgsql"                  +
              |                |          |         |       | "opscode-pgsql"=CTc/"opscode-pgsql"+
              |                |          |         |       | opscode_chef=CTc/"opscode-pgsql"   +
              |                |          |         |       | opscode_chef_ro=CTc/"opscode-pgsql"
 postgres    | opscode-pgsql  | SQL_ASCII | C      | C     |
 template0   | opscode-pgsql  | SQL_ASCII | C      | C     | =c/"opscode-pgsql"                   +
              |                |          |         |       | "opscode-pgsql"=CTc/"opscode-pgsql"
 template1   | opscode-pgsql  | SQL_ASCII | C      | C     | =c/"opscode-pgsql"                   +
              |                |          |         |       | "opscode-pgsql"=CTc/"opscode-pgsql"
(4 rows)

opscode_chef=#
```

Figure 2-4. *Structure of database*

Ports

Table 2-1 shows the list of ports that the chef server utilizes.

Table 2-1. *Ports Used by Chef*

Service	Port Used
Erchef	8000
ChefServer-WebUI	9462
Postgresql	5432
RabbitMQ	5672
Chef Solr	8983
Bookshelf	4321
Nginx	443/80

■ ■ ■

## CHAPTER 3

Installation

This chapter discusses the Installation and configuration of open source chef server.

Install the Chef Server
Prerequisite
System Requirements

Some of the important system requirements that need to be fulfilled before we install the chef server are

- Users: Chef server requires a local user and group to be created. It will create them automatically if proper privileges are given, but if we don't have a restricted access to the environment then we need to create them manually.

- FQDN: The server should have a complete and fully qualified domain name (FQDN), and it should be resolvable. If we are working in a production environment we should go for a DNS (Domain Name System) entry.

- Git: Git must be installed on the server so that it is able to maintain the revisions of internal services.

- NTP: As the chef server is sensitive to click drift, the server should be connected to an NTP server.

- Apache Qpid: The daemon should be disabled on CentOS and Red Hat systems.

- Make sure your firewall is configured properly.

Hardware Prerequisite

If we are going to use our chef server for testing purposes, it can be installed on an m1.small instance on AWS (Amazon Web Services). It can also be installed on a local virtual machine with 1GB of RAM.

If we are going for a production environment, then the desired configuration is

- RAM—4GB

- Cores—4 with 2.0GHz Intel/AMD CPUs

- Disk space—5GB in /opt and 5GB free in /var

The following operating systems support the chef server:

Operating System	Version	Architecture
Ubuntu	10.04, 10.10, 11.04, 11.10, 12.04, 12.10	X86_64 and i686
Enterprise Linux	5,6	X86_64

Hostname

The main prerequisite for chef server is that the hostname of the server should be set before installing the server. The hostname should meet certain conditions.

1. The hostname should be an FQDN and should include the domain suffix as well.

2. It should be resolvable. For a production environment, we should go for a DNS entry; in a testing environment we can make an entry in /etc/hosts to ensure that the hostname is resolvable.

To check whether you have configured the hostname properly, run the "hostname" command. The output should be similar to what we see in Figure 3-1.

```
[root@googler ~]# hostname
googler.com
[root@googler ~]# 
```

Figure 3-1. Verifying a hostname

To check whether your hostname is resolvable, run the "hostname -f" command. The output should be similar to what we see in Figure 3-2.

```
[root@googler ~]# hostname -f
googler.com
[root@googler ~]# 
```

Figure 3-2. Verifying that a hostname is resolvable

Installation

In this section we demonstrate the Installation of chef server version 11.x.

Steps

Several steps need to be taken to install the open source chef server.

The first step is to download the chef server installer available on the chef web site.

Go to the following link and download the OS-relevant setup as shown in Figure 3-3.

```
www.getChef.com/Chef/install/
```

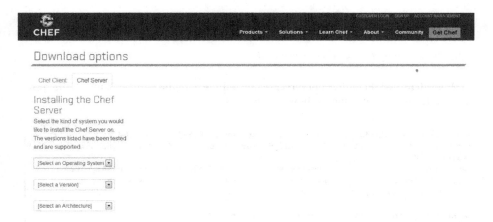

Figure 3-3. *Downloading the chef server(1)*

In the chef server tab, select the operating system (OS), its version, and its architecture. A list of the chef server versions will come up. Select a version. The download link for the selected version will come up as shown in Figure 3-4. Click the link to start downloading. Make the selections as shown in Figure 3-4 as we will be installing the chef open source version on RHEL (Red Hat Enterprise Linux).

29

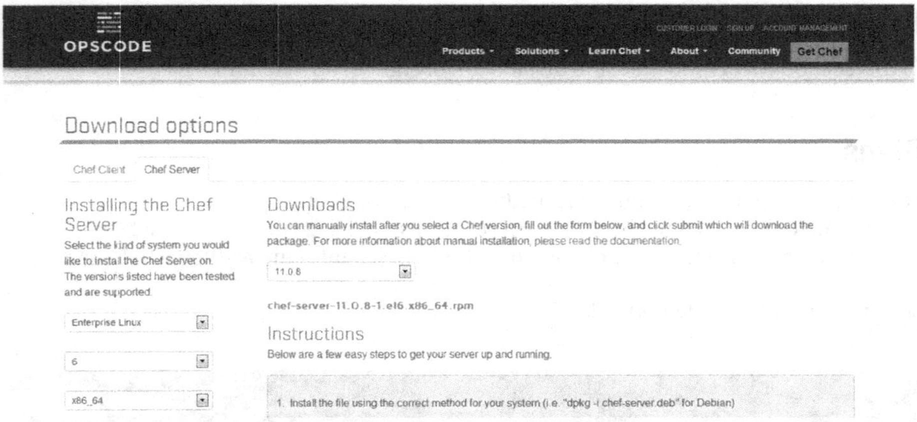

Figure 3-4. *Downloading the chef server(2)*

We will be installing the chef server on a machine with the RHEL OS. Install the rpm downloaded on the machine as shown in Figure 3-5.

```
[root@ip-10-252-103-30 ~]# rpm -ivh chef-server-11.0.8-1.el6.x86_64.rpm
warning: chef-server-11.0.8-1.el6.x86_64.rpm: Header V4 DSA/SHA1 Signature, key ID 8
3ef826a: NOKEY
Preparing...                ########################################### [100%]
   1:chef-server           ########################################### [100%]
Thank you for installing Chef Server!

The next step in the install process is to run:

sudo chef-server-ctl reconfigure
```

Figure 3-5. *Installing the chef server*

When the rpm is installed the next step is to run a command that will configure the chef server. Run the following command (see Figure 3-6):

```
$ Chef-server-ctl reconfigure
```

```
root@ip-10-252-196-87:~# chef-server-ctl reconfigure
Starting Chef Client, version 11.4.0
Compiling Cookbooks...
Recipe: chef-server::default
  * directory[/etc/chef-server] action create
    - create new directory /etc/chef-server
    - change mode from '' to '0775'
    - change owner from '' to 'root'
    - change group from '' to 'root'

[2013-12-18T13:04:57+00:00] WARN: Cloning resource attributes for directory[/va
/opt/chef-server/chef-server-webui/etc] from prior resource (CHEF-3694)
[2013-12-18T13:04:57+00:00] WARN: Previous directory[/var/opt/chef-server/chef-
erver-webui/etc]: /opt/chef-server/embedded/cookbooks/chef-server/recipes/chef-
erver-webui.rb:31:in `block in from_file'
[2013-12-18T13:04:57+00:00] WARN: Current  directory[/var/opt/chef-server/chef-
erver-webui/etc]: /opt/chef-server/embedded/cookbooks/chef-server/definitions/u
icorn_config.rb:21:in `block in from_file'
Generating RSA private key, 2048 bit long modulus
..................................................................+++
..................................+++
e is 65537 (0x10001)
Converging 203 resources
  * directory[/etc/chef-server] action nothing (up to date)
```

Figure 3-6. *Configuring the chef server*

The foregoing command will install the chef server with default settings. If we need some custom settings, then we need to create a file from which the chef server will fetch the settings. We discuss this topic in detail in the section "Configuration." When the configuration is complete you will see a screen similar to the one in Figure 3-7.

```
+        "checkpoint_timeout": "5min",
+        "checkpoint_completion_target": 0.9,
+        "checkpoint_warning": "30s"
+     }
+   },
+   "run_list": [
+      "recipe[chef-server]"
+   ]
+}

Recipe: chef-server::erchef
  * service[erchef] action restart
    - restart service service[erchef]

Chef Client finished, 268 resources updated
chef-server Reconfigured!
```

Figure 3-7. \Configuration completed

31

To check whether our Installation completed successfully, run the following command (see Figure 3-8):

```
$ Chef-server-ctl test
```

```
[root@ip-10-255-28-106 bin]# chef-server-ctl test
Configuring logging...
Creating platform...
Starting Pedant Run: 2013-12-17 10:36:06 UTC
setting up rspec config for #<Pedant::OpenSourcePlatform:0x00000002a2f498>
Configuring RSpec for Open-Source Tests
```

Figure 3-8. *TestingInstallation of chef server*

This is a built-in command that comes with chef. Whenever you invoke the command, it will run a test against the installed chef server and verify whether everything is working fine.

A screen similar to the one in Figure 3-9 will let you know if the Installation is working properly.

```
/opt/chef-server/embedded/service/gem/ruby/1.9.1/gems/rspec-core-2.11.1/lib/rspe
c/core/hooks.rb:72:in `each'
/opt/chef-server/embedded/service/gem/ruby/1.9.1/gems/rspec-core-2.11.1/lib/rspe
c/core/hooks.rb:72:in `run'
/opt/chef-server/embedded/service/gem/ruby/1.9.1/gems/rspec-core-2.11.1/lib/rspe
c/core/hooks.rb:424:in `run_hook'
/opt/chef-server/embedded/service/gem/ruby/1.9.1/gems/rspec-core-2.11.1/lib/rspe
c/core/command_line.rb:27:in `block in run'
/opt/chef-server/embedded/service/gem/ruby/1.9.1/gems/rspec-core-2.11.1/lib/rspe
c/core/reporter.rb:34:in `report'
/opt/chef-server/embedded/service/gem/ruby/1.9.1/gems/rspec-core-2.11.1/lib/rspe
c/core/command_line.rb:25:in `run'
/opt/chef-server/embedded/service/gem/ruby/1.9.1/gems/rspec-core-2.11.1/lib/rspe
c/core/runner.rb:69:in `run'
./bin/chef-pedant:29:in `<main>'

Finished in 0.11654 seconds
0 examples, 0 failures   _
```

Figure 3-9. *Testing successful*

Now, open the WebUI of the chef server using the IP (Internet protocol) address or the FQDN of the server. You will find a screen similar to the one in Figure 3-10.

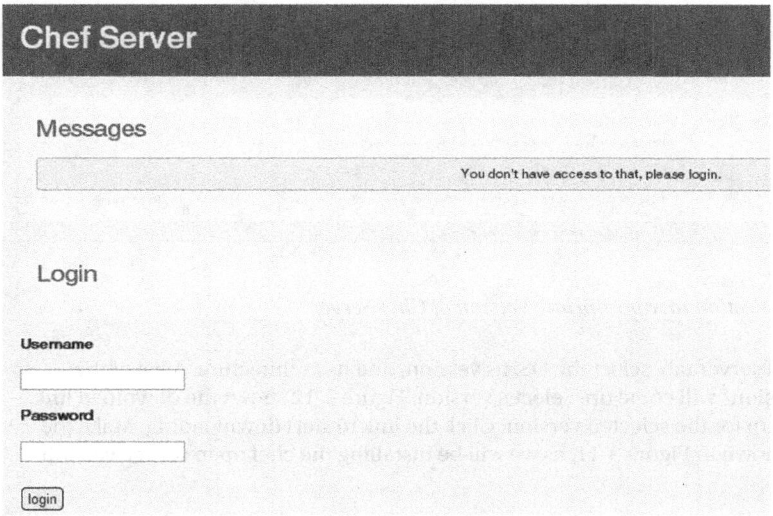

Figure 3-10. *Web interface of chef server*

Installation on a Virtual Machine

In this scenario we will install the chef server on a virtual machine. The following requirements are necessary to proceed with the Installation:

- A computer running VMware workstation with a configured virtual machine running RHEL 6.0.

- A working browser on the computer running the workstation.

- A bridged adaptor to configure our chef server.

- The IP or the FQDN of the virtual machine in order to access the chef server.

Steps

The steps are similar to those of installing the chef server on a server.
First, download the chef server package on the virtual machine.
Go to the following link and download the OS-relevant setup as shown in Figure 3-11.

```
www.getChef.com/Chef/install/
```

Chef Client	Chef Server

Installing the Chef Server

Select the kind of system you would like to install the Chef Server on. The versions listed have been tested and are supported.

Enterprise Linux ▼

6 ▼

x86_64 ▼

Downloads

You can manually install after you select a Chef version, fill out the form below, and click submit which will download the package. For more information about manual installation, please read the documentation.

11.0.10 ▼

chef-server-11.0.10-1.el6.x86_64.rpm

Instructions

Below are a few easy steps to get your server up and running.

1. Install the file using the correct method for your system (i.e. "dpkg -i chef-server.deb" for Debian)

2. sudo chef-server-ctl reconfigure

Figure 3-11. Selection an appropriate Version of Chef-Server

In the chef server tab, select the OS, its version, and its architecture. A list of the chef server versions will come up. Select a version. Figure 3-12 shows the download link that will come up for the selected version. Click the link to start downloading. Make the selections as shown in Figure 3-11, as we will be installing the chef open source version on RHEL.

```
[root@virtualchefserver ~]# wget https://opscode-omnibus-packages.s3.amazonaws.c
om/el/6/x86_64/chef-server-11.0.10-1.el6.x86_64.rpm
--2014-03-06 16:16:16--  https://opscode-omnibus-packages.s3.amazonaws.com/el/6/
x86_64/chef-server-11.0.10-1.el6.x86_64.rpm
Resolving opscode-omnibus-packages.s3.amazonaws.com... 176.32.102.89
Connecting to opscode-omnibus-packages.s3.amazonaws.com|176.32.102.89|:443... co
nnected.
HTTP request sent, awaiting response... 200 OK
Length: 204490087 (195M) [application/x-redhat-package-manager]
Saving to: "chef-server-11.0.10-1.el6.x86_64.rpm"

 0% [                                    ] 143,599     53.4K/s
```

Figure 3-12. Downloading the chef server

We would be installing the chef server on a machine with RHEL OS. Install the rpm downloaded on the machine as shown in Figure 3-13.

```
[root@virtualchefserver ~]# rpm -ivh chef-server-11.0.6-1.el6.x86_64.rpm
warning: chef-server-11.0.6-1.el6.x86_64.rpm: Header V4 DSA/SHA1 Signature, key
ID 83ef826a: NOKEY
```

Figure 3-13. *Installing the chef server*

Once you have installed the rpm, the next step is to run a command that will configure the chef server. Use the following command, as shown in Figure 3-14:

```
$ Chef-server-ctl reconfigure
```

```
[root@virtualchefserver ~]# chef-server-ctl reconfigure
```

Figure 3-14. *Configuring the chef server*

The aforementioned command will install the chef server with default settings. If we need some custom settings we need to create a file from which the chef server will fetch the settings. We discuss this topic in detail in the section "Configuration." When the configuration is complete you will get a screen similar to the one in Figure 3-15.

```
* directory[/var/opt/chef-server/erchef] action create
  - create new directory /var/opt/chef-server/erchef
  - change mode from '' to '0700'
  - change owner from '' to 'chef_server'

* directory[/var/opt/chef-server/erchef/etc] action create
  - create new directory /var/opt/chef-server/erchef/etc
  - change mode from '' to '0700'
  - change owner from '' to 'chef_server'

* directory[/var/log/chef-server/erchef] action create
  - create new directory /var/log/chef-server/erchef
  - change mode from '' to '0700'
  - change owner from '' to 'chef_server'

* directory[/var/log/chef-server/erchef/sasl] action create
  - create new directory /var/log/chef-server/erchef/sasl
  - change mode from '' to '0700'
  - change owner from '' to 'chef_server'

* link[/opt/chef-server/embedded/service/erchef/log] action create
  - create symlink at /opt/chef-server/embedded/service/erchef/log
```

Figure 3-15. *Configuration completed*

To check whether our Installation completed successfully, run the following command as shown in figure 3-16:

```
$ Chef-server-ctl test
```

```
[root@virtualchefserver ~]# chef-server-ctl test
```

Figure 3-16. *TestingInstallation of chef server*

This is a built-in command that comes with chef. Whenever the command is invoked, it will run a test against the installed chef server and will verify whether everything is working fine or not.

You will see a screen similar to the one in Figure 3-17 if the Installation is working properly.

```
/opt/chef-server/embedded/service/gem/ruby/1.9.1/gems/rspec-core-2.11.1/lib/rspe
c/core/hooks.rb:72:in `each'
/opt/chef-server/embedded/service/gem/ruby/1.9.1/gems/rspec-core-2.11.1/lib/rspe
c/core/hooks.rb:72:in `run'
/opt/chef-server/embedded/service/gem/ruby/1.9.1/gems/rspec-core-2.11.1/lib/rspe
c/core/hooks.rb:424:in `run_hook'
/opt/chef-server/embedded/service/gem/ruby/1.9.1/gems/rspec-core-2.11.1/lib/rspe
c/core/command_line.rb:27:in `block in run'
/opt/chef-server/embedded/service/gem/ruby/1.9.1/gems/rspec-core-2.11.1/lib/rspe
c/core/reporter.rb:34:in `report'
/opt/chef-server/embedded/service/gem/ruby/1.9.1/gems/rspec-core-2.11.1/lib/rspe
c/core/command_line.rb:25:in `run'
/opt/chef-server/embedded/service/gem/ruby/1.9.1/gems/rspec-core-2.11.1/lib/rspe
c/core/runner.rb:69:in `run'
./bin/chef-pedant:29:in `<main>'

Finished in 0.11654 seconds
0 examples, 0 failures
```

Figure 3-17. *Testing successful*

Now the next step would be to set the network adapter of your virtual machine to bridged. It should look similar to what we see in Figure 3-18.

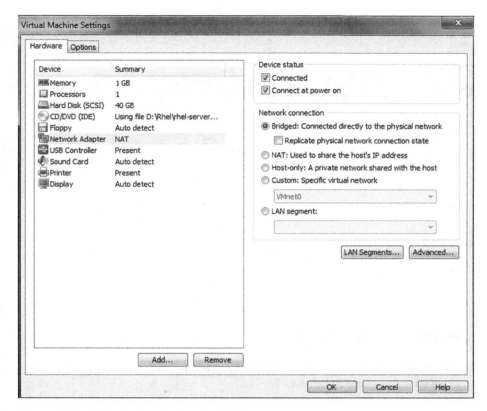

Figure 3-18. *Set network adapter as bridged*

Restart the network services of the virtual machine and run `ifconfig` command to get the IP address of the virtual machine as shown in Figure 3-19.

```
[root@virtualchefserver ~]# ifdown eth1
[root@virtualchefserver ~]# ifup eth1

Determining IP information for eth1... done.
[root@virtualchefserver ~]# ifconfig
eth1      Link encap:Ethernet  HWaddr 00:0C:29:8C:FB:2A
          inet addr:10.33.66.124  Bcast:10.33.66.255  Mask:255.255.255.0
          inet6 addr: fe80::20c:29ff:fe8c:fb2a/64 Scope:Link
          UP BROADCAST RUNNING MULTICAST  MTU:1500  Metric:1
          RX packets:322924 errors:0 dropped:0 overruns:0 frame:0
          TX packets:43964 errors:0 dropped:0 overruns:0 carrier:0
          collisions:0 txqueuelen:1000
          RX bytes:220292884 (210.0 MiB)  TX bytes:2988645 (2.8 MiB)
          Interrupt:19 Base address:0x2000
```

Figure 3-19. *Restarting network services*

Open the web browser and access your chef server. You will see a screen similar the one in Figure 3-20.

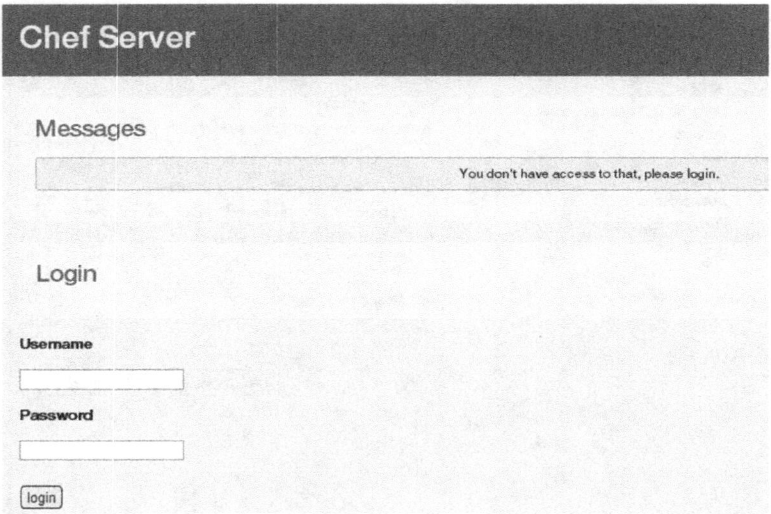

Figure 3-20. *Web interface of the chef server*

Use the default login credentials available to access the chef server. Now we have set up a chef server on a virtual machine.

File System locations

Chef server uses the following file locations for installing chef.

- /opt/Chef-server: This directory is used for Installation.

- /etc/Chef-server: This directory is used for storing the key files and the API configuration.

- /var/opt/Chef-server: All the services in chef are here.

- /var/log/Chef-server: This directory is used for storing the logs.

Configuration

The chef server is installed with default configuration settings. If we need to update any configuration settings, then we need to create a Chef-server.rb file and specify the settings that we need to modify.

After specifying the settings, we need to run the Chef-server-ctl reconfigure command to apply these settings.

The configuration file is located at /etc/Chef-server/Chef-server.rb.

These settings are optional and are required only if we want to change the default settings.

Some of the important settings that can be modified are mentioned in the Table 3-1.

The following settings can be added to the Chef-server.rb file to tune it:

Table 3-1. *Settings available in chef-server.rb*

Setting	Description
api_fqdn	It is used to define the FQDN of the server. The value should be same as the FQDN for the server.
bookshelf['vip']	The virtual IP address. Default value: node['fqdn']. (This setting is related to the **bookshelf** service.)
Bootstrap	Default value: true.
notification_email	Default value: info@example.com.

Optional Settings

The following settings are often used for performance tuning open source chef in largerInstallations. When changes are made to the Chef-server.rb file, the open source chef must be reconfigured by running the Chef-server-ctl reconfigure command.

Bookshelf

Bookshelf services can be tuned by changing the following setting:

Setting	Description
bookshelf['vip']	The virtual IP address. Default value:node['fqdn'].

Chef Expander

The following setting is often modified from the default as part of the tuning effort for the **opscode-expander** service:

Setting	Description
Chef_expander['nodes']	The number of allowed worker processes. The **opscode-expander** service runs on the back end and feeds data to the **opscode-solr** service, which creates and maintains search data used by the server. Additional memory may be required by these worker processes depending on the frequency and volume of chef client runs across the organization, but only if the back-end machines have available CPU and RAM. Default value: 2.

Chef Solr

The following settings are often modified from the default as part of the tuning effort for the **opscode-solr** service:

Setting	Description
Chef_solr['heap_size']	The amount of memory available to Apache Solr. If there is not enough memory available, search queries made by nodes to Apache Solr may fail. The amount of memory that must be available also depends on the number of nodes in the organization, the frequency of search queries, and other characteristics that are unique to each organization. In general, as the number of nodes increases, so will the amount of memory.
	If Apache Solr is running out of memory, the /var/log/opscode/Chef_solr-solr/current log file will contain SEVERE: java.lang.OutOfMemoryError: Javaheap space.
	The default value should work for many organizations with fewer than 25 nodes. Suggested value: 256 for every 25 nodes. For example, an organization with 300 nodes should have this value should set to 3072.
Chef_solr['max_field_length']	The maximum field length (in number of tokens/terms). If a field length exceeds this value, Apache Solr may not be able to complete the building of the index. Default value: 100000 (increased from the Apache Solr default value of 10000).

Update Frequency

At the end of every chef client run, the node object is saved to the server. From the server, each node object is then added to the SOLR search index. This process is asynchronous. By default, node objects are committed to the search index every 60 seconds or every 1000 node objects, whichever occurs first.

When data is committed to the Apache Solr index, all incoming updates are blocked. If the duration between updates is too short, it is possible for the rate at which updates are asked to occur to be faster than the rate at which objects can be actually committed.

For open source chef, the following settings are configurable in the Chef-server.rb file:

Setting	Description
Chef_solr['commit_interval']	The frequency (in seconds) at which node objects are added to the Apache Solr search index. Default value: 60000 (every 60 seconds).
Chef_solr['max_commit_docs']	The frequency (in documents) at which node objects are added to the Apache Solr search index. Default value: 1000 (every 1000 documents).

erChef

To tune the **opscode-erChef** service, the following settings can be changed:

Setting	Description
erChef['db_pool_size']	This setting specifies the number of open connections to the database server that are maintained by opscode-erChef service. The default value is 20. This should be changed along with the postgresql['max_connections'] setting.
erChef['s3_url_ttl']	This setting specifies the timeout for chef client. The default time out is 900.

Postgresql

The tuning of **postgresql** service can be done by changing the following settings:

Setting	Description
postgresql ['max_connections']	The setting specifies the maximum number of allowed concurrent connections to the database server. This value should only be tuned when the ErChef['db_pool_size'] value used by the **opscode-erChef** service is modified. Default value for the max_connections is 200.

WebUI

The following setting can be modified from the default as part of the tuning effort for the
opscode-webui service:

Setting	Description
Chef_server_webui ['worker_processes']	This setting specifies the number of allowed worker processes. This setting should be increased or decreased based on the number of users in an organization who use the server web user interface. The default value for the worker_processes is 2.

CHAPTER 4

■ ■ ■

Workstation

A workstation can be defined as a system on which we have chef client installed, and which has knife configured properly. A workstation holds a local repository for chef server. It is a place where all the development work takes place, and then that work is uploaded to the chef server. It provides an interface to interact with the chef server. The main functions of a workstation can be

- Uploading the items from the local chef repository to the chef server.

- Installing chef on the nodes using a knife bootstrap operation.

- Creating cookbooks.

- Creating roles/environments or any other policies and then uploading them to the chef server.

- Managing nodes using knife.

Prerequisite

Before we start with the installation, we must make sure we meet the prerequisites required to install and configure a workstation properly.

- A working chef server with which we will configure our workstation.

- Chef client requires at least 512MB of RAM, 15GB storage, and one vCPU (virtual CPU) running properly.

- The node should be able to interact with the chef server via HTTPS.

- Ruby should be installed (1.8.7 + versions).

For testing purposes we can use a t1.micro instance on AWS (Amazon Web Services) to run chef client. However, for a production client we should use instances with at least 2GB of RAM and 15GB of storage.

Operating System Support

Table 4-1 lists the operating systems (OSs) that currently support chef client.

Table 4-1. *List of Operating Systems That Support Chef Client*

Operating System	Version	Architecture
Debian	6 and above	i686, x86_64
Enterprise Linux	5.x, 6.x	i686, x86_64
Mac OS X	10.6, 10.7	x86_64
openSUSE	12.1	i686, x86_64
Solaris	5.9	Sparc
	5.10. 5.11	i386, sparc
SUSE Enterprise	11.2	i686, x86_64
Ubuntu	10.04, 10.10, 11.04, 11.10, 12.04, 12.10	i686, x86_64
Windows	2003 R2, 2008	i686, x86_64
	2008 R2, 2012	x86_64

Install and Configure a Workstation

In order to configure a workstation properly, several steps are necessary. Here we demonstrate the configuration of a workstation on an Enterprise Linux-based OS. The same steps can be used to configure it on any other OS.

1. Identify the operating system.

2. Install the chef client package.

3. Copy the `validator.pem` and `admin.pem` from to the chef server.

4. Configure knife.

5. Install git (optional).

6. Copy the knife configuration and key files in the chef repository.

7. Verify the workstation configuration.

We cover each and every step in detail in the upcoming sections.

Identify the Operating System

This step mainly includes identifying the OS, which will help us in installing the relevant package on the system.

Install the Chef Client Package

There are two options to install the chef client package.

1. Use the script provided by chef, which will install the latest version available.

2. Download the relevant version and install it using a suitable method.

Go to www.getChef.com/Chef/install/.

Visit the chef client tab and select your OS and its architecture. You will find two ways to install the package, as shown in Figure 4-1, and you can use either method to install the package. We demonstrate here by using the second method.

Download options

Chef Client	Chef Server

Installing the Chef Client

Select the kind of system you would like to install the Chef Client on. The versions listed have been tested and are supported.

Enterprise Linux ▼

6 ▼

x86_64 ▼

Quick Installation Instructions

Open a root shell on the target system and run the following client:

```
curl -L https://www.opscode.com/chef/install.sh | bash
```

Downloads

You can install manually by downloading the package below about manual installation, please read the documentation.

Chef Version ▼

Figure 4-1. *Downloading the chef package*

Select the chef version and download it to the machine on which we will configure the workstation.

After downloading the installer, run it using a relevant method based upon your OS. For Windows, right-click and run as administrator and install (see Figure 4-2). For Enterprise Linux, download the rpm and install it.

```
~]# rpm -ivh chef-11.8.2-1.el6.x86_64.rpm
warning: chef-11.8.2-1.el6.x86_64.rpm: Header V4 DSA/SHA1 Signature, key ID 83ef
826a: NOKEY
Preparing...                ########################################### [100%]
   1:chef                   ########################################### [100%]
Thank you for installing Chef!
~]# ▓t@chef-testing
```

Figure 4-2. *Installing the chef package*

Verify the installation by typing chef client –v at the command line. It should return something like what we see in Figure 4-3.

```
~]# chef-client -v
Chef: 11.8.2
~]# ▓t@chef-testing
```

Figure 4-3. *Verifying installation*

Copy the Key Files from the Chef Server

The workstation needs some keys and configuration files to connect and authenticate with the chef server. The following items are required:

- Knife configuration file (Knife.rb): It can be created using the knife configure command. We demonstrate this in the next section.

- Knife user key file: It can be created using the knife configure command.

- Chef validator key: This is a private key that is generated by the chef server when we configure it for the first time. We need to manually copy this file to .chef folder on the workstation.

Configure Knife

We demonstrate by configuring knife to an open source chef server. Run the knife configure command to configure the workstation and create the knife configuration file. Figure 4-4 shows this operation.

```
~]# knife configure
WARNING: No knife configuration file found
Where should I put the config file? [/root/.chef/knife.rb]
Please enter the chef server URL: [https://localhost:443] https://chef-server:44
3
Please enter an existing username or clientname for the API: [root] admin
Please enter the validation clientname: [chef-validator]
Please enter the location of the validation key: [/etc/chef-server/chef-validato
r.pem]
Please enter the path to a chef repository (or leave blank):
*****

You must place your client key in:
  /root/.chef/admin.pem
Before running commands with Knife!

*****

You must place your validation key in:
  /etc/chef-server/chef-validator.pem
Before generating instance data with Knife!

*****
Configuration file written to /root/.chef/knife.rb
```

Figure 4-4. *Configuring knife*

The following inputs are required to configure knife:

- The path (for Linux `/root/.chef` and for Windows c:/users/user/. chef) to keep the configuration file.

- The URL (uniform resource locator) of the chef server: It can be the IP (Internet provider) or the FQDN (fully qualified domain name) of the server. FQDN is preferred over IP.

- Client name for API (application programming interface). The admin user to be used with knife.

- Validation client name: Chef validator client that is automatically created with chef.

- Location of validation key.

- Path to a chef repository.

Install Git (Optional)

Git is required on the workstation if we want to clone the repository on github provided by Opscode. If we don't want to do so, then we can create our own chef repository. This step is an optional, required only if we want to clone the repository provided by chef.

Place the Knife Configuration and Key Files in the .Chef Directory

By default, Chef looks for the knife configuration in the .Chef directory (for Linux /root/.chef and for Windows c:/users/user/.chef). So, you need to place the following items in that directory:

- The knife configuration file

- The chef validator key file

- The user to be used to make the API calls

Verify the Workstation Configuration

To verify that our workstation is properly configured we run a test command.

Knife client list.

The command will list all the clients registered with chef server. The output will be similar to what we see in Figure 4-5.

```
[root@chef-testing ~]# knife client list
1C659D33D4B8
DS-485B393A1
LP-0022645A3
LP-2C27D7DC8
RHEL6-manak
chef-testing
chef-validator
chef-webui
[root@chef-testing ~]#
```

Figure 4-5. *Verifying that chef is installed properly*

## CHAPTER 5

Nodes

A node can be defined as a server that is managed by chef. It can be either a virtual or a physical server. "Managed by chef" means that the server has a chef client installed on it and that it is able to communicate with the chef server.

In this chapter, we try to cover all aspects related to a node. We also cover the installation and configuration of a node.

Types of Nodes

Nodes can be of different types. They can be virtual, physical, or cloud based. We consider two types of nodes here: cloud based and physical or virtual servers.

Cloud-based nodes refer to the nodes that are hosted on any of the cloud providers, such as AWS (Amazon Web Services), Microsoft Windows Azure, or any other cloud provider. We can provision these types of nodes using knife. Once the nodes are created chef can easily manage them.

A physical server can be a virtual machine or a server or any device that can send, receive, and forward information. In simpler terms, it is a device that can communicate with the chef server and has chef client installed and configured.

Node Names

The node_name is used as a part of the authentication process of the chef server.

The node name can be anything, but should be unique within a chef organization.

We can provide the node name in the client configuration file (client.rb). By default, chef uses Ohai to get the node name and it is the FQDN (fully qualified domain name) of the server.

Using the FQDN as the node name, and then allowing Ohai to collect this information during each chef run is the recommended approach and the easiest way to ensure that the names of all nodes across the chef organization are unique.

Manage Nodes

Nodes can be managed in chef using various approaches. They can be managed using knife or using the management console that chef provides.

- We can use knife to manage the nodes. Managing covers creating, editing, tagging, listing, and so on.

- We can use knife plug-ins to provision nodes.

- We can also manage nodes using the management console.

Chef Client

Chef client is an agent installed on the node, and with its help, the nodes communicate with the chef server. Whenever chef client is run on a node, it follows certain steps.

The Chef Run

Chef run basically defines the steps that take place whenever chef client is invoked. Figure 5-1 shows the various steps that occur during a typical chef run.

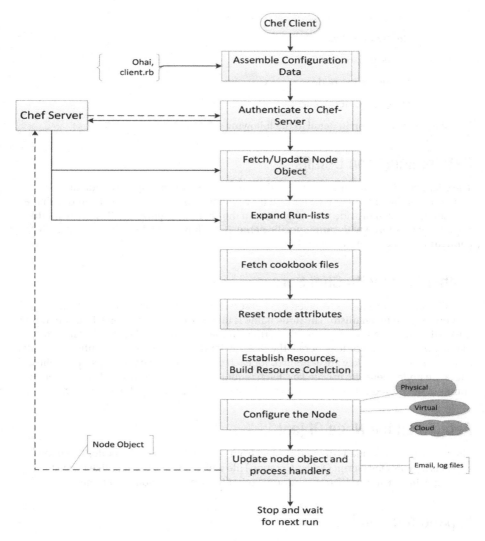

Figure 5-1. *Chef run*

We discuss each step in detail.

Whenever chef client is run, the following steps occur:

1. Get configuration details

2. Authenticate with chef server

3. Rebuild on the node object

4. Expand the run list

5. Download the cookbooks on the node

6. Reset node attributes

7. Identify resources

8. Configure the node

9. Update the node object

We cover each step in detail in the following sections.

Get Configuration Details

The client configuration file (Client.rb) is used to store the configuration details. The configuration includes the node name with which the node (client) is registered with the chef server. We can provide the node name in the client configuration file if we want the node to be registered with some specific name. If we don't provide anything in the client configuration file, then the node is registered with the FQDN.

Authenticate with Chef Server

To make sure that requests received by chef server are from a known source, it uses an RSA encryption mechanism. The node name is taken into consideration while generating the certificate. Whenever the chef client runs for the first time on the node, it takes the identity of chef validator to generate the RSA key for the node. When we configure a node, a public and a private key are generated for each node and the server keeps the public key while the node keeps the private key. Each request that comes from a node to the server comes in encrypted HTTP headers form which is decrypted using the public key.

Rebuild on the Node Object

The chef client downloads the node object from the chef server to the node. The node object is a JSON (JavaScript Object Notation) file which contains details like run list, node-specific attributes (if any), and some other information about that node.

Expand the Run List

The run list in the node object containing the details about every role/recipe that will be applied to the node is expanded and then placed in the order in which it will be applied to the node. The recipe that occurs first in the run list will be applied first, and so on.

Download the Cookbooks on the Node

In chef, the processing takes place at the client. So whenever the chef client runs, it downloads all the cookbooks in the run list of the node to the local cache of the node and then compiles them. If any file has changed, chef client downloads the new version of the file and deletes the previous version. The files include recipes, resources, libraries, and so on.

Reset Node Attributes

The next step in the chef run is to reset all the node attributes. The attributes are loaded from roles, environments, recipes, Ohai, and attribute files according to their precedence level and are updated on the node object. Chef has various types of precedence levels. Attributes are applied in chef in the following order, 1 being the lowest precedence and 16 the highest. Table 5-1 also describes the same thing in a different way, where 1 is the lowest precedence level and 15 is the highest.

Table 5-1. *Attribute precedence level*

	Attribute Files	Node/Recipe	Environment	Role
Default	1	2	3	4
Force_default	5	6		
Normal	7	8		
Override	9	10	11	12
Force_override	13	14		
Automatic			15	

Identify Resources

The next step is to identify the resources that would be required for successful compilation of the recipes. All the definitions and libraries are loaded so that the Ruby classes and the pseudo resources are available at the time of compilation. The recipe/recipes are loaded and the blocks within these recipes are evaluated. The recipes are evaluated in a top-down approach.

Configure the Node

The next step is to configure the node using the information that has been collected in the aforementioned steps. The resources that were identified in the previous steps are now mapped to a provider that will perform the desired action. The provider is responsible for completing the necessary action.

Update the Node Object

The final step is for the chef run to update the node object on the chef server. This action takes place when all the other actions have been completed. The chef client updates the node object that was built during the chef run on the chef server. This object would be used during the next chef run. Thus, the latest version information on a node is available in the chef server after every configuration of the node.

Install and Configure the Node

In order to configure a node properly, several steps are necessary. We demonstrate the configuration of a node on an Enterprise Linux-based operating system. The same steps can be used to configure it on any other operating system:

1. Identify the operating system

2. Install the chef client package

3. Copy the key files from the chef server

Identify the Operating System

This step mainly includes identifying the operating system (OS) which will help us in installing the relevant package on the system.

The OSs listed in Table 5-2 currently support chef client.

Table 5-2. *Operating Systems Supporting Chef Client*

Operating System	Version	Architecture
Debian	6	i686, x86_64
Enterprise Linux	5, 6	i686, x86_64
Mac OS X	10.6, 10.7	x86_64
openSUSE	12.1	i686, x86_64
Solaris	5.9	sparc
	5.10. 5.11	i386, sparc
SUSE Enterprise	11.2	i686, x86_64
Ubuntu	10.04, 10.10, 11.04, 11.10, 12.04, 12.10	i686, x86_64
Windows	2003 R2, 2008	i686, x86_64
	2008 R2, 2012	x86_64

Install the Chef Client Package

There are two options to install the chef client package:

1. We can directly use the script provided by chef, which will install the latest version available.

2. We can download the relevant version and install it using a suitable method.

Go to www.getchef.com/chef/install/.

Visit the chef client tab and select your OS and its architecture.

You can use any of the methods just described to install the chef client.

Figure 5-2 demonstrates installation using the second method. Select the chef version and download it to the machine on which we will configure the node.

Download options

| Chef Client | Chef Server |

Installing the Chef Client

Select the kind of system you would like to install the Chef Client on.
The versions listed have been tested and are supported.

| Enterprise Linux ▼ |

| 6 ▼ |

| x86_64 ▼ |

Quick Installation Instructions

Open a root shell on the target system and run the following client:

```
curl -L https://www.opscode.com/chef/install.sh | bash
```

Downloads

You can install manually by downloading the package below about manual installation, please read the documentation.

| Chef Version ▼ |

Figure 5-2. *Downloading the chef package*

After downloading the installer, run it using a relevant method based upon your OS. For Windows, double-click and install (see Figure 5-3). For Enterprise Linux, download the rpm and install it.

```
~]# rpm -ivh chef-11.8.2-1.el6.x86_64.rpm
warning: chef-11.8.2-1.el6.x86_64.rpm: Header V4 DSA/SHA1 Signature, key ID 83ef
826a: NOKEY
Preparing...                ########################################### [100%]
   1:chef                   ########################################### [100%]
Thank you for installing Chef!
~]# at@chef-testing
```

Figure 5-3. *Installing the chef package*

Verify the installation by typing chef-client –v at the command line. It should return something like what we see in Figure 5-4.

```
~]# chef-client -v
Chef: 11.8.2
~]# ▓t@chef-testing
```

Figure 5-4. *Verifying installation*

Copy the Key Files from the Chef Server

The node needs some keys and configuration files to connect and authenticate with the chef server. The following items are required:

- Client configuration file (Client.rb): You can create it using the knife configure command.

- Chef validator key: This is a private key that is generated by the chef server when we configure it for the first time. We need to manually copy this file to the workstation.

Bootstrap

Bootstrapping is a process whereby when a new node gets into the environment. It gets configured based on the policies and configuration required for that role.

As explained in earlier chapters, the chef server is the centralized location where all data is stored. The data stored includes the node object and the cookbooks that define the configuration and policies.

Thus, the client node uses the chef client to connect to the chef server and download the configuration details from the chef server. The chef client does the heavy lifting and processing to do the configuration changes required on the node. Thus, at the end of configuration, the chef node has the desired configuration based on the policies and role. The chef client only makes the required changes to the node and does not make any changes if nothing is required to be changed on the node.

The steps required to bootstrap a node are as follows:

1. Identify the FQDN or IP address for the node.

2. Run the knife bootstrap command.

3. Verify the node on the chef server.

The first step in bootstrapping is to identify the configured FQDN or IP address assigned to a node.

The knife bootstrap command requires the FQDN or the IP address of the node in order to complete the bootstrap operation.

After you identify the IP address and FQDN, the administrator has to run the knife bootstrap command.

knife bootstrap IP –x username –P password –sudo.

The command installs chef on the end client and runs chef client on the node.

The last step in this exercise is to verify that the client is now configured and available in the chef server for further management (see Figure 5-5). The following command is used to verify the installation of chef-client and its configuration in the chef-server.

```
~]# knife node show chef-testing
Node Name:    chef-testing
Environment:  _default
FQDN:
IP:           10.98.241.28
Run List:
Roles:
Recipes:      locale
Platform:     centos 6.0
Tags:
```

Figure 5-5. *Verifying bootstrapping*

knife client show name_of_node.

The chef server will return something as shown in Figure 5-5.

If something similar to what is shown in Figure 5-5 is returned, then chef has successfully been installed on your node.

Configuring

Chef client uses a configuration file (Client.rb) to store the configuration. This file is loaded every time we run chef client. If we are working on a Linux-based box, this file is normally stored at /etc/chef/client.rb and on a Windows-based server the location is c:/chef/client.rb.

Various settings can be done via this file. Table 5-3 discusses some of the important options available in the configuration file.

Table 5-3. *Configuration settings available*

Setting	Description
• chef_server_url	This is one of the important options of this file. It is used to specify the address of the chef server.
	chef_server_url "https://10.98.241.28"
client_key	Chef uses a key to authenticate itself to the chef server. Client key will be generated during the first chef client run. This option is used to specify the location of the key file. For example:
	client_key "/etc/chef/client.pem"
client_registration_retries	This option is used to specify the number the number of attempts that should be made by a chef client to register itself with the chef server. The default value is 5.
environment	This option is used if we want our node to be in a specific environment. For example,
	environment "testing."

(*continued*)

Table 5-3. (*continued*)

Setting	Description
http_proxy	This option is used if our environment is using a proxy for http connections. For example: http_proxy "http://yourproxy.com:8080"
http_proxy_pass	If our proxy is using a password for connection, then we need to specify this option. There is no default value for this option. For example: http_proxy_pass "1234567890."
http_proxy_user	If our proxy is using a username for connection, then we need to specify this option. There is no default value for this option. For example: http_proxy_user "my_username"
http_retry_count	The number of retry attempts. Default value: 5. For example: http_retry_count 5
http_retry_delay	The delay (in seconds) between retry attempts. Default value: 5. For example: http_retry_delay 5
https_proxy	This option is used if our environment is using a proxy for https connections. For example: https_proxy "http://yourproxy.com:8080"
interval	This option is used to specify the time after which chef client should run. For example: interval 3000
json_attribs	Use to override attributes that are set from other locations, such as from within a cookbook or by a role. The value must be entered as JSON data. For example: json_attribs nil
log_level	It is used to specify the level at which logging should be done. For example: log_level :debug

(*continued*)

Table 5-3. (*continued*)

Setting	Description
log_location	This option is used to specify the location of the log file. The default value is STDOUT. For example: log_location STDOUT
no_proxy	This option is used to specify the list of URLs that do not need a proxy. For example: no_proxy "test.com"
node_name	This option is used to specify the name with which the node would be registered with the chef server. If we do not supply this value, then the FQDN of the server is taken. For example: node_name "mynode.com"
node_path	The location in which to look for node-specific recipes. This has the default value of :/var/chef/node. For example: node_path "/var/chef/node"
rest_timeout	The time (in seconds) after which an HTTP REST request will time out. This has the default value: 300. For example: rest_timeout 300
splay	A number (in seconds) to add to the interval that is used to determine the frequency of chef client runs. This number can help prevent server load when there are many clients running at the same time. Default value: nil. For example: Splay
ssl_ca_file	The file in which the OpenSSL key is saved. This setting is generated automatically by chef and most users will not need to modify it. For example: ssl_ca_file nil
ssl_ca_path	The path to where the OpenSSL key is located. This setting is generated automatically by chef and most users will not need to modify it. For example: ssl_ca_path nil "/etc/ssl/certs"

(*continued*)

Table 5-3. (*continued*)

Setting	Description
ssl_client_cert	The OpenSSL X509 certificate. This setting is generated automatically by chef and most users will not need to modify it. For example: ssl_client_cert ""
ssl_client_key	The OpenSSL X509 key. This setting is generated automatically by chef and most users will not need to modify it. For example: ssl_client_key ""
umask	The file mode creation mask. This has the default value: 0022. For example: umask 0022
validation_client_name	This option is used to specify the name of the validation client. A validation client is created automatically when we install the chef server. This client is used to register any node on the chef server. For example: validation_client_name "chef-validator"
validation_key	This option is used to specify the location of the validation key. For example: validation_key "/etc/chef/validation.pem"

CHAPTER 6

■ ■ ■

Working with Knife

Knife is a command line utility that comes with chef and is used to interact with the chef server which is used to manage chef. Management in chef includes many tasks.

- Managing nodes

- Uploading cookbooks and recipes from the local chef repository to the chef server

- Managing roles

- Managing environments

- Managing cloud resources which include provisioning on AWS (Amazon Web Services), Azure, or any other cloud provider

- Bootstrapping chef on nodes

Along with the aforementioned tasks, chef can be used to perform many other tasks which we discuss in the upcoming sections of this chapter.

Working with Knife

Knife executes its functions from a workstation and is used to interact with the chef server and also with your infrastructure (see Figure 6-1). The interaction with the workstation and the chef server is done using the REST API (application programming interface) that is used by a chef client. The workstation configuration includes knife configuration, but if we want to change or modify anything, we can directly do it in the knife configuration file.

```
~]# knife -help
ERROR: You need to pass a sub-command (e.g., knife SUB-COMMAND)

Usage: knife sub-command (options)
    -s, --server-url URL            Chef Server URL
        --chef-zero-port PORT       Port to start chef-zero on
    -k, --key KEY                   API Client Key
        --[no-]color                Use colored output, defaults to false on Wi
ndows, true otherwise
    -c, --config CONFIG             The configuration file to use
        --defaults                  Accept default values for all questions
    -d, --disable-editing           Do not open EDITOR, just accept the data as
 is
    -e, --editor EDITOR             Set the editor to use for interactive comma
nds
    -E, --environment ENVIRONMENT   Set the Chef environment
    -F, --format FORMAT             Which format to use for output
    -z, --local-mode                Point knife commands at local repository in
stead of server
    -u, --user USER                 API Client Username
        --print-after               Show the data after a destructive operation
    -V, --verbose                   More verbose output. Use twice for max verb
osity
    -v, --version                   Show chef version
```

Figure 6-1. *List of options available with knife*

There are many subcommands available with knife that are used to manage chef (Figures 6-2 and 6-3). We discuss some of them in the following sections. Knife -help can be used to see options common to all subcommands.

```
Available subcommands: (for details, knife SUB-COMMAND --help)

** BOOTSTRAP COMMANDS **
knife bootstrap FQDN (options)

** CLIENT COMMANDS **
knife client bulk delete REGEX (options)
knife client create CLIENT (options)
knife client delete CLIENT (options)
knife client edit CLIENT (options)
knife client list (options)
knife client reregister CLIENT (options)
knife client show CLIENT (options)

** CONFIGURE COMMANDS **
knife configure (options)
knife configure client DIRECTORY

** COOKBOOK COMMANDS **
knife cookbook bulk delete REGEX (options)
knife cookbook create COOKBOOK (options)
knife cookbook delete COOKBOOK VERSION (options)
knife cookbook download COOKBOOK [VERSION] (options)
knife cookbook list (options)
```

Figure 6-2. *List of commands available with knife (1)*

```
** DATA BAG COMMANDS **
knife data bag create BAG [ITEM] (options)
knife data bag delete BAG [ITEM] (options)
knife data bag edit BAG ITEM (options)
knife data bag from file BAG FILE|FOLDER [FILE|FOLDER..] (options)
knife data bag list (options)
knife data bag show BAG [ITEM] (options)

** ENVIRONMENT COMMANDS **
knife environment create ENVIRONMENT (options)
knife environment delete ENVIRONMENT (options)
knife environment edit ENVIRONMENT (options)
knife environment from file FILE [FILE..] (options)
knife environment list (options)
knife environment show ENVIRONMENT (options)

** EXEC COMMANDS **
knife exec [SCRIPT] (options)

** HELP COMMANDS **
knife help [list|TOPIC]
```

Figure 6-3. *List of commands available with knife (2)*

You can use the knife subcommand –help to see the options available to that subcommand.

All the commands in knife are structured in a similar way. They have the form NOUN verb NOUN (options). Chef server uses RESTful API. The chef server API is RESTful. The options available for the verb part are

- Create (create)
- List and show (read)
- Edit (update)
- Delete (destroy)

```
knife sub-command [argument] [options]
```

Some of the knife commands require the environment variable EDITOR to edit or create some objects, so it's recommended to have it before using knife.

```
export EDITOR=vi
```

Bootstrap

A bootstrap is a process by which we install chef client on a target node. This command takes the IP (Internet provider) or the FQDN (fully qualified domain name) of the node as an input and installs the chef client package on it.

The syntax for this command is as follows:

```
knife bootstrap FQDN_or_IP_ADDRESS (options)
```

We will discuss some of the important options available in the bootstrap command.

```
--bootstrap-proxy PROXY_URL
```

This command requires Internet connectivity to be present on the node system. If the node is using proxy to connect to the Internet, then we need to specify this option.

```
--bootstrap-version VERSION
```

We use this option if we want to install a specific version of chef. By default, it installs the latest version.

```
-G GATEWAY, --ssh-gateway GATEWAY
```

The bootstrap command uses SSH to install chef. We use this option if our network has SSH, an SSH gateway configured, and direct SSH to our target node is blocked or not allowed.

```
-i IDENTITY_FILE, --identity-file IDENTITY_FILE
```

We adopt this option if we are using key-based authentication for SSH rather than a username and password.

```
-j JSON_ATTRIBS, --json-attributes JSON_ATTRIBS
```

We use this option if we want to specify some custom attributes on the first chef run.

```
-N NAME, --node-name NAME
```

We use this option to specify the node name by which it would be registered with the chef server. If we don't specify this option, the FQDN of the node would be used.

```
--[no-]host-key-verify
```

We use this option to skip the host key verifications. It is enabled by default.

```
-p PORT, --ssh-port PORT
```

We use this option to specify the port to be used for SSH. If we don't specify anything, Port 22 would be used.

`-P PASSWORD, --ssh-password PASSWORD`

We use this option to provide the password that would be used to log in to the instance.

`-r RUN_LIST, --run-list RUN_LIST`

We use this option to specify the list of recipes/roles or both to be applied to the node in a comma-separated format.

`--sudo`

If you use this option, then the bootstrap operation will be executed using sudo.

`-x USERNAME, --ssh-user USERNAME`

We use this option to specify the username that would be used by knife to log in to the instance.

Figure 6-4 shows the list of options available with the bootstrap subcommand.

```
~]# knife bootstrap -help
knife bootstrap FQDN (options)
        --bootstrap-no-proxy [NO_PROXY_URL|NO_PROXY_IP]
                                  Do not proxy locations for the node being b
ootstrapped
        --bootstrap-proxy PROXY_URL  The proxy server for the node being bootstr
apped
        --bootstrap-version VERSION  The version of Chef to install
    -N, --node-name NAME          The Chef node name for your new node
        --server-url URL          Chef Server URL
        --chef-zero-port PORT     Port to start chef-zero on
    -k, --key KEY                 API Client Key
        --[no-]color              Use colored output, defaults to false on Wi
ndows, true otherwise
    -c, --config CONFIG           The configuration file to use
        --defaults                Accept default values for all questions
        --disable-editing         Do not open EDITOR, just accept the data as
 is
    -d, --distro DISTRO           Bootstrap a distro using a template
    -e, --editor EDITOR           Set the editor to use for interactive comma
nds
    -E, --environment ENVIRONMENT  Set the Chef environment
    -j JSON_ATTRIBS,              A JSON string to be added to the first run
of chef-client
```

Figure 6-4. *List of options available with knife bootstrap subcommand*

Client

We use the client subcommand to manage the clients that are registered with the chef server. Many options are available, which we discuss here one by one.

The syntax for this command is as follows:

```
knife client (options)
```

Figure 6-5 shows the options available in knife client subcommand.

```
** CLIENT COMMANDS **
knife client bulk delete REGEX (options)
knife client create CLIENT (options)
knife client delete CLIENT (options)
knife client edit CLIENT (options)
knife client list (options)
knife client reregister CLIENT (options)
knife client show CLIENT (options)
```

Figure 6-5. *List of options available with knife client subcommand*

Bulk Delete

We use this option to delete any client registered with the chef server that matches a regular expression. Figure 6-6 shows an example.

```
~]# knife client bulk delete test
The following clients will be deleted:

chef-testing

Are you sure you want to delete these clients? (Y/N) ▌
```

Figure 6-6. *Deleting multiple clients*

Create

We use the create option to create a new client. Whenever we run this command, it generates a new RSA key pair for the client. The server will store the public key and the private would be displayed as an output. Figure 6-7 shows an example.

```
~]# knife client create test-client
{
  "name": "test-client",
  "public_key": null,
  "validator": false,
  "admin": false,
  "json_class": "Chef::ApiClient",
  "chef_type": "client"
}
```

***Figure 6-7.** Creating an API client*

The following details are required in order to create an API client:

Name – The name with which the client would be registered.

Public-key – A RSA key pair that would be auto-generated.

Validator – Whether the client would be a validator or not. A validator is a special type of client which is used to register new clients to the chef server.

Admin – Whether the client would have administration privileges or not. It can either be true or false.

Delete

This argument is passed if we want to delete only a single registered API client. We need to provide the name with which the client is registered. Figure 6-8 shows an example.

```
~]# knife client delete chef-testing
Do you really want to delete chef-testing? (Y/N)
```

***Figure 6-8.** Deleting a client*

The syntax for this command is as follows:

```
knife client delete client_name
```

Edit

We use this option if we want to edit the details of an already registered API client. We need to set the environment editor variable before using this option. Knife will use that editor to open the node object and we can edit the detail we want to. Knife then directly uploads the changes to the server. Figure 6-9 shows an example.

```
~]# knife client edit chef-testing

  "name": "chef-testing",
  "public_key": "-----BEGIN PUBLIC KEY-----\nMIIBIjANBgkqhkiG9w0BAQEFAAOCAQ8AMII
BCgKCAQEAtOXRTSB3fbb5oe1Me5je\nwA8CQdEXL+TOC/Exxmfp+QkwOukmfQqbQcvRWQm5YvONqYe51
ALMJM6ihmXsYJF2\nRlVrupfVlCVljnrA433c4pDB2oGToI5P4smjMJuA7oZdFF4FRorFVatY9+segyt
l\ndmXAQTrtT/cJnfw6KpbzXDywwW1WJtr7+UzPdMFS6qHwMJjFeY6a/EAHSQrs+Q4l\nCAGvOnTu+xU
XD19UXyGWroa+1eytm6ubCjTr8BMwDZ9r1U+eC4f45DzW7OkXyNhR\nnoCI3zKrAqI+r5vHuxTd7wHwUL
jGTfocONCDWs54AjMEmA4U4uKehFfMIvkOR7mGG\n2wIDAQAB\n-----END PUBLIC KEY-----\n",
  "validator": false,
  "admin": false,
  "json_class": "Chef::ApiClient",
  "chef_type": "client"
~
~
~
~
~
~
~
```

Figure 6-9. *Editing a client*

The syntax for this command is as follows:

`knife client edit client_name`

List

We use this option to view the list of clients registered with the chef server. Using his option will return a list of registered clients. Figure 6-10 shows an example.

```
~]# knife client list
1C659D33D4B8.HCLC.CORP.HCL.IN
DS-485B393A1E2C.HCLC.CORP.HCL.IN
LP-0022645A35FB.HCLC.CORP.HCL.IN
LP-2C27D7DC8BC6.HCLC.CORP.HCL.IN
RHEL6-manak
chef-testing
chef-validator
chef-webui
scom2012b.scvmm.local
  ~]# t@chef-testing
```

Figure 6-10. *List of registered clients*

The syntax for this command is as follows:

`knife client list`

Reregister

We normally use this option when we delete the client key from the client and we want a new key to be generated. It will regenerate the RSA key pair for the client. Figure 6-11 shows an example.

```
~]# knife client reregister chef-testing
-----BEGIN RSA PRIVATE KEY-----
MIIEogIBAAKCAQEAwgz/3plsZaB89cLODnOROBZdnRYGQFwFjDcGySUF85CkvPjX
NKkU4NsvfTIQeCbboxU9KHIWmECmxOdUnCVXsCdXhlCvMxs06mSy+cMQ09jbsoAJ
D1PrbD1XklWtYgDzYztbEn4CcH4WRY93k6CbKrJkce43X8wOzmhQGtmK/PQBw67F
Dr4+LYHGr4mDbzCrDRelQjDzuYFwqbFxS4QmMT8EvByjWtlLEN2UA+T4ZeI0CfFS
e2ijHEnHfmonjBuOZ/Ni+N4kwCskHKe9zKbfVy3lRpYLCrIFxf7ZpNORJwrm/Agv
t6nxKMJpipoGxDXaAlJHyInhR0yomat1zHHutQIDAQABAoIBACrteUUjJ6mrwTkU
6USlKFgD2p2/m45tTQThv2yL9i8Vlnv/iIwrw2Si2HSXuLD716bSMf9ajckMtFfm
3P7V+/oKGgCqpLdnk2Mu97DtCDH1TVTFojtz0ybUwySqM3r0vuL65IDIw31jR0YI
IOnVo73kTPgvPKzClZvv05i8+1RNuzH+wM0M95maggMKf+TxNbB1+2+MsaacLil1
QvuYmhbnzzZPmURw1dRUlF15rqgT8wBPyDJ7WXjc1TPtoCX1646g8NRzchycg9M+
hypATFeyL/TD0Rzuhpzk9sxlWZUGIRE0DfjOAbMstwV5TkI45QTfKPl9jWuLF6Sd
YZpzr8ECgYEA+rtbSrCO2d2Qc4XP+Yk2OPfzVG4vfta6pwSAMOC+j2rhpIATaDQz
pWYbZZRp8xuW2FOF3xA31qrSMCnRQrZo4yTk9cjprjs/d6lVTDaEFMFWYpo9K/nW
IP/o5zyPmI/B4xhFzKw/ukzEm0WX8uE0syan1fuPCd10qFZ27DkMzu0CgYEAxiDD
301hEaEYWt6itWGY7d5Ej3NGZ+/8xU7SPvQ52io8602//qfB9xVVJqpHkGatVsOL
DIpz3O6DUIuajWbOk5dPRlnwmoor54Bz/GWWQvmZFEvet9pNpulojft1YK0LY3bl
5KvsRXv/1Tkr91xBr6NVud4ZMkuj49/PZAnj3ekCgYAhBzciYpmet2IE5bacv2dm
H7ts/srA4ZZa0+vzBFf12nV4zuo/isjW2912CxPd01+OhYoX9TH11DC16XxIVnEA
ouaKPfoSWnmkOKiMzo2dkk5H1NuEBHghhrRuaXrc9OrseFERggsvBXyaG5PFiccA
ZnIrbOTNvt9UIXeu7GD0jQKBgFhgKx7DFEZZ1lRKNMe1ZhLMb0aRg9k+6kBUnWGp
```

Figure 6-11. *Reregistering a client*

The syntax for this command is as follows:

```
knife client reregister client_name
```

Show

This option will display the information available about a client. Figure 6-12 shows what this information will look like.

```
~]# knife client show chef-testing
admin:          false
chef_type:      client
json_class:     Chef::ApiClient
name:           chef-testing
public_key:     -----BEGIN PUBLIC KEY-----
MIIBIjANBgkqhkiG9w0BAQEFAAOCAQ8AMIIBCgKCAQEAtOXRTSB3fbb5oe1Me5je
wA8CQdEXL+T0C/Exxmfp+QkwOukmfQqbQcvRWQm5Yv0NqYe5lALMJM6ihmXsYJF2
RlVrupfVlCVljnrA433c4pDB2oGToI5P4smjMJuA7oZdFF4FRorFVatY9+segyt1
dmXAQTrtT/cJnfw6KpbzXDywwW1WJtr7+UzPdMFS6qHwMJjFeY6a/EAHSQrs+Q4l
cAGvOnTu+xUXD19UXyGWroa+1eytm6ubCjTr8BMwDZ9r1U+eC4f45DzW7OkXyNhR
oCI3zKrAqI+r5vHuxTd7wHwULjGTfocONCDWs54AjMEmA4U4uKehFfMIvkOR7mGG
2wIDAQAB
-----END PUBLIC KEY-----

validator:      false
 ~]# @t@chef-testing
```

Figure 6-12. *Viewing a client*

The syntax for this command is as follows:

`knife client show client_name`

Configure

We can use the configure command to configure a workstation and client. We have already covered these things in previous chapters. We can create the knife configuration file (`Knife.rb`) and client configuration file (`Client.rb`) using this command. Figures 6-13 and 6-14 show how to use the command and the options available with the command.

```
~]# knife configure
WARNING: No knife configuration file found
Where should I put the config file? [/root/.chef/knife.rb]
Please enter the chef server URL: [https://localhost:443] https://chef-server:44
3
Please enter an existing username or clientname for the API: [root] admin
Please enter the validation clientname: [chef-validator]
Please enter the location of the validation key: [/etc/chef-server/chef-validato
r.pem]
Please enter the path to a chef repository (or leave blank):
*****

You must place your client key in:
  /root/.chef/admin.pem
Before running commands with Knife!

*****

You must place your validation key in:
  /etc/chef-server/chef-validator.pem
Before generating instance data with Knife!

*****
Configuration file written to /root/.chef/knife.rb
```

Figure 6-13. *Configuring a client*

```
~]# knife configure -help
knife configure (options)
        --admin-client-key PATH         The path to the admin client's private key
(usually a file named admin.pem)
        --admin-client-name NAME        The existing admin clientname (usually admi
n)
    -s, --server-url URL                Chef Server URL
        --chef-zero-port PORT           Port to start chef-zero on
    -k, --key KEY                       API Client Key
        --[no-]color                    Use colored output, defaults to false on Wi
ndows, true otherwise
    -c, --config CONFIG                 The configuration file to use
        --defaults                      Accept default values for all questions
    -d, --disable-editing               Do not open EDITOR, just accept the data as
 is
    -e, --editor EDITOR                 Set the editor to use for interactive comma
nds
    -E, --environment ENVIRONMENT       Set the Chef environment
    -F, --format FORMAT                 Which format to use for output
    -i, --initial                       Create an initial API User
    -z, --local-mode                    Point knife commands at local repository in
stead of server
    -u, --user USER                     API Client Username
        --print-after                   Show the data after a destructive operation
```

Figure 6-14. *Listing of options available with knife configure*

The syntax for this command is as follows:

knife configure (options)

The following options are available in this command.

--client DIRECTORY

We use this option to specify the client directory where the client configuration file would be placed. It reads from the knife configuration file and writes relevant information to the client configuration file.

-i, --initial

We use this option to create an API client that would be used by knife for authorization.

-r REPO, --repository REPO

We use this option to provide the path of the local chef repository.

Cookbook

We use the cookbook subcommand to interact with cookbooks that are located on the chef server or on the local chef repository (see Figure 6-15).

```
~]# knife cookbook -help
FATAL: Cannot find sub command for: 'cookbook -help'
Available cookbook subcommands: (for details, knife SUB-COMMAND --help)

** COOKBOOK COMMANDS **
knife cookbook bulk delete REGEX (options)
knife cookbook create COOKBOOK (options)
knife cookbook delete COOKBOOK VERSION (options)
knife cookbook download COOKBOOK [VERSION] (options)
knife cookbook list (options)
knife cookbook metadata COOKBOOK (options)
knife cookbook metadata from FILE (options)
knife cookbook show COOKBOOK [VERSION] [PART] [FILENAME] (options)
knife cookbook test [COOKBOOKS...] (options)
knife cookbook upload [COOKBOOKS...] (options)
```

Figure 6-15. *Listing of options available with the knife cookbook subcommand*

The syntax for this command is as follows:

```
knife cookbook [Argument] (options)
```

We discuss the arguments available in this subcommand one by one in the following sections.

Bulk Delete

We use this argument if we want to delete cookbooks that match certain patterns. The Regex should be written within quotes.

The syntax for this argument is as follows:

```
knife cookbook bulk delete "REGEX"
```

Create

We use this argument to create a cookbook in the local repository (see Figure 6-16). It will create a list of directories and files necessary for a cookbook. We can then upload the cookbook to the chef server.

```
~]# knife cookbook create test
** Creating cookbook test
** Creating README for cookbook: test
** Creating CHANGELOG for cookbook: test
** Creating metadata for cookbook: test
~]#
```

Figure 6-16. *Creating a cookbook*

The syntax for this command is as follows:

```
knife cookbook create COOKBOOK_NAME (options)
```

Delete

We use this subcommand if we want to delete a cookbook or any version of a cookbook from the chef server (see Figure 6-17).

```
~]# knife cookbook delete test
Do you really want to delete test version 0.1.0? (Y/N) ▊
```

Figure 6-17. *Deleting a cookbook*

The syntax for this command is as follows:

```
knife cookbook delete cookbook_name
```

Download

We use this subcommand to download a cookbook from the chef server (see Figure 6-18).

```
~]# knife cookbook download test
Downloading test cookbook version 0.1.0
Downloading resources
Downloading providers
Downloading recipes
```

Figure 6-18. *Downloading a cookbook*

The syntax for this command is as follows:

```
knife cookbook download COOKBOOK_NAME [COOKBOOK_VERSION] (options)
```

List

We use this argument to list the cookbooks that are present on the chef server. It will list the latest versions of the cookbooks that are available (see Figure 6-19).

73

```
~]# knife cookbook list
123                          0.1.0
Adobe                        9.3.1
activemq                     5.5.0
ad_rodc                      0.1.0
ant                          0.1.0
apache2                      1.5.0
apache2-1.5.0                1.5.0
build-essential              1.3.4
check_free_port              0.0.0
chef_handler                 1.1.4
copy_a_file                  0.0.0
couchdb                      0.1.0
dire                         0.1.0
dotnet                       0.1.0
drbd-master                  0.8.0
file_copy                    0.1.0
file copy1                   0.1.0
```

Figure 6-19. *Listing cookbooks*

The syntax is as follows:

```
knife cookbook list
```

Show

We used this argument to view the information about a cookbook or any file associated with the cookbook present on the chef server (see Figure 6-20).

```
~]# knife cookbook show test
test    0.1.0
```

Figure 6-20. *Viewing a version*

The syntax for this argument is as follows:

```
knife cookbook show COOKBOOK_NAME [COOKBOOK_VERSION] [PART...] [FILE_NAME]
(options)
```

Test

We use this argument if we want to check a cookbook for syntax errors. This argument verifies every file present in the cookbook directory ending with a `.rb` or a `.erb` extension.

Figure 6-21 shows the syntax for this argument.

```
~]# knife cookbook test test
checking test
Running syntax check on test
Validating ruby files
Validating templates
```

Figure 6-21. *Testing a cookbook*

Upload

We require the upload argument if we want to upload any cookbook or associated files from the local repository to the chef server (see Figure 6-22).

```
~]# knife cookbook upload test
Uploading test              [0.1.0]
Uploaded 1 cookbook.
~]# t@chef-testing
```

Figure 6-22. *Uploading a cookbook*

The syntax for the upload argument is as follows:

```
knife cookbook upload [COOKBOOK_NAME...] (options)
```

Cookbook Site

We use this subcommand if we want to directly use the cookbooks that Opscode provides.

The syntax for this command is as follows:

```
knife cookbook site [argument] (options)
```

The following arguments are available in this subcommand:

- Download
- Install
- List
- Search

- Share

- Show

- UnShare

Download

We use this argument if we want to download any cookbook available on the chef server.
This argument has the following syntax:

```
knife cookbook site download COOKBOOK_NAME [COOKBOOK_VERSION] (options)
```

It will download the cookbook in the directory we are working as a tar file. Extract the file and upload it to the chef server for further use.

Install

We use this argument if we want to install any cookbook to a local git repository.
Using this argument does the following:

- Creates a new branch for tracking the upstream.

- Removes all the previous versions of cookbook from the branch (if any).

- Downloads the cookbook from https://cookbooks.opscode.com in the tar.gz format.

- Untars the downloaded cookbook and commits its contents to git and creates a tag.

- Merges the newly created branch into the master branch.

This process allows the upstream cookbook in the master branch to be modified while letting git maintain changes as a separate patch. When an updated upstream version becomes available, those changes can be merged while maintaining any local modifications.
This argument has the following syntax:

```
knife cookbook site install COOKBOOK_NAME [COOKBOOK_VERSION] (options)
```

List

It is used to view the list of cookbooks that are available in the community.
This argument has the following syntax:

```
knife cookbook site list
```

Search

This is used in case we want to search any cookbook available. It will return a list of cookbooks that match the search criteria.

The syntax for this argument is as follows:

```
knife cookbook site search SEARCH_QUERY (options)
```

Show

It can be used to view any information about any cookbook that Opscode provides.

The syntax for this argument is as follows:

```
knife cookbook site show COOKBOOK_NAME [COOKBOOK_VERSION]
```

Data Bag

Data bags are objects that are stored as a global variable and can be accessed from the chef server. This subcommand allows us to create or edit a data bag or any data bag item (see Figure 6-23).

```
~]# knife data bag -help
FATAL: Cannot find sub command for: 'data bag -help'
Available data bag subcommands: (for details, knife SUB-COMMAND --help)

** DATA BAG COMMANDS **
knife data bag create BAG [ITEM] (options)
knife data bag delete BAG [ITEM] (options)
knife data bag edit BAG ITEM (options)
knife data bag from file BAG FILE|FOLDER [FILE|FOLDER..] (options)
knife data bag list (options)
knife data bag show BAG [ITEM] (options)
```

Figure 6-23. *List of options available with knife data bag subcommand*

The syntax for this command is as follows:

```
knife data bag [Argument] (options)
```

Delete

This command is used in case we want to delete any object from the chef server. It can be any node, any cookbook, or anything else (see Figure 6-24).

```
~]# knife delete -help
knife delete [PATTERN1 ... PATTERNn]
        --both                          Delete both the local and remote copies.
        --chef-repo-path PATH           Overrides the location of chef repo. Defaul
t is specified by chef_repo_path in the config
    -s, --server-url URL                Chef Server URL
        --chef-zero-port PORT           Port to start chef-zero on
    -k, --key KEY                       API Client Key
        --[no-]color                    Use colored output, defaults to false on Wi
ndows, true otherwise
        --concurrency THREADS           Maximum number of simultaneous requests to
send (default: 10)
    -c, --config CONFIG                 The configuration file to use
        --defaults                      Accept default values for all questions
    -d, --disable-editing               Do not open EDITOR, just accept the data as
 is
    -e, --editor EDITOR                 Set the editor to use for interactive comma
nds
    -E, --environment ENVIRONMENT       Set the Chef environment
    -F, --format FORMAT                 Which format to use for output
        --local                         Delete the local copy (leave the remote cop
y).
    -z, --local-mode                    Point knife commands at local repository in
stead of server
```

Figure 6-24. *List of options available with knife delete subcommand*

The syntax for this command is as follows:

knife delete [pattern...] (options)

This subcommand has the following options:

Download

The download subcommand can be used to download any data that exists on the chef server (see Figure 6-25). This data can include cookbooks, nodes, roles, and environments.

```
~]# knife download -help
knife download PATTERNS
        --chef-repo-path PATH        Overrides the location of chef repo. Defaul
t is specified by chef_repo_path in the config
    -s, --server-url URL             Chef Server URL
        --chef-zero-port PORT        Port to start chef-zero on
    -k, --key KEY                    API Client Key
        --[no-]color                 Use colored output, defaults to false on Wi
ndows, true otherwise
        --concurrency THREADS        Maximum number of simultaneous requests to
send (default: 10)
    -c, --config CONFIG              The configuration file to use
        --cookbook-version VERSION   Version of cookbook to download (if there a
re multiple versions and cookbook_versions is false)
        --defaults                   Accept default values for all questions
        --[no-]diff                  Turn off to avoid uploading existing files;
 only new (and possibly deleted) files with --no-diff
    -d, --disable-editing            Do not open EDITOR, just accept the data as
 is
    -n, --dry-run                    Don't take action, only print what would ha
ppen
    -e, --editor EDITOR              Set the editor to use for interactive comma
nds
    -E, --environment ENVIRONMENT    Set the Chef environment
```

Figure 6-25. *List of options available with the knife download subcommand*

The syntax for this command is as follows:

```
knife download [PATTERN...] (options)
```

Environment

Environments in chef are a way to group nodes in chef. We can have environment-specific attributes. The environment subcommand can be used to manage the environments that already exist on the chef server or can be used to create new servers also (see Figure 6-26).

```
~]# knife environment -help
FATAL: Cannot find sub command for: 'environment -help'
Available environment subcommands: (for details, knife SUB-COMMAND --help)

** ENVIRONMENT COMMANDS **
knife environment create ENVIRONMENT (options)
knife environment delete ENVIRONMENT (options)
knife environment edit ENVIRONMENT (options)
knife environment from file FILE [FILE..] (options)
knife environment list (options)
knife environment show ENVIRONMENT (options)
```

Figure 6-26. *List of options available with knife environment subcommands*

The syntax for this command is as follows:

```
knife environment [Argument] (options)
```

Node

Any server registered with the chef server can be referred to as a node. The node subcommand of knife can be used to manage the nodes that are registered with the chef server (see Figure 6-27). It can also be used to create a new node.

```
~]# knife node -help
FATAL: Cannot find sub command for: 'node -help'
Available node subcommands: (for details, knife SUB-COMMAND --help)

** NODE COMMANDS **
knife node bulk delete REGEX (options)
knife node create NODE (options)
knife node delete NODE (options)
knife node edit NODE (options)
knife node from file FILE (options)
knife node list (options)
knife node run_list add [NODE] [ENTRY[,ENTRY]] (options)
knife node run_list remove [NODE] [ENTRIES] (options)
knife node run_list set NODE ENTRIES (options)
knife node show NODE (options)
knife node status [<node> <node> ...]
```

Figure 6-27. *List of options available with knife node subcommand*

The syntax for this command is as follows:

```
knife node [argument] (options)
```

Recipe List

This subcommand is used to view the recipes that are present on the chef server (see Figure 6-28). By default, it will return all the recipes present and we can reduce the count by providing a Regex in the search query.

```
~]# knife recipe list -help
knife recipe list [PATTERN]
        -s, --server-url URL                Chef Server URL
            --chef-zero-port PORT           Port to start chef-zero on
        -k, --key KEY                       API Client Key
            --[no-]color                    Use colored output, defaults to false on Wi
ndows, true otherwise
        -c, --config CONFIG                 The configuration file to use
            --defaults                      Accept default values for all questions
        -d, --disable-editing               Do not open EDITOR, just accept the data as
 is
        -e, --editor EDITOR                 Set the editor to use for interactive comma
nds
        -E, --environment ENVIRONMENT       Set the Chef environment
        -F, --format FORMAT                 Which format to use for output
        -z, --local-mode                    Point knife commands at local repository in
stead of server
        -u, --user USER                     API Client Username
            --print-after                   Show the data after a destructive operation
        -V, --verbose                       More verbose output. Use twice for max verb
osity
        -v, --version                       Show chef version
        -y, --yes                           Say yes to all prompts for confirmation
        -h, --help                          Show this message
```

Figure 6-28. *List of options available with knife recipe subcommands*

The syntax for this command is as follows:

```
knife recipe list REGEX
```

Role

Roles are a way to define certain process or patterns. A role is a collection of run list and some attributes. For example, a MySQL server role can consist of a MySQL server recipe and any custom attributes.

We use the knife subcommand to manage the roles that exist on the chef server (see Figure 6-29).

```
~]# knife role -help
FATAL: Cannot find sub command for: 'role -help'
Available role subcommands: (for details, knife SUB-COMMAND --help)

** ROLE COMMANDS **
knife role bulk delete REGEX (options)
knife role create ROLE (options)
knife role delete ROLE (options)
knife role edit ROLE (options)
knife role from file FILE [FILE..] (options)
knife role list (options)
knife role show ROLE (options)
```

Figure 6-29. *List of options available with the knife role subcommand*

Usage is as follows:
The syntax for this command is as follows:

```
Knife role [Argument] (options)
```

Search

We use the search command to search the information that is indexed on the chef server (see Figure 6-30). Searches can be employed using the management console.

```
knife search INDEX QUERY (options)
    -a ATTR1 [--attribute ATTR2] ,   Show one or more attributes
        --attribute
    -s, --server-url URL             Chef Server URL
        --chef-zero-port PORT        Port to start chef-zero on
    -k, --key KEY                    API Client Key
        --[no-]color                 Use colored output, defaults to false on Wi
ndows, true otherwise
    -c, --config CONFIG              The configuration file to use
        --defaults                   Accept default values for all questions
    -d, --disable-editing            Do not open EDITOR, just accept the data as
 is
    -e, --editor EDITOR              Set the editor to use for interactive comma
nds
    -E, --environment ENVIRONMENT    Set the Chef environment
    -F, --format FORMAT              Which format to use for output
    -i, --id-only                    Show only the ID of matching objects
    -z, --local-mode                 Point knife commands at local repository in
stead of server
    -l, --long                       Include all attributes in the output
    -m, --medium                     Include normal attributes in the output
    -u, --user USER                  API Client Username
        --print-after               Show the data after a destructive operation
    -q, --query QUERY               The search query; useful to protect queries
```

Figure 6-30. *List of options available with knife search subcommand*

Show

We use the show command if we want to view anything that is stored on the chef server (see Figure 6-31).

```
knife show [PATTERN1 ... PATTERNn]
            --chef-repo-path PATH             Overrides the location of chef repo. Defaul
t is specified by chef_repo_path in the config
     -s, --server-url URL                     Chef Server URL
            --chef-zero-port PORT             Port to start chef-zero on
     -k, --key KEY                            API Client Key
            --[no-]color                      Use colored output, defaults to false on Wi
ndows, true otherwise
            --concurrency THREADS             Maximum number of simultaneous requests to
send (default: 10)
     -c, --config CONFIG                      The configuration file to use
            --defaults                        Accept default values for all questions
     -d, --disable-editing                    Do not open EDITOR, just accept the data as
 is
     -e, --editor EDITOR                      Set the editor to use for interactive comma
nds
     -E, --environment ENVIRONMENT            Set the Chef environment
     -F, --format FORMAT                      Which format to use for output
            --local                           Show local files instead of remote
     -z, --local-mode                         Point knife commands at local repository in
stead of server
     -u, --user USER                          API Client Username
            --print-after                     Show the data after a destructive operation
            --repo-mode MODE                  Specifies the local repository layout.  Val
```

Figure 6-31. *List of options available with knife show subcommand*

The syntax for this command is as follows:

```
knife show [PATTERN...] (options)
e.g. - knife show roles,
Knife show cookbooks
```

SSH

We use this command if we want to invoke parallel SSH commands on a number of nodes, based upon a search query (see Figure 6-32).

```
knife ssh QUERY COMMAND (options)
    -a, --attribute ATTR              The attribute to use for opening the connec
tion - default depends on the context
    -s, --server-url URL              Chef Server URL
        --chef-zero-port PORT         Port to start chef-zero on
    -k, --key KEY                     API Client Key
        --[no-]color                  Use colored output, defaults to false on Wi
ndows, true otherwise
    -C, --concurrency NUM             The number of concurrent connections
    -c, --config CONFIG               The configuration file to use
        --defaults                    Accept default values for all questions
    -d, --disable-editing             Do not open EDITOR, just accept the data as
 is
    -e, --editor EDITOR               Set the editor to use for interactive comma
nds
    -E, --environment ENVIRONMENT     Set the Chef environment
    -F, --format FORMAT               Which format to use for output
    -A, --forward-agent               Enable SSH agent forwarding
        --[no-]host-key-verify        Verify host key, enabled by default.
    -i IDENTITY_FILE,                 The SSH identity file used for authenticati
on
        --identity-file
    -z, --local-mode                  Point knife commands at local repository in
stead of server
```

Figure 6-32. *List of options available with the knife SSH subcommand*

The syntax for this command is as follows:

```
knife ssh Search_Query SSH_Command (options)
```

Following are the options available with the subcommand:

```
-a SSH_ATTR, --attribute SSH_ATTR
```

We us this option to specify the attributes that would be used for opening SSH connections.

```
-C NUM, --concurrency NUM
```

This option is used to specify the maximum number of concurrent connections.

```
-G GATEWAY, --ssh-gateway GATEWAY
```

We use this option if our network has an SSH gateway configured.

```
-i IDENTITY_FILE, --identity-file IDENTIFY_FILE
```

We use this option if we are using key-based authentication.

```
-p PORT, --ssh-port PORT
```

We use this option to specify the port that would be used for SSH. By default, a 22 port is used.

```
-P PASSWORD, --ssh-password PASSWORD
```

We use this option to pass the password that would be used for SSH into the node.

```
-x USER_NAME, --ssh-user USER_NAME
```

We use this option to pass the username that would be used for SSH.

Tag

We use this subcommand if we want to add a custom description to our nodes on the chef server, to group them based on the custom description (see Figure 6-33).

```
~]# knife recipe list -help
knife recipe list [PATTERN]
     -s, --server-url URL          Chef Server URL
         --chef-zero-port PORT     Port to start chef-zero on
     -k, --key KEY                 API Client Key
         --[no-]color              Use colored output, defaults to false on Wi
ndows, true otherwise
     -c, --config CONFIG           The configuration file to use
         --defaults                Accept default values for all questions
     -d, --disable-editing         Do not open EDITOR, just accept the data as
 is
     -e, --editor EDITOR           Set the editor to use for interactive comma
nds
     -E, --environment ENVIRONMENT Set the Chef environment
     -F, --format FORMAT           Which format to use for output
     -z, --local-mode              Point knife commands at local repository in
stead of server
     -u, --user USER               API Client Username
         --print-after            Show the data after a destructive operation
     -V, --verbose                 More verbose output. Use twice for max verb
osity
     -v, --version                 Show chef version
     -y, --yes                     Say yes to all prompts for confirmation
     -h, --help                    Show this message
```

Figure 6-33. *List of options available with knife tag subcommands*

The syntax for this command is as follows:

```
knife tag [arguments]
```

- create—knife tag create NODE_NAME
- delete—knife tag delete NODE_NAME
- list—knife tag list NODE_NAME

Upload

This subcommand is used to upload anything from the local chef repository to the chef server (see Figure 6-34).

```
knife upload PATTERNS
        --chef-repo-path PATH           Overrides the location of chef repo. Defaul
t is specified by chef_repo_path in the config
    -s, --server-url URL                Chef Server URL
        --chef-zero-port PORT           Port to start chef-zero on
    -k, --key KEY                       API Client Key
        --[no-]color                    Use colored output, defaults to false on Wi
ndows, true otherwise
        --concurrency THREADS           Maximum number of simultaneous requests to
send (default: 10)
    -c, --config CONFIG                 The configuration file to use
        --defaults                      Accept default values for all questions
        --[no-]diff                     Turn off to avoid uploading existing files;
 only new (and possibly deleted) files with --no-diff
    -d, --disable-editing               Do not open EDITOR, just accept the data as
 is
    -n, --dry-run                       Don't take action, only print what would ha
ppen
    -e, --editor EDITOR                 Set the editor to use for interactive comma
nds
    -E, --environment ENVIRONMENT       Set the Chef environment
        --[no-]force                    Force upload of files even if they match (q
uicker for many files).  Will overwrite frozen cookbooks.
    -F, --format FORMAT                 Which format to use for output
```

Figure 6-34. *List of options available with knife upload subcommands*

The syntax for this command is as follows:

```
knife upload [Pattern..] (options)
```

■ ■ ■

## CHAPTER 7

Cookbooks

This chapter covers different aspects related to cookbooks.

Cookbooks are the fundamental unit of configuration in chef. Cookbooks determine what gets deployed on the client.

Basics of Cookbooks

A cookbook is the basic unit of configuration and policy definition in chef. It defines a complete scenario for the deployment and configuration of an application.

As an example, a cookbook for Apache or Tomcat would provide all details to install and configure a fully configured Apache or Tomcat server.

A complete cookbook is one that contains all the components required to support the installation and configuration of an application or component.

- It defines the files that need to be distributed for that component onto the client.

- It defines the attribute values that should be present on the nodes.

- It provides definitions for reusability of code.

- It provides libraries which can be used to extend the functionality of chef.

- It provides recipes that specify the resources and the order of execution of code on the client.

- It provides templates for file configurations.

- It provides metadata which can be used specify any kind of dependency, version constraints, and so on.

We use Ruby as the reference library in chef. For writing specific resources we can use extended DSL (Domain Specific Language).

Let's discuss the structure and content of a cookbook in detail.

Cookbook Directory Structure

Figure 7-1 shows the typical directory structure of any cookbook.

```
drwxr-xr-x 2 root root 4096 Dec 17 14:28 attributes
-rw-r--r-- 1 root root  425 Dec 17 14:28 CHANGELOG.md
drwxr-xr-x 2 root root 4096 Dec 17 14:28 definitions
drwxr-xr-x 3 root root 4096 Dec 17 14:28 files
drwxr-xr-x 2 root root 4096 Dec 17 14:28 libraries
-rw-r--r-- 1 root root  254 Dec 17 14:28 metadata.rb
drwxr-xr-x 2 root root 4096 Dec 17 14:28 providers
-rw-r--r-- 1 root root   88 Dec 17 14:28 README.md
drwxr-xr-x 2 root root 4096 Dec 17 14:28 recipes
drwxr-xr-x 2 root root 4096 Dec 17 14:28 resources
drwxr-xr-x 3 root root 4096 Dec 17 14:28 templates
```

Figure 7-1. *Directory structure of a cookbook*

The following sections cover all aspects related to the cookbook.
Figure 7-2 shows the working of a cookbook.

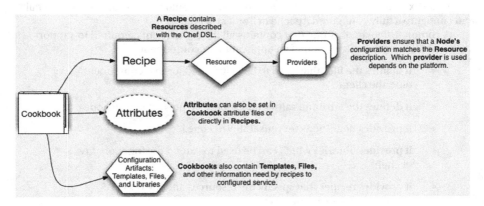

Figure 7-2. *Working of a cookbook*

Recipes

Recipes are the configuration units in chef that are actually deployed on the client and are used to configure the system. They are written in Ruby DSL. Recipes are normally a collection of resources with a bit of Ruby code.

A recipe

- Helps in configuring the nodes.

- Is stored in a cookbook.

- Can be used in any other recipe.

- Is authored in Ruby.

- Is executed in a top-down approach.

Working with Recipes

In this section we discuss the various approaches that are useful while creating recipes.

Using Data Bags in a Recipe

- Data bags are a global JSON (JavaScript Object Notification) variable that can store any kind of data but are normally used to store passwords. We can access data bags from the chef server. Chef also indexes them so that they can be easily accessed.

- The content of a data bag can be used within a recipe. Figure 7-3 shows what the data inside a data bag looks like.

```
{
    "id":    "my_application"
    "repository":   "git://github.com/test/my_application.git"
}
```

Figure 7-3. *Contents of a data bag*

We can access the created data bag in the recipe using the following syntax:

```
item = data_bag_item("application", "my_application")
```

where application is the name of the data bag and my_application is the object name. We can use a Ruby hash to access data bag items.

```
item["repository"]  #=> "git://github.com/test/my_application.git"
```

We can also create a data bag using knife as shown in Figure 7-4.

```
~]# knife data bag create test
Created data_bag[test]
~]# ⬛t@chef-testing
```

Figure 7-4. *Creating a databag*

Encrypting Data Bag items

Any item created in a data bag is not encrypted by default, but for creating any sort of secured environment we should encrypt our data bag items. We can achieve the same by creating a secret key. Here we use open SSL to create a secret key.

```
openssl rand -base64 512 | tr -d '\r\n' > Secret_key
```

The foregoing command will create a secret key named Secret_key by generating a random number.

Store Keys on Nodes

We can store the encryption key in a file and copy the file to the node that requires it (see Figure 7-5). We need to pass the location of the file inside an attribute.

```
# inside your attribute file:
# default[:sql][:secretpath] = "C:\\chef\\any_secret_filename"
#
# inside your recipe:
# look for secret in file pointed to by sql attribute :secretpath
sql_secret = Chef::EncryptedDataBagItem.load_secret("#{node[:sql][:secretpath]}"
)
sql_creds = Chef::EncryptedDataBagItem.load("passwords", "sql", sql_secret)
sql_creds["pass"] # will be decrypted
⬛
```

Figure 7-5. *Storing keys*

The `EncryptedDataBagItem.load` method expects the secret key as the third argument; we can use `EncryptedDataBagItem.load_secret` to use the secret file contents and then pass them.

Using Search Results in a Recipe

Chef server maintains an index of your data (environments, nodes, roles). Search index easily allows you to query the data that is indexed and then use it within a recipe.

There is a specified query syntax that supports range, wildcard, exact, and fuzzy.

Search can be done from various places in chef; it can be within a recipe, it can be from the management console.

The search engine in a chef installation is based on Apache Solr.

We can use the result of a search query in a recipe. The following code shows an example of using a simple search query in a recipe:

```
search(:node, "attribute:value")
```

The result of a search query can be stored in variable and then can be used anywhere within a recipe.

The search query in Figure 7-6 will return the servers with the role dbserver and then will render the template for all those servers.

```
dbservers = search(:node, "role:dbserver")

template "/tmp/list_of_dbservers" do
        source "list_of_dbservers.erb"
        variables(:dbservers => dbservers)
end
```

Figure 7-6. *Searching in a recipe*

Use Ruby in Recipes

Recipes are written in Ruby, so anything that can be done within Ruby can be done within a recipe. We cover some of the important concepts in the following sections.

Assign a Value to a Variable

We use the '=' operator to assign a value.
The following code shows an example of the '=' operator.

```
package_name = "apache2"
```

It will create a variable named package_name with value "apache2".

Using the Case Statement

We use the case statement when we need to compare an expression and, based upon it, execute certain code.
Figure 7-7 shows a piece of code that demonstrates the use of case statement within a recipe.

```
package "apache2" do
  case node[:platform]
  when "centos","redhat","fedora","suse"
    package_name "httpd"
  when "debian","ubuntu"
    package_name "apache2"
  when "arch"
    package_name "apache"
  end
  action :install
end
```

Figure 7-7. Using case statement

Check for a Condition

We use the 'if' expression to check the 'true or false' condition in a chef recipe.

Figure 7-8 shows a piece of code that checks if the node platform is Ubuntu or Debian and will execute the code accordingly.

```
if platform?("debian", "ubuntu")
  # do something if node['platform'] is debian or ubuntu
else
  # do other stuff
end
```

Figure 7-8. Checking for a condition

Unless Expression

We use the 'unless' expression to execute a piece of code when the result is FALSE.

Figure 7-9 shows an example. If the platform version is anything other than 5.0, then the code will be executed.

```
unless node[:platform_version] == "5.0"
  # do stuff on everything but 5.0
end
```

Figure 7-9. Using 'unless' statement

Include Recipes in Recipes

A recipe can be included in any other recipe by using the include_recipe keyword.

The resources of the recipe that is included will be executed in the same order in which they appear in the original recipe. A recipe can be included in another recipe using the following syntax:

```
include_recipe "apache2::mod_ssl"
```

We can include a recipe within a recipe any number of times, but it will be processed only for the first time and after that it will be ignored.

Apply Recipes to Run List

If we need to apply any recipe then it needs to be added to the run list using a suitable name which is defined by the cookbook directory structure.

For example, a cookbook might have the following structure:

```
cookbooks/
        mysql/
                recipes/
                        default.rb
                        server.rb
```

One is the default recipe which has the same name as that of the cookbook and other recipe is server.rb. Figure 7-10 shows the syntax of a run list.

```
{
  "run_list": [
  "recipe[mysql]",
  "recipe[mysql::server]"
  ]
}
```

Figure 7-10. *Specifying the run list*

Exception Handlers and Log Files

We can write the output of a recipe to a log file. This can be achieved using the Chef::Log. There can be various levels of logging which include debug, warn, info, fatal, and error.

The following code can be used to capture some information:

```
Chef::Log.info('some useful information')
```

Tags

A tag describes a node in a customized way and then we can group our nodes based on that description.

You can check whether or not your machines have a tag. You can also add or remove tags at any point by using the following command.

```
tag('mytag')
```

Tagging can be done using various modes including from knife and from within a recipe. We can use the following code to check whether or not a machine is tagged:

```
tagged?('mytag')
```

To return true or false use

```
tagged?[array of nodes]
```

We can use the following untag command to remove the tag from any node:

```
untag('mytag')
```

See Figure 7-11 for an example.

```
tag("machine")
if tagged?("server")
    Chef::Log.info("Hey I'm a #{node[:tags]}")
end
untag("machine")
if not tagged?("machine")
    Chef::Log.info("I don't have a tag")
end
```

Figure 7-11. *Example*

The output would be as follows:

```
[Wed, 12Jul 2014 22:23:45 +0000] INFO: Hey I'm a server
[Wed, 12 Jul 2014 22:23:45 +0000] INFO: I don't have a tag.
```

Recipe DSL

Recipe DSL is mainly Ruby DSL and we use it to declare resources within a recipe.

We use the methods in the recipe DSL to find out the value of a specific parameter, and then, based on that value, chef takes an action. Anything that can be done with Ruby can be done in a recipe.

We can use attributes, search results, and data bags in the recipe DSL. We can also use the helper methods available. The helper methods are

- platform?
- platform_family?
- value_for_platform
- value_for_platform_family

Let's discuss these four helper methods in detail.

Platform?

We use Ohai to detect the value of the node['platform'] parameter during every chef run. We use the platform method in a recipe to run platform-specific actions.

We can use the "platform" method in a recipe with the following syntax:

platform?("parameter","parameter")

We can provide one or more than one parameter in a comma-separated list. Typically, we use this method along with conditional Ruby (Case, if, or elseif) (e.g., see Figure 7-12).

```
if platform? ("redhat", "centos")
        # code to execute
end
```

Figure 7-12. *Using platform? method in a recipe*

With this method we can create a single cookbook which can be used on multiple operating systems (OSs).

platform_family?

We use the platform_family? method when we want to execute some actions for a specific platform family. We use Ohai to detect the platform_family? attribute. The actions will be executed if one of the listed parameters matched the node['platform_family'].

We can use it in the recipe with the following syntax:

platform_family?("parameter","parameter")

We can provide more than one value of parameters using a comma-separated list.

We also use this method along with conditional Ruby, so that a single cookbook is used on multiple platforms (e.g., see Figure 7-13).

```
if platform_family? ("rhel")
        # code to execute
end
```

Figure 7-13. *Using* platform_family? *method in a recipe*

value_for_platform?

We use this method in a recipe with a hash of a particular value based on node['platform'] and node['platform_version']. Ohai provides the value during each chef run.

We can use it in the recipe with the following syntax:

```
value_for_platform( ["platform"] => { ["version"] => value } )
```

We can provide one or more than one value for platform in a comma-separated list, and version specifies the version of that platform.

If each value only has a single platform, then the syntax is as shown in Figure 7-14.

```
value_for_platform(
        "platform" => { "version" => "value" },
        "platform" => "value"
)
```

Figure 7-14. *Using* value_for_platform? *method in a recipe*

It there is more than one platform, the syntax will be as shown in Figure 7-15.

```
value_for_platform(
["platform", "platform", "platform", "platform" ] => {
"version" => "values"
},
["platform", "platform"] => {
        "version" => "value"
}
)
```

Figure 7-15. *Using* value_for_platform? *method in a recipe*

The code shown in Figure 7-16 will set the value of package_name variable as httpd if that platform is CentOS or Red Hat and Apache2 if platform is Debian or Ubuntu.

```
package_name = value_for_platform(
        ["centos", "redhat ] => {
        "default" => "httpd"
        },
        ["Ubuntu", "debian"] => {
        "default" => "apache2"
        }
)
```

Figure 7-16. *Using value_for_platform? method in a recipe*

value_for_platform_family?

We use this method in a recipe with a hash to select value based on node ['platform_family'] attribute detected by Ohai.

We can use it in a recipe with the following syntax:

value_for_platform_family({ platform_family => value })

We can provide one or more than one platform_family using a comma-separated list. If there is a single platform for each value, then the syntax is as shown in Figure 7-17.

```
value_for_platform_family(
        "platform" => { "version" => "value"},
"platform" => { "version" => "value"},
"platform" => "value"
)
```

Figure 7-17. *Using value_for_platform_family? method in a recipe*

If the value has more than one platform, then the syntax is as shown in Figure 7-18.

```
value_for_platform_family(
["platform", "platform", "platform", "platform" ] => "value",
["platform", "platform"] => "value",
"default" => "value"
)
```

Figure 7-18. *Using value_for_platform_family? method in a recipe*

The code shown in Figure 7-19 will set the value of the package variable to httpd-devel if the platform_family is Red Hat or Fedora or Suse and the value would be "apache-dev" if the platform_family is Debian.

```
package = value_for_platform_family(
["rhel", "fedora", "suse"] => "httpd-devel",
"debian" => "apache2-dev"
)
```

Figure 7-19. *Using value_for_platform_family? method in a recipe*

Resources and Providers

Resources are the chunks of Ruby blocks that you declare in your recipe and that actually help in configuring the system. A resource helps us to define the actions that we want our recipe to do. These actions can be anything like installing a package or starting a service. The action is completed with the help of a provider.

During a chef run the resources are identified and mapped to a provider. The provider then executes that action. The resources define the current state of system and the state in which we want the system to be. Providers are used to define the steps to bring the system into that state.

An action is decoupled from the steps required to complete that action, which means that a provider exists for each of the paths that are required to complete the action. This is important because a single action may require different steps, depending on the platform of the system on which the action is being taken.

For example, "install a package" is a single action. To install a package onto various platforms, the steps required for each of those platforms may be different and may require different providers. On a Red Hat or CentOS machine a provider will use the Yum package provider to get the package installed and on a Debian or an Ubuntu machine, a provider will use the APT package installer.

The Chef::Platform class maps providers to platforms (and platform versions).

We use Ohai to get the information about the platform. Based upon that data we can identify the correct provider and then execute the action.

For example, see the resource shown in Figure 7-20.

```
directory "/tmp/folder" do
        owner "root"
        group "root"
        mode 0755
        action :create
end
```

Figure 7-20. *Example of a resource*

Resources Syntax

A resource has four components.

- Type

- Name

- Attribute (one or more)

- Action (one or more)

The syntax for a resource is as follows:

```
type "name" do
        attribute "value"
        action :type_of_action
end
```

The code in Figure 7-21 can be used to install version 1.16.1 of the tar package.

```
package "tar" do
        version "1.16.1"
        action :install
end
```

Figure 7-21. *Example of a resource used for installing a package*

There are predefined actions and attributes for each resource in chef and there is a default value for most of the attributes.

Some attributes are available to all resources; these are sometimes referred to as "meta" attributes and they are commonly used to send notifications to other resources or to set up conditional execution rules.

There is a default value for each action. We need to specify only the nondefault behaviors of actions and attributes.

Attributes associated with resources are not the same as attributes associated with nodes.

Resources

We can use a number of inbuilt chef resources in configuration. We discuss some of the important chef resources here.

Cookbook_file

We use this resource if we want to transfer any file with our cookbook. It transfers the files available in the files/default subdirectory of the cookbook to any specified path. We can use this resource on any platform.

We can use the cookbook_file resource in a recipe as shown in Figure 7-22.

```
cookbook_file "name" do
        some_attribute "value" # see attributes
        action :action # see actions
end
```

Figure 7-22. Using the cookbook_file resource

For example,

```
cookbook_file "test" do
  path "/root/test"
  action :create
end
```

This would copy the test file to /root/test.
where

- cookbook_file is an inbuilt chef resource and it will use Chef::Provider::CookbookFile provider during the chef run.

- "name" is used to specify the name with which the file will be stored on the node.

- attribute is used to provide any attributes that are available with this resource.

- action is the execution that will be done on the node.

The following actions are available with this resource:

- Create: This is the default action. We use it to create a file.

- Create_if_missing: We use this action when we need to create a file only when it doesn't already exist.

- Delete: We use this action if we want to delete a file.

There are many attributes available with the resource. Some of the important attributes are

- Backup. We use this attribute to specify the number of backups that should be kept for a file. The default value is 5.

- Cookbook. We use this attribute to specify the name of the cookbook, if the file is present in some other cookbook.

- Path. We use this attribute to specify the path of the file.

cron

We use this resource to manage the cron entries. This resource requires access to a crontab program to work properly.

We can use the cron resource can be used in a recipe as shown in Figure 7-23.

```
cron "name" do
        some_attribute "value" # see attribute section below
        ...
        action :action # see actions sections below
end
```

Figure 7-23. *Using the cron resource*

For example,

```
cron "test" do
  hour "3"
  minute "30"
  command "/bin/test"
end
```

This would run a program at the specified interval.
where

- cron is an inbuilt chef resource and it will use the
  Chef::Provider::Cron provider during the chef run.

- "name" is used to provide the name with which the cron entry will
  be created.

- attribute is used to provide one or more attributes that the
  resource will use.

- action is the actual execution that will be done on the node.

The following actions are available in the cron resource:

- Create: We use this action to create in the crontab file.

- Delete: We use this action to delete any entry from the
  crontab file.

Some of the important attributes available with the cron resource are:

- Day: We use this option to specify the day of the month on which
  the job should run. The options available are 1–31.

- Hour: We use this option to specify at which hour (0–23) your job
  should run. Ute

- Minute: We use this option to specify the minute (0–59) at which
  the cron entry should run.

- Weekday: We use this option to specify the day of the week on
  which your job should run. The value can vary from 0–6 where
  0 = Sunday.

Directory

We use this resource to manage a directory. Chef should have the permission to the
directory that will be managed.

We can use the directory resource in a recipe with the syntax shown in Figure 7-24.

```
directory "name" do

some_attribute "value" # see attributes section below
...
action :action # see actions section below
end
```

Figure 7-24. Using the directory resource

where

- directory is an inbuilt chef resource and it will use the Chef::Provider::Directory provider during the chef run.

- "name" is used to provide the complete path to the directory.

- attribute is used to provide one or more attributes that the resource will use.

- action is the actual execution that will be done on the node.

The following actions are available in the directory resource:

- Create: We use this action to create any directory.

- Delete: We use this action to delete any directory.

Some of the important attributes available with this resource are

- Mode: We use the mode attribute to set the permission of the directory. We need to specify the permissions in octal mode.

- Owner: We use the owner attribute to specify the user who will be the owner of that directory.

- Recursive: The value for this attribute can be true or false. We use it to specify whether the directory created or deleted will be done recursively or not.

env

The env resource is a Windows-specific resource and we use it to manage environment variables.

We can use the env resource in a recipe with the syntax shown in Figure 7-25.

```
env "name" do
some_attribute "value" # see attributes section below
...
action :action # see actions section below
end
```

Figure 7-25. *Using the env resource*

For example,

```
env "Test" do
  value "C:\\test\\test.exe"
end
```

It would create an environment variable named Test with the provided value. where

- env is an inbuilt chef resource and it will use the
  Chef::Provider::env provider during the chef run.

- "name" is used to provide the name with which the variable will
  be created.

- attribute is used to provide one or more attributes that the
  resource will use.

- action is the actual execution that will be done on the node.

The following actions are available in this resource:

- Create: We use this action if we want to create a new environment
  variable.

- Delete: We use this action if we want to delete any environment
  variable.

- Modify: We use this action in case we want to edit an environment
  variable that already exists.

Some of the important attributes available with this resource are

- Delim: We use this attribute to specify the delimiter that will be
  used to separate multiple values.

- Key_name: We use this attribute to specify the name of the key
  which be managed.

- Value: We use this attribute to set the value of key_name.

execute

We use the execute resource in case we want to execute a command. Idempotency is not maintained by this resource by default. If we want to maintain the idempotency we need to use the not_if and only_if parameters.

We can use the execute resource in a recipe with the syntax shown in Figure 7-26.

```
execute "name" do
some_attribute "value" # see attributes section below
...
action :action # see actions section below
end
```

Figure 7-26. *Using the execute resource*

For example,

```
execute "environment" do
  command "source /etc/environment"
end
```

This would reload the /etc/environment file.
where

- execute is an inbuilt chef resource and it will use the Chef::Provider::execute provider during the chef run.

- "name" is used to provide the name of the command that will run.

- attribute is used to provide one or more attributes that the resource will use.

- action is the actual execution that will be done on the node.

The following actions are available with this resource:

- Run: This is the default action and it indicates that the command should run.

- Nothing: This action specifies that the command should not run directly but should run only if some other resource specifies it.

Some of the important attributes available with this resource are

- Command: The command that will be executed.

- Cwd: We use this option if we want a command to be executed from a certain directory.

- Environment: We use this option to set the environment variable that will be set before running the commands.

- Timeout: We use this option to specify the time a command will wait before timing out.

- User: We use this option to specify the user with which the command should run.

file

We use this resource in case we need to manage the files that are present on a node. We can use the file resource in a recipe (as shown in Figure 7-27).

```
file "name" do
some_attribute "value" # see attributes section below
      ...
action :action # see actions section below
end
```

Figure 7-27. *Using the file resource*

where

- file is an inbuilt chef resource and it will use the Chef::Provider::file provider during the chef run.

- "name" is used to provide the name of the file.

- attribute is used to provide one or more attributes that the resource will use.

- action is the actual execution that will be done on the node.

The screenshot in Figure 7-28 shows how we can use the file resource.

```
file "/tmp/something" do
        owner "root"
        group "root"
        mode "0755"
       action :create
end
```

Figure 7-28. *Using the file resource*

The following actions are available in the file resource:

- Create: This is the default action and we use it to create a file.

- create_if_missing: We use this action in case we want to create a file only if it is not present.

- Delete: We use this action to delete a file.

- Touch: We use this action to update the access and the file modification time for a file.

Some of the important attributes available with this resource are

- Backup: We use this attribute to specify the number of backups that should be kept for a file.

- Content: We use this attribute to specify the string that will be written to a file.

- Path: We use this attribute to specify the complete path of the file.

package

We use this resource to manage packages. The resource uses the native functionality of the OS to install the packages on the nodes. Although there are OS-specific chef resources that can be used to manage packages, we recommend using the package resource wherever possible.

We can use the package resource in a recipe with the syntax shown in Figure 7-29

```
package "name" do
        some_attribute "value" # see attributes section below
        ...
        action :action # see actions section below
end
```

Figure 7-29. *Using the package resource*

where

- package is an inbuilt chef resource and it will use the Chef::Provider::package provider during the chef run.

- "name" is used to provide the name of the package.

- attribute is used to provide one or more attributes that the resource will use.

- action is the actual execution that will be done on the node.

The following actions are available with the package resource:

- Install: This is the default action and we use it to install any package.

- Upgrade: We use this action in case we want to upgrade any package to the latest version.

- Reconfig: We use this action in case we want to reconfigure any package. There should be a response file for this action.

- Remove: We use this action in case we want remove any installed package.

- Purge: We use this action if we want to purge a package. If used, it will remove the package as well as the configuration file related to the package.

Some of the important attributes that are available with this resource are

- Flush_cache: We use this attribute if we want to flus the yum cache before or after any installation.

- Package_name: We use this option to specify the name of the package to be installed.

- Source: This is an optional attribute and we use it to specify the source for providers that use a local file.

- Version: We use this option if we want to install any specific version of a package.

powershell_script

This is a Windows-specific resource. We use this resource if we want execute a script using powershell. This resource is similar to many chef resources with small tweaks. This resource will create a temporary file rather than running it inline. The commands executed with this resource are not idempotent by default; we can use the not_if and only_if meta parameters to maintain the idempotency.

We can use the powershell_script resource in a recipe with the syntax shown in Figure 7-30.

```
powershell_script "name" do
        some_attribute "value" # see attributes section below
        ...
        action :action # see actions section below
end
```

Figure 7-30. *Using the powershell_script resource*

where

- powershell_script is an inbuilt chef resource and it will use the Chef::Provider::PowershellScript provider during the chef run.

- "name" is used to provide the name of the PowerShell Script.

- attribute is used to provide one or more attributes that the resource will use.

- action is the actual execution that will be done on the node.

The screenshot in Figure 7-31 shows how to use the powershell_script resource.

```
powershell "name_of_script" do
        cwd Chef::Config[:file_cache_path]
        code <<-EOH
    # some script goes here
        EOH
end
```

Figure 7-31. *Using the powershell_script resource*

The following actions are available in the powershell_script resource:

- Run: This is the default action. It will run the specified script.

- Nothing: We use this action if we do not want the resource to be executed directly.

Some of the important attributes available with this resource are

- Code: We use the attribute to specify the set of commands to be executed.

- Command: We use this attribute to specify the name of the command to execute.

- Flags: We use this option to pass the command line flags.

remote_file

We use this resource if we want to transfer a file from a remote location to the node. The functioning of this resource is similar to that of the file resource.

We can use it in a recipe with the syntax shown in Figure 7-32

```
remote_file "name" do
        some_attribute "value" # see attributes section below
        ...
        action :action # see actions section below
end
```

Figure 7-32. *Using the remote_file resource*

where

- remote_file is an inbuilt chef resource and it will use the Chef::Provider::RemoteFile provider during the chef run.

- "name" is used to provide the name and location of the remote file.

- attribute is used to provide one or more attributes that the resource will use.

- action is the actual execution that will be done on the node.

The screenshot in Figure 7-33 shows how we can use this resource in a recipe.

```
remote_file "#{Chef::Config[:file_cache_path]}/large-file.tar.gz" do
     source "http://www.example.org/large-file.tar.gz"
end
```

Figure 7-33. *Using the remote_file resource*

The following actions are available in the remote_file resource:

- Create: We use this action to download the file from the remote source to the node.

- Create_if_missing: We also use it to download the file from the remote source to the node but only if the file is missing.

Some of the important attributes available with this resource are

- Backup: We use this attribute to specify the number of backups that should be kept for the file.

- Checksum: This is an optional setting and we use it if we don't need the file to be downloaded again. It will check the checksum.

- Source: We use this attribute to specify the source from which the file should be downloaded.

script

We use this resource to execute the scripts. We can choose the interpreter we want to use. It creates a temporary file and executes the file rather than running it inline.

The commands that are executed by this resource are not idempotent by nature; to maintain idempotency we need to use the not_if and only_if meta parameters.

We can use script in a recipe with the syntax shown in Figure 7-34

```
script "name" do
        some_attribute "value" # see attributes section below
        ...
        action :action # see actions section below
end
```

Figure 7-34. *Using the script resource*

where

- script is an inbuilt chef resource and it will use the Chef::Provider::Script provider during the chef run.

- "name" is used to provide the name with which the script will run.

- attribute is used to provide one or more attributes that the resource will use.

- action is the actual execution that will be done on the node.

The following actions are available with this resource:

- Run: This is the default action and it indicates that the command should run.

- Nothing: This action specifies that the command should not run directly but should run only if some other resource specifies it.

Some of the important attributes available with this resource are

- Command: The command that will be executed.

- Cwd: We use this option if we want a command to be executed from a certain directory.

- Environment: We use this option to set the environment variable that will be set before running the commands.

- Timeout: We use this option to specify the time a command will wait before timing out.

- User: We use this option to specify the user with which the command should run.

service

We use this resource to manage any service on a node.

The syntax for using the service resource in a recipe is shown in Figure 7-35.

```
service "name" do
        some_attribute "value" # see attributes section below
        ...
        action :action # see actions section below
end
```

Figure 7-35. *Using the service resource*

where

- service is an inbuilt chef resource and it will use the provider based on the OS of the node.

- "name" is used to provide the name of the service.

- attribute is used to provide one or more attributes that the resource will use.

- action is the actual execution that will be done on the node.

The following actions are available with this resource:

- Enable: We use this action if we want to enable a service on startup.

- Disable: We use this action to disable a service.

- Start: We use this action to start a service.

- Stop: We use this action to stop a service.

- Restart: We use this action to restart a service.

- Reload: We use this action to reload the configuration files for a service.

Some of the important attributes available with this resource are

- Reload_commmand: The command that will be used to reload the service.

- Restart_command: The command that will be used to restart the service.

- Service_name: The name of the service that will be managed.

- Start_command: The command that will be used to start the service.

- Stop_command: The command that will be used to stop the service.

Template

We use this resource if we want to manage the contents of a file. It stores files in an erb (Embedded Ruby) template. We normally store templates in the template/default available in the cookbook subdirectory.

We can use the template resource in the recipe as shown in Figure 7-36.

```
template "name" do
  some_attribute "value" # see attributes section below
  ...
  action :action # see actions section below
end
```

Figure 7-36. *Using the template resource*

For example,

```
template "/etc/nginx.conf" do
  source "nginx.conf.erb"
end
```

We use this resource to configure a file from a template where

- template is an inbuilt chef resource and it will use the Chef::Provider::Template provider during the chef run.

- "name" is used to provide the name of the template file.

- attribute is used to provide one or more attributes that the resource will use.

- action is the actual execution that will be done on the node.

Following are the actions that are available with this resource:

- Create: This is the default action and we use it to create a file.

- Create_if_missing: This action will create a file if the file doesn't exist.

Some of the important attributes available with this resource are

- Backup: We use this option to specify the number of backups that should be kept for a file.

- Path: We use this attribute to provide the complete path to the file.

- Source: We use this option to specify the location of the source file.

- Variable: We use this option to provide variables in the template file.

Attributes Files

Attribute are used to override the settings on any node. During each chef run, the attributes on a node are compared to those in the cookbook and then, depending upon the precedence level, the settings are done.

The attribute file is located in the attributes subdirectory of the cookbook. During each chef run, the attributes in the attributes files are evaluated against the node object.

For example, the mysql cookbook contains the following attribute file (called default.rb):

```
default["mysql"]["data_dir"]          = "/opt/local/lib/mysql"
default["mysql"]["port"] = ""3306"
```

The use of the node object is implicit here. The following example is equivalent to the previous one:

```
node.default["mysql"]["data_dir"]          = "/etc/apache2"
node.default["mysql"]["port"] = '3306'
```

Chef server keeps the attributes indexed so that they are easy to access.

Attributes Types

The following types of attributes are available:

- Default
- Force_default
- Force_override
- Normal
- Override
- Automatic

Attributes Methods

Various attribute methods can be used in the attribute files of the cookbook or directly in a recipe. The various attribute methods that are available are

- Override
- Default
- Normal

There is one more method, attribute?, that is available and is used to check the value of an attribute.

We can use the attribute?() method in an attributes file as shown in Figure 7-37.

```
if attribute?("ec2")
# ... set stuff related to EC2
end
■
```

Figure 7-37. *Using attributes*

Similarly, we can use it in a recipe as shown in Figure 7-38.

```
if node.attribute?("ec2")
# ... do stuff on EC2 nodes
end
■
```

Figure 7-38. *Using attributes in recipes*

Precedence

During a chef run, saved attributes are retrieved from the chef server and are merged with the attributes on the local system. The attribute type and the source of the attribute determine which attribute values have priority over others.

In general, use the default attributes as much as possible (or even all the time).

The merge order for attribute precedence will do most of the work, yet leaving many levels of precedence available for the situations in which they are truly necessary.

Attribute values are applied in the following order (from low to high priority): 1 being the lowest and 15 being the highest.

	Attribute Files	Node/ Recipe	Environment	Role
Default	1	2	3	4
Force Default	5	6		
Normal	7	8		
Override	9	10	12	11
Force Override	13	14		
Automatic	15			

In other words, an automatic attribute takes precedence over a forced override attribute, a forced override attribute takes precedence over an override attribute, an override attribute takes precedence over a normal attribute, and so on.

Definitions

Definitions are used to create new resources by combing the existing resources. Usually we use definitions when we are repeating a pattern of resources. Definition is not a resource or a lightweight resource but is actually a collection of two or more resource declarations.

There is a separate directory where we create definitions.

A definition is never declared into a cookbook.

There are mainly three components of a definition.

- The name of the resource.

- The arguments (one or more than one) that will be used to set the value for the parameters.

- A hash that would be used to accessing parameters and their values.

If we do not set any value for a parameter, we use the default value.

The syntax of a definition is as shown in Figure 7-39.

```
define :resource_name, :parameter => :argument, :parameter => :argument do
       params_hash
end
```

Figure 7-39. *Using definitions*

Figure 7-40 shows an example of a definition with name apache_site with 'action' as a parameter and 'enable' as its argument.

```
define :apache_site, :action => :enable do
if params[:action] == :enable
...
                else
                ...
end
end
```

Figure 7-40. *Using definitions*

Libraries

A library is a way to increase chef functionality. We can implement a Ruby class directly and then use it in our recipe. There is a separate directory for library where we create libraries. A library once defined is available to be used anywhere in the cookbook.

The basic syntax of a library is shown in Figure 7-41.

```
# define a module to mix into Chef::Recipe::namespace

module YourExampleLibrary
  def your_function()
    # ... do something useful
  end
end
```

Figure 7-41. Defining libraries

This syntax can be used in a recipe with the code shown in Figure 7-42.

```
# open the Chef::Recipe class and mix in the library module

class Chef::Recipe::namespace
  include YourExampleLibrary
end

your_function()
```

Figure 7-42. Using libraries

For example, we could create a simple library that extends Chef::Recipe::, as shown in Figure 7-43.

```
class Chef
  class Recipe
    # A shortcut to a customer
    def customer(name)
      node[:mycompany_customers][name]
    end
  end
end
```

Figure 7-43. Creating a library

We can use this library in a recipe as shown in Figure 7-44.

```
directory customer(:bob)[:webdir] do
  owner "bob"
  group "bob"
  action :create
end
```

Figure 7-44. *Using Library in recipe*

Metadata

We use metadata to store certain information about the cookbook. We use the file
`metadata.rb` to provide this information. The file is located in the cookbook directory.

The following things can be specified in the cookbook. Figure 7-45 shows the
metadata file of the build-essential cookbook.

```
name               'build-essential'
maintainer         'Opscode, Inc.'
maintainer_email   'cookbooks@opscode.com'
license            'Apache 2.0'
description        'Installs C compiler / build tools'
version            '1.4.4'
recipe             'build-essential', 'Installs packages required for compiling C
  software from source.'

%w{ fedora redhat centos ubuntu debian amazon suse scientific oracle smartos}.ea
ch do |os|
  supports os
end

supports 'mac_os_x', '>= 10.6.0'
supports 'mac_os_x_server', '>= 10.6.0'
suggests 'pkgutil' # Solaris 2
```

Figure 7-45. *Metadata*

A metadata can be used to specify the following important things:

- Dependencies: If the cookbook is dependent on any other
  cookbook.

- Description: What is the cookbook actually doing.

- Supported OS list.

- Name of the cookbook.

- Version of the cookbook.

■ ■ ■

## CHAPTER 8

Using Cookbooks

In the previous chapter, we discussed the important components related to a cookbook. In this chapter we use some cookbooks available from the community. We download and deploy these cookbooks on a node. We have picked up important cookbooks from the community and will try to explain exactly how to use them.

MySQL(4.1.2)

This program installs and configures the MySQL client or server. Different recipes are defined for installing and configuring the MySQL server on different platform machines.

Platform

The following platforms support this cookbook:

- Debian/Ubuntu
- CentOS 5.x,6.x, Red Hat 5.x,6.x, Fedora(18.x,19.x,20.x)
- Mac OS X (Using homebrew)

Dependencies

- Requires Opscode's OpenSSL cookbook for secure password generation.

Prerequisite

- Client machine must have a running Internet connection.

Cookbook Download

You can download the cookbook on the workstation in your corresponding cookbooks directory, inside your chef repo, on your knife workstation from the Opscode community web site (see Figure 8-1), by running the following command on your knife workstation:

```
Knife cookbook site download mysql
```

```
c:\chef-repo>knife cookbook site download mysql
Downloading mysql from the cookbooks site at version 5.0.0 to c:/chef-repo/mysql
-5.0.0.tar.gz
Cookbook saved: c:/chef-repo/mysql-5.0.0.tar.gz
```

Figure 8-1. *Download MySQL cookbook from Opscode community*

The downloaded cookbook will be in '.tar.gz'. The cookbook can be extracted from here (see Figure 8-2).

```
c:\chef-repo>tar -xvf mysql-5.0.0.tar.gz
x mysql/
x mysql/CHANGELOG.md
x mysql/README.md
x mysql/attributes
x mysql/attributes/default.rb
x mysql/libraries
x mysql/libraries/helpers.rb
x mysql/libraries/matchers.rb
x mysql/libraries/provider_mysql_client.rb
x mysql/libraries/provider_mysql_client_debian.rb
x mysql/libraries/provider_mysql_client_fedora.rb
x mysql/libraries/provider_mysql_client_omnios.rb
x mysql/libraries/provider_mysql_client_rhel.rb
x mysql/libraries/provider_mysql_client_smartos.rb
x mysql/libraries/provider_mysql_client_ubuntu.rb
x mysql/libraries/provider_mysql_service.rb
x mysql/libraries/provider_mysql_service_debian.rb
x mysql/libraries/provider_mysql_service_fedora.rb
x mysql/libraries/provider_mysql_service_omnios.rb
x mysql/libraries/provider_mysql_service_rhel.rb
x mysql/libraries/provider_mysql_service_smartos.rb
x mysql/libraries/provider_mysql_service_ubuntu.rb
x mysql/libraries/resource_mysql_client.rb
x mysql/libraries/resource_mysql_service.rb
```

Figure 8-2. *Extracting the cookbook*

Once we extract the cookbook, we can move to the next step of uploading the cookbook to the chef server.

Cookbook Upload

For setting up a MySQL server on a node, we first have to set the attribute values according to our setup. Certain attributes need to be changed before running the chef client on the node.

In your chef repo directory on your knife workstation, go to the cookbooks folder and open the MySQL cookbook directory, open 'attributes/server.rb' file in the editor of your choice. Set the values for the following attributes:

Default ['mysql']['port'] = 3306 (or any other as per your settings)

In the 'attributes/server_rhel.rb', set the values for following attributes:

- default ['mysql']['server']['basedir'] = '/usr'

- default ['mysql']['server']['tmpdir'] = ['/tmp']

- default ['mysql']['server']['directories']['run_dir']
  = '/var/run/mysqld'

- default ['mysql']['server']['directories']['log_dir']
  = '/var/lib/mysql'

- default ['mysql']['server']['directories']['slow_log_dir']
  = '/var/log/mysql'

- default ['mysql']['server']['directories']['confd_dir']
  = '/etc/mysql/conf.d'

- default ['mysql']['server']['service_name'] = 'mysqld'

- default ['mysql']['server_root_password'] = 'rootpass'

You upload the cookbook (see Figure 8-3) to the chef server using knife (see Figure 8-3). Once you upload the cookbook (along with its dependencies), you can add it to the run list of the node.

```
Knife cookbook upload mysql
```

```
c:\chef-repo\cookbooks>knife cookbook upload mysql
Uploading mysql            [4.1.2]
Uploaded 1 cookbook.

c:\chef-repo\cookbooks>
```

Figure 8-3. *Uploading the cookbook*

Client Run

For the purpose of this book, a node 'chef testing' has been preconfigured and is utilized here.

Add the recipe to the run list of the node from your knife workstation (see Figure 8-4), and run chef client on the configured node.

```
c:\chef-repo>knife node run_list add chef-testing 'recipe[mysql]'
chef-testing:
  run_list: recipe[mysql]

c:\chef-repo>
```

Figure 8-4. *Adding cookbook to the run list*

Knife node run_list add node_name 'recipe[mysql]'
Now, we run the chef client on the configured node (see Figure 8-5).

```
~]# chef-clientting
Starting Chef Client, version 11.8.2
resolving cookbooks for run list: ["mysql"]
Synchronizing Cookbooks:
  - chef_handler
  - windows
  - homebrew
  - build-essential
  - openssl
  - mysql
Compiling Cookbooks...
```

Figure 8-5. *Running chef client*

```
    - create new directory /var/log/mysql[2014-03-07T15:23:45+05:30] INFO: direc
tory[/var/log/mysql] owner changed to 501
[2014-03-07T15:23:45+05:30] INFO: directory[/var/log/mysql] group changed to 501
[2014-03-07T15:23:45+05:30] INFO: directory[/var/log/mysql] mode changed to 755

    - change mode from '' to '0755'
    - change owner from '' to 'mysql'
    - change group from '' to 'mysql'
    - restore selinux security context

  * directory[/etc/mysql/conf.d] action create[2014-03-07T15:23:46+05:30] INFO:
Processing directory[/etc/mysql/conf.d] action create (mysql::_server_rhel line
11)
[2014-03-07T15:23:46+05:30] INFO: directory[/etc/mysql/conf.d] created directory
/etc/mysql/conf.d
```

Figure 8-6. *Creating log directory for MySQL*

```
    - create new directory /etc/mysql/conf.d[2014-03-07T15:23:46+05:30] INFO: di
rectory[/etc/mysql/conf.d] owner changed to 501
[2014-03-07T15:23:46+05:30] INFO: directory[/etc/mysql/conf.d] group changed to
501
[2014-03-07T15:23:46+05:30] INFO: directory[/etc/mysql/conf.d] mode changed to 7
55

    - change mode from '' to '0755'
    - change owner from '' to 'mysql'
    - change group from '' to 'mysql'
    - restore selinux security context
```

Figure 8-7. *Creating MySQL configuration file*

```
- update content in file /etc/my.cnf from 98bb7a to 762753
    --- /etc/my.cnf 2013-07-01 14:51:13.080894427 +0530
    +++ /tmp/chef-rendered-template20140307-17748-1ot1bgr    2014-03-07 15:23
:46.504424479 +0530
    @@ -1,5 +1,6 @@
    -#chef for chef-testing
     #
    +# Generated by Chef for chef-testing
    +#
     # Local modifications will be overwritten.
     #
     # The MySQL database server configuration file.
    @@ -19,11 +20,19 @@
     # It has been reported that passwords should be enclosed with ticks/quo
tes
     # escpecially if they contain "#" chars...
     # Remember to edit /etc/mysql/debian.cnf when changing the socket locat
ion.
    .. -.. ..
```

Figure 8-8. *Updating the content of my.conf (from template)*

```
- start service service[mysql-start]

 * service[mysql-start] action nothing[2014-03-07T15:23:49+05:30] INFO: Process
ing service[mysql-start] action nothing (mysql::_server_rhel line 38)
 (skipped due to action :nothing)
 * execute[/usr/bin/mysql_install_db] action run[2014-03-07T15:23:49+05:30] INF
O: Processing execute[/usr/bin/mysql_install_db] action run (mysql::_server_rhel
 line 43)
 (skipped due to only_if)
 * execute[assign-root-password] action run[2014-03-07T15:23:49+05:30] INFO: Pr
ocessing execute[assign-root-password] action run (mysql::_server_rhel line 50)
[2014-03-07T15:23:49+05:30] INFO: execute[assign-root-password] ran successfully

   - execute /usr/bin/mysqladmin -u root password dO2k1pFHwOP3n7OmfoJE
```

Figure 8-9. *Starting MySQL service and setting root password*

After the client run has been ended (see Figure 8-10), we can check on the specified port to see whether the MySQL service is running (see Figure 8-11).

```
lsof -i :3306
```

```
   - restart service service[mysql]

  * execute[install-grants] action nothing[2014-03-07T15:23:52+05:30] INFO: Proc
essing execute[install-grants] action nothing (mysql::_server_rhel line 66)
 (skipped due to action :nothing)
  * template[final-my.cnf] action create[2014-03-07T15:23:52+05:30] INFO: Proces
sing template[final-my.cnf] action create (mysql::_server_rhel line 73)
 (up to date)
  * service[mysql] action enable[2014-03-07T15:23:52+05:30] INFO: Processing ser
vice[mysql] action enable (mysql::_server_rhel line 82)
[2014-03-07T15:23:53+05:30] INFO: service[mysql] enabled

   - enable service service[mysql]

  * service[mysql] action start[2014-03-07T15:23:53+05:30] INFO: Processing serv
ice[mysql] action start (mysql::_server_rhel line 82)
 (up to date)
[2014-03-07T15:23:53+05:30] INFO: Chef Run complete in 23.761338341 seconds
[2014-03-07T15:23:53+05:30] INFO: Running report handlers
[2014-03-07T15:23:53+05:30] INFO: Report handlers complete
Chef Client finished, 9 resources updated
```

Figure 8-10. *Chef client run end*

```
~]# lsof -i :3306
COMMAND  PID  USER    FD    TYPE DEVICE SIZE/OFF NODE NAME
mysqld  2266 mysql    4u    IPv4 14589       0t0  TCP chef-testing:mysql (LISTEN)
~]# ■t@chef-testing
```

Figure 8-11. *Checking MySQL service*

Once the cookbook has been converged and all the resources have been updated, you can access your MySQL database admin by logging in as user `'mysql'`.

Figure 8-12 is a snapshot of the `'/etc/mysql_grants.sql'` file which sets the password for the root user and also specifies other grant table permissions.

```
▊ Generated by Chef for chef-testing.
# Local modifications will be overwritten.

# Grant replication for a slave user. 9_syM2KrAo33nVBWvrKB
GRANT REPLICATION SLAVE ON *.* TO 'repl'@'%' identified by 'replpass';

# remove remote access for root user and set password for local root userSLWZuXTI6IP
AH4dnPdfO
DELETE FROM mysql.user WHERE User='root' AND Host NOT IN ('localhost', '127.0.0.1',
'::1');
UPDATE mysql.user SET Password=PASSWORD('rootpass') WHERE User='root';

# Remove test database and access to it

# Set the password for root@localhost.SLWZuXTI6IPAH4dnPdfO
SET PASSWORD FOR 'root'@'localhost' = PASSWORD('rootpass');
SET PASSWORD FOR 'root'@'127.0.0.1' = PASSWORD('rootpass');
```

Figure 8-12. `Mysql_grants` *file*

You can see the password you specified in the attributes. Now you can log in to the MySQL console using this password and user as root (see Figure 8-13).

```
mysql -u root -p 'your_password_here'
```

```
[root@chef-testing ~]# mysql -u root -p
Enter password:
Welcome to the MySQL monitor.  Commands end with ; or \g.
Your MySQL connection id is 2
Server version: 5.1.73 Source distribution

Copyright (c) 2000, 2013, Oracle and/or its affiliates. All rights reserved.

Oracle is a registered trademark of Oracle Corporation and/or its
affiliates. Other names may be trademarks of their respective
owners.

Type 'help;' or '\h' for help. Type '\c' to clear the current input statement.

mysql> []
```

Figure 8-13. *Log in to the MySQL console*

Nginx(2.4.2)

Platform

This cookbook is supported on the following platforms:

- Ubuntu 10.04, Ubuntu 12.04
- CentOS 5.8, 6.3

Dependencies

The following cookbooks are direct dependencies because they're used for common "default" functionality:

- Build essential (for nginx::source)
- Ohai (for nginx::ohai_plugin)

Prerequisite

- Client machine must have a running Internet connection.

Cookbook Download

You can download the cookbook (see Figure 8-14) in your corresponding cookbooks directory inside your chef repo on the workstation, from the Opscode community web site, by running the following command on your knife workstation:

```
knife cookbook site download nginx
```

```
c:\chef-repo\cookbooks>knife cookbook site download nginx
Downloading nginx from the cookbooks site at version 2.4.2 to c:/chef-repo/cookb
ooks/nginx-2.4.2.tar.gz
Cookbook saved: c:/chef-repo/cookbooks/nginx-2.4.2.tar.gz

c:\chef-repo\cookbooks>
```

Figure 8-14. *Downloading the cookbook*

The downloaded cookbook will be in '.tar.gz'. You can extract the cookbook from here (see Figure 8-15).

```
tar -xvf nginx-2.5.0.tar.gz
```

```
c:\chef-repo>tar -xvf nginx-2.5.0.tar.gz
x nginx/
x nginx/CHANGELOG.md
x nginx/README.md
x nginx/attributes
x nginx/attributes/auth_request.rb
x nginx/attributes/default.rb
x nginx/attributes/devel.rb
x nginx/attributes/echo.rb
x nginx/attributes/geoip.rb
x nginx/attributes/headers_more.rb
x nginx/attributes/lua.rb
x nginx/attributes/naxsi.rb
x nginx/attributes/openssl_source.rb
x nginx/attributes/passenger.rb
x nginx/attributes/rate_limiting.rb
x nginx/attributes/repo.rb
x nginx/attributes/source.rb
x nginx/attributes/status.rb
x nginx/attributes/upload_progress.rb
x nginx/definitions
x nginx/definitions/nginx_site.rb
x nginx/files
x nginx/files/default
```

Figure 8-15. *Extracting the cookbook*

Once you extract the cookbook, we can move to the next step of uploading the cookbook to the chef server.

Cookbook Upload

Edit the following configuration attributes on your cookbook and upload them to the chef server once again, before running the chef client.

In your chef repo directory on your knife workstation, go to the cookbooks folder and open Nginx cookbook directory and open 'attributes/default.rb' file in the editor of your choice. Set the values of the following attributes (these are the values used for the purpose of this book) according to your settings:

- default['nginx']['dir']   = '/etc/nginx'
- default['nginx']['script_dir']   = '/usr/sbin'
- default['nginx']['log_dir']   = '/var/log/nginx'
- default['nginx']['binary']   = '/usr/sbin/nginx'
- default['nginx']['default_root'] = '/var/www/nginx-default'
- default['nginx']['upstart']['foreground'] = true
- default['nginx']['pid'] = '/var/run/nginx.pid'

We upload the cookbook to the chef server using knife (see Figure 8-16). Once you upload the cookbook (along with its dependencies), you can add it to the run list of the node.

```
knife cookbook upload nginx
```

```
c:\chef-repo>knife cookbook upload nginx
Uploading nginx            [2.4.2]
Uploaded 1 cookbook.

c:\chef-repo>
```

Figure 8-16. *Uploading the cookbook*

Client Run

Add the recipe to the run list of the node from your knife workstation, and run chef client on the configured client node.

```
knife node run_list add node_name 'recipe[nginx]'
```

```
c:\chef-repo>knife node run_list add chef-testing 'recipe[nginx]'
chef-testing:
  run_list: recipe[nginx]
```

Figure 8-17. *Adding the recipe to the run_list*

There's some redundancy in that the config handling hasn't been separated from the installation method (yet), so use only one of the recipes, default or source.

For the purpose of this book, we have used the default recipe. Run the chef client on the node.

Chef client (see Figures 8-18 – 8-21)

```
   - nginx
Compiling Cookbooks...
[2014-03-11T14:34:27+05:30] INFO: ohai plugins will be at: /etc/chef/ohai_plugin
s
Recipe: ohai::default
  * remote_directory[/etc/chef/ohai_plugins] action create[2014-03-11T14:34:27+0
5:30] INFO: Processing remote_directory[/etc/chef/ohai_plugins] action create (o
hai::default line 33)
[2014-03-11T14:34:27+05:30] INFO: remote_directory[/etc/chef/ohai_plugins] creat
ed directory /etc/chef/ohai_plugins

    - create new directory /etc/chef/ohai_plugins[2014-03-11T14:34:27+05:30] INF
O: remote_directory[/etc/chef/ohai_plugins] mode changed to 755

    - change mode from '' to '0755'
    - restore selinux security contextRecipe: <Dynamically Defined Resource>
  * cookbook_file[/etc/chef/ohai_plugins/README] action create[2014-03-11T14:34:
28+05:30] INFO: Processing cookbook_file[/etc/chef/ohai_plugins/README] action c
reate (dynamically defined)
[2014-03-11T14:34:28+05:30] INFO: cookbook_file[/etc/chef/ohai_plugins/README] c
reated file /etc/chef/ohai_plugins/README
```

Figure 8-18. *- Creating ohai_plugins directory*

```
[2014-03-11T14:34:29+05:30] INFO: template[/etc/chef/ohai_plugins/nginx.rb] mode
 changed to 755

    - change mode from '' to '0755'
    - change owner from '' to 'root'
    - change group from '' to 'root'
    - restore selinux security context

[2014-03-11T14:34:29+05:30] INFO: template[/etc/chef/ohai_plugins/nginx.rb] send
ing reload action to ohai[reload_nginx] (immediate)
  * ohai[reload_nginx] action reload[2014-03-11T14:34:29+05:30] INFO: Processing
ohai[reload_nginx] action reload (nginx::ohai_plugin line 22)
[2014-03-11T14:34:29+05:30] INFO: ohai[reload_nginx] reloaded

    - re-run ohai and merge results into node attributes
```

Figure 8-19. *Setting up directory permissions and merging into node attributes*

```
Recipe: yum-epel::default
  * yum_repository[epel] action create[2014-03-11T14:34:29+05:30] INFO: Processi
ng yum_repository[epel] action create (yum-epel::default line 25)
Recipe: <Dynamically Defined Resource>
  * template[/etc/yum.repos.d/epel.repo] action create[2014-03-11T14:34:29+05:30
] INFO: Processing template[/etc/yum.repos.d/epel.repo] action create (/var/chef
/cache/cookbooks/yum/providers/repository.rb line 39)
[2014-03-11T14:34:29+05:30] INFO: template[/etc/yum.repos.d/epel.repo] backed up
 to /var/chef/backup/etc/yum.repos.d/epel.repo.chef-20140311143429.616026
[2014-03-11T14:34:29+05:30] INFO: template[/etc/yum.repos.d/epel.repo] updated f
ile contents /etc/yum.repos.d/epel.repo

    - update content in file /etc/yum.repos.d/epel.repo from 6156ce to 759e91
        --- /etc/yum.repos.d/epel.repo   2013-07-08 20:51:06.448027536 +0530
        +++ /tmp/chef-rendered-template20140311-28083-1v3sggm    2014-03-11 14:34
:29.613410708 +0530
```

Figure 8-20. *Creating and updating content of epel definition file in /etc/yum.repos.d*

```
[2014-03-11T14:37:15+05:30] INFO: template[/etc/yum.repos.d/epel.repo] sending c
reate action to ruby_block[yum-cache-reload-epel] (immediate)
  * ruby_block[yum-cache-reload-epel] action create[2014-03-11T14:37:15+05:30] I
NFO: Processing ruby_block[yum-cache-reload-epel] action create (/var/chef/cache
/cookbooks/yum/providers/repository.rb line 59)
[2014-03-11T14:37:15+05:30] INFO: ruby_block[yum-cache-reload-epel] called

    - execute the ruby block yum-cache-reload-epel
```

Figure 8-21. *Enabling the epel repository*

Now, the code to install and configure Nginx will run and all the required directories and configuration files will be created. (see Figures 8-22 – 8-29).

```
Recipe: nginx::package
  * package[nginx] action install[2014-03-11T14:37:15+05:30] INFO: Processing pa
ckage[nginx] action install (nginx::package line 39)
 (up to date)
  * service[nginx] action enable[2014-03-11T14:37:35+05:30] INFO: Processing ser
vice[nginx] action enable (nginx::package line 43)
 (up to date)
Recipe: nginx::commons_dir
  * directory[/etc/nginx] action create[2014-03-11T14:37:36+05:30] INFO: Process
ing directory[/etc/nginx] action create (nginx::commons_dir line 22)
 (up to date)
  * directory[/var/log/nginx] action create[2014-03-11T14:37:36+05:30] INFO: Pro
cessing directory[/var/log/nginx] action create (nginx::commons_dir line 29)
[2014-03-11T14:37:36+05:30] INFO: directory[/var/log/nginx] owner changed to 495

    - change owner from 'root' to 'nginx'
    - restore selinux security context
```

Figure 8-22. *Creating and configuring directory settings*

```
[2014-03-11T14:37:36+05:30] INFO: directory[/etc/nginx/sites-available] created
directory /etc/nginx/sites-available

    - create new directory /etc/nginx/sites-available[2014-03-11T14:37:36+05:30]
 INFO: directory[/etc/nginx/sites-available] owner changed to 0
[2014-03-11T14:37:36+05:30] INFO: directory[/etc/nginx/sites-available] group ch
anged to 0
[2014-03-11T14:37:36+05:30] INFO: directory[/etc/nginx/sites-available] mode cha
nged to 755

    - change mode from '' to '0755'
    - change owner from '' to 'root'
    - change group from '' to 'root'
    - restore selinux security context
```

Figure 8-23. *Creating sites-available directory*

```
[2014-03-11T14:37:37+05:30] INFO: template[/usr/sbin/nxensite] created file /usr
/sbin/nxensite

    - create new file /usr/sbin/nxensite[2014-03-11T14:37:37+05:30] INFO: templa
te[/usr/sbin/nxensite] updated file contents /usr/sbin/nxensite

    - update content in file /usr/sbin/nxensite from none to fa46fb
        --- /usr/sbin/nxensite    2014-03-11 14:37:37.153449806 +0530
        +++ /tmp/chef-rendered-template20140311-28083-hubxk7      2014-03-11 14:37
:37.157410528 +0530
```

Figure 8-24. *Creating/updating nxensite file*

```
[2014-03-11T14:37:37+05:30] INFO: template[/usr/sbin/nxensite] mode changed to 7
55

    - change mode from '' to '0755'
    - change owner from '' to 'root'
    - change group from '' to 'root'
    - restore selinux security context
```

Figure 8-25. *Setting directory permissions on /usr/sbin/nxensite file*

```
[2014-03-11T14:37:37+05:30] INFO: template[/usr/sbin/nxdissite] created file /us
r/sbin/nxdissite

    - create new file /usr/sbin/nxdissite[2014-03-11T14:37:37+05:30] INFO: templ
ate[/usr/sbin/nxdissite] updated file contents /usr/sbin/nxdissite

    - update content in file /usr/sbin/nxdissite from none to cc16ec
        --- /usr/sbin/nxdissite 2014-03-11 14:37:37.652439643 +0530
        +++ /tmp/chef-rendered-template20140311-28083-6runoo      2014-03-11 14:37
```

Figure 8-26. *Creating/updating nxdissite template*

```
[2014-03-11T14:37:38+05:30] INFO: template[nginx.conf] updated file contents /et
c/nginx/nginx.conf

    - update content in file /etc/nginx/nginx.conf from 2bf3a3 to 161383
        --- /etc/nginx/nginx.conf        2013-04-05 12:51:27.042231463 +0530
        +++ /tmp/chef-rendered-template20140311-28083-192n5fg    2014-03-11 14:37
:38.060413250 +0530
        @@ -9,6 +9,7 @@
            }
```

Figure 8-27. *Creating/updating nginx.conf file*

```
    - create new file /etc/nginx/sites-available/default[2014-03-11T14:37:38+05:
30] INFO: template[/etc/nginx/sites-available/default] updated file contents /et
c/nginx/sites-available/default

    - update content in file /etc/nginx/sites-available/default from none to 0a0
e55
        --- /etc/nginx/sites-available/default  2014-03-11 14:37:38.404413387 +0
530
        +++ /tmp/chef-rendered-template20140311-28083-13oau6a    2014-03-11 14:37
:38.405444644 +0530
        @@ -1 +1,12 @@
        +server {
        +  listen    80;
        +  server_name   chef-testing;
        +
        +  access_log  /var/log/nginx/localhost.access.log;
```

Figure 8-28. *Sites-available configuration file*

```
Recipe: nginx::default                   --        -
  * service[nginx] action start
    - start service service[nginx]

Chef Client finished, 2 resources updated
~]# ▓t@chef-testing
```

Figure 8-29. *Client finish*

At the end of client run, the recipe starts the nginx service.

We can check (see Figure 8-30) that Nginx is listening on port 80 by running the following command:

```
lsof -i :80
```

```
~]# lsof -i :80
COMMAND    PID    USER    FD    TYPE    DEVICE SIZE/OFF NODE NAME
nginx    25048    root    7u    IPv4 69154089      0t0   TCP *:http (LISTEN)
nginx    25050   nginx    7u    IPv4 69154089      0t0   TCP *:http (LISTEN)
~]# ▓t@chef-testing
```

Figure 8-30. *Checking if the service is running*

Figure 8-31 shows the configuration directory which is created at 'etc/nginx' location. In the configuration directory, we can see different directories such as sites available, sites enabled, and the Nginx configuration file that were created by the recipes during the chef client run.

```
cd /etc/nginx
ls
```

```
nginx]# cd /etc/nginx/
nginx]# ls[root@chef-testing
conf.d              koi-utf  mime.types  scgi_params   sites-enabled  win-utf
fastcgi_params  koi-win  nginx.conf  sites-available  uwsgi_params
nginx]# ▌
```

***Figure 8-31.** Nginx Configuration directory*

We create the log directory (see Figure 8-32) for nginx server at '/var/log/nginx'.

```
cd /var/log/nginx
```

```
~]# cd /var/log/nginx/
nginx]# ls
access.log                error.log-20131112.gz  error.log-20140131.gz
error.log                 error.log-20140123.gz  error.log-20140307.gz
error.log-20130407.gz  error.log-20140124.gz  error.log-20140312.gz
error.log-20130504.gz  error.log-20140128.gz  error.log-20140322
error.log-20130806.gz  error.log-20140130.gz  localhost.access.log
nginx]# /nginx[root@chef-testing
```

***Figure 8-32.** Nginx log directory*

Finally, to confirm that the Nginx server is successfully installed and working, you can visit the Nginx web page (see Figure 8-33) by entering the IP address of the node on which the n.ginx server is installed.

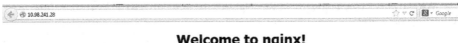

Welcome to nginx!

If you see this page, the nginx web server is successfully installed and working. Further configuration is required.

For online documentation and support please refer to nginx.org. Commercial support is available at nginx.com.

Thank you for using nginx.

***Figure 8-33.** Verifying Nginx install*

Squid(0.4.0)

Platform

The following platforms support this cookbook:

- Amazon (> = 0.0.0)
- CentOS (> = 0.0.0)
- Debian (> = 0.0.0)
- Fedora (> = 0.0.0)
- Red Hat (> = 0.0.0)
- Scientific (> = 0.0.0)
- Suse (> = 0.0.0)
- Ubuntu (> = 0.0.0)

Cookbook Download

You can download the cookbook for installing and configuring the Squid proxy server in the corresponding cookbooks directory inside your chef repo on your knife workstation, from the Opscode community web site, by running the following command on your knife workstation:

```
Knife cookbook site download squid
```

```
c:\chef-repo\cookbooks>knife cookbook site download squid
Downloading squid from the cookbooks site at version 0.4.0 to c:/chef-repo/cookb
ooks/squid-0.4.0.tar.gz
Cookbook saved: c:/chef-repo/cookbooks/squid-0.4.0.tar.gz

c:\chef-repo\cookbooks>
```

Figure 8-34. *Downloading the Squid cookbook*

The cookbook you downloaded is in 'tar.gz' format. You have to extract the cookbook from here (see Figure 8-35), as follows:

```
tar -xvf squid-0.4.0.tar.gz
```

```
c:\chef-repo>tar -xvf squid-0.4.0.tar.gz
x squid/
x squid/CHANGELOG.md
x squid/README.md
x squid/attributes
x squid/attributes/default.rb
x squid/files
x squid/files/default
x squid/files/default/mime.conf
x squid/libraries
x squid/libraries/default.rb
x squid/metadata.json
x squid/metadata.rb
x squid/recipes
x squid/recipes/default.rb
x squid/templates
x squid/templates/default
x squid/templates/default/redhat
x squid/templates/default/redhat/sysconfig
x squid/templates/default/redhat/sysconfig/squid.erb
x squid/templates/default/squid.conf.erb

c:\chef-repo>
```

Figure 8-35. *Extracting the file*

Cookbook Upload

In your chef repo directory on your knife workstation, go to the cookbooks folder and open Squid cookbook directory and open 'attributes/default.rb' file in the editor of your choice. Set the values of the attributes according to your settings. Following are the values used for the purpose of this book.

- node['squid']['port']=' 3128'

- Network caching proxy: node['squid']['network'] = 'your ip address range'

You can also change the listen interface and cache memory size for the proxy server by changing the following attributes in default.rb:

- default ['squid']['listen_interface'] = 'eth0'

- default ['squid']['cache_size'] = '100'

- default ['squid']['cache_mem'] = '2048'

Upload the cookbook (see Figure 8-36) to the chef server from your knife workstation, from inside the chef repo directory.

```
knife cookbook upload squid
```

```
c:\chef-repo>knife cookbook upload squid
Uploading squid              [0.4.0]
Uploaded 1 cookbook.

c:\chef-repo>
```

Figure 8-36. *Uploading the cookbook*

Add the cookbook to the run list of the node (see Figure 8-37), and run chef client to install and configure Squid cache.

```
Knife node run_list add node_name 'recipe[squid]'
```

```
c:\chef-repo>knife node run_list add chef-testing 'recipe[squid]'
chef-testing:
  run_list: recipe[squid]
  . . .
```

Figure 8-37. *Adding the cookbook to the run_list*

Client Run

Now, we run the chef client (see Figure 8-38) on the node on which we want to install and configure the Squid proxy server (see Figure 8-39).

```
~]# chef-client
Starting Chef Client, version 11.8.2
resolving cookbooks for run list: ["squid"]
Synchronizing Cookbooks:
  - squid
Compiling Cookbooks...
Converging 7 resources
```

Figure 8-38. *Chef client run start*

```
Converging 7 resources
Recipe: squid::default
  * package[squid] action install[2014-03-11T12:26:37+05:30] INFO: Processing pa
ckage[squid] action install (squid::default line 43)
[2014-03-11T12:26:53+05:30] INFO: package[squid] installing squid-3.1.10-20.el6_
5 from updates repository

   - install version 3.1.10-20.el6_5 of package squid

  * template[/etc/sysconfig/squid] action create[2014-03-11T12:27:58+05:30] INFO
: Processing template[/etc/sysconfig/squid] action create (squid::default line 4
6)
[2014-03-11T12:28:00+05:30] INFO: template[/etc/sysconfig/squid] backed up to /v
ar/chef/backup/etc/sysconfig/squid.chef-20140311122800.488386
[2014-03-11T12:28:00+05:30] INFO: template[/etc/sysconfig/squid] updated file co
ntents /etc/sysconfig/squid

   - update content in file /etc/sysconfig/squid from 8199a6 to 480edf
       --- /etc/sysconfig/squid        2014-01-21 16:11:58.000000000 +0530
       +++ /tmp/chef-rendered-template20140311-4227-uca5mo        2014-03-11 12:28
:00.480411917 +0530
       @@ -1,9 +1,8 @@
       # default squid options
```

Figure 8-39. Squid install

```
       # default squid conf file
       SQUID_CONF="/etc/squid/squid.conf"
   - restore selinux security context

  * directory[/etc/squid] action create[2014-03-11T12:28:00+05:30] INFO: Process
ing directory[/etc/squid] action create (squid::default line 54)
  (up to date)
  * cookbook_file[/etc/squid/mime.conf] action create[2014-03-11T12:28:00+05:30]
  INFO: Processing cookbook_file[/etc/squid/mime.conf] action create (squid::defa
ult line 62)
  (up to date)
  * file[/etc/squid/msntauth.conf] action delete[2014-03-11T12:28:00+05:30] INFO
: Processing file[/etc/squid/msntauth.conf] action delete (squid::default line 6
8)
```

Figure 8-40. Create mime.conf

```
[2014-03-11T12:28:00+05:30] INFO: file[/etc/squid/msntauth.conf] backed up to /v
ar/chef/backup/etc/squid/msntauth.conf.chef-20140311122800.799285
[2014-03-11T12:28:00+05:30] INFO: file[/etc/squid/msntauth.conf] deleted file at
 /etc/squid/msntauth.conf

   - delete file /etc/squid/msntauth.conf

  * template[/etc/squid/squid.conf] action create[2014-03-11T12:28:00+05:30] INF
O: Processing template[/etc/squid/squid.conf] action create (squid::default line
 73)
[2014-03-11T12:28:00+05:30] INFO: template[/etc/squid/squid.conf] backed up to /
var/chef/backup/etc/squid/squid.conf.chef-20140311122800.918881
[2014-03-11T12:28:00+05:30] INFO: template[/etc/squid/squid.conf] updated file c
ontents /etc/squid/squid.conf

   - update content in file /etc/squid/squid.conf from 10841e to d4d0ae
       --- /etc/squid/squid.conf        2014-01-21 16:11:53.000000000 +0530
       +++ /tmp/chef-rendered-template20140311-4227-tu7ey6        2014-03-11 12:28
:00.910410730 +0530
```

Figure 8-41. Create squid.conf

```
    - change mode from '0640' to '0644'
    - restore selinux security context

  * service[squid] action enable[2014-03-11T12:28:01+05:30] INFO: Processing ser
vice[squid] action enable (squid::default line 85)
[2014-03-11T12:28:01+05:30] INFO: service[squid] enabled

    - enable service service[squid]

  * service[squid] action start[2014-03-11T12:28:01+05:30] INFO: Processing serv
ice[squid] action start (squid::default line 85)
```

Figure 8-42. *Setting directory permissions and enabling service*

```
:08.979633316 +0100
        @@ -56,9 +56,9 @@
        # refresh_pattern           \.$                    1440    20%      10080
        # refresh_pattern           .                         0    20%          4
320
          hosts_file /etc/hosts
         -cache_dir ufs /var/spool/squid  16 256
         +cache_dir ufs /var/spool/squid 100 16 256
          coredump_dir /var/spool/squid                  •
          refresh_pattern deb$ 1577846 100% 1577846
          maximum_object_size 1024 MB
         -cache_mem 1024 MB
         +cache_mem 2048 MB
    - restore selinux security context

  * service[squid] action enable (up to date)
  * service[squid] action start
    - start service service[squid]

  * service[squid] action reload
    - reload service service[squid]

Chef Client finished, 3 resources updated
 ~]# ■t@chef-testing
```

Figure 8-43. *Chef client finish*

Once the client run has finished, we can determine if the Squid server was installed successfully by checking the Squid service (see Figure 8-44).

```
service squid status
```

```
 ~]# service squid status
squid (pid  4664) is running...
```

Figure 8-44. *Service status*

Wordpress(2.1.0)
Platform

The following operating systems support this cookbook:

- CentOS (> = 0.0.0)
- Debian (> = 0.0.0)
- Fedora (> = 0.0.0)
- Oracle (> = 0.0.0)
- Red Hat (> = 0.0.0)
- Scientific (> = 0.0.0)
- Ubuntu (> = 0.0.0)
- Windows (> = 0.0.0

Dependencies

This cookbook is dependent on the following cookbooks:

- MySQL, Version > = 1.0.5
- PHP, Version > = 0.0.0
- Apache2, Version > = 0.99.4
- IIS, Version > = 1.6.2
- OpenSSL, Version > = 0.0.0
- Database, Version > = 1.6.0
- Build essential, Version > = 0.0.0

Prerequisite

- Client machine must have a running Internet connection.

Cookbook Download

You can download the cookbook (see Figure 8-45) in your corresponding cookbooks directory inside your chef repo, on the knife workstation, from the Opscode community web site, by running the following command on your knife workstation:

```
knife cookbook site download wordpress
```

```
c:\chef-repo\cookbooks>knife cookbook site download wordpress
Downloading wordpress from the cookbooks site at version 2.1.0 to c:/chef-repo/c
ookbooks/wordpress-2.1.0.tar.gz
Cookbook saved: c:/chef-repo/cookbooks/wordpress-2.1.0.tar.gz

c:\chef-repo\cookbooks>_
```

Figure 8-45. *Downloading the cookbook*

The cookbook that is downloaded is in 'tar.gz' format. The cookbook has to be extracted from here (see Figure 8-46), as follows:

```
tar -xvf wordpress-2.1.0.tar.gz
```

```
c:\chef-repo>tar -xvf wordpress-2.1.0.tar.gz
x wordpress/
x wordpress/CHANGELOG.md
x wordpress/README.md
x wordpress/attributes
x wordpress/attributes/default.rb
x wordpress/libraries
x wordpress/libraries/helpers.rb
x wordpress/metadata.json
x wordpress/metadata.rb
x wordpress/recipes
x wordpress/recipes/database.rb
x wordpress/recipes/default.rb
x wordpress/recipes/languages.rb
x wordpress/templates
x wordpress/templates/default
x wordpress/templates/default/wordpress.conf.erb
x wordpress/templates/default/wp-config.php.erb
```

Figure 8-46. *Extracting the cookbook*

Cookbook Upload

In your chef repo directory on your knife workstation, go to the cookbooks folder and open Wordpress cookbook directory and open 'attributes/default.rb' file in the editor of your choice. Set the values of the attributes according to your settings. Following are the values used for the purpose of this book.

You can mention your own database name, user, and password, or you can use the defaults.

- default ['wordpress']['db']['name'] = "wordpressdb"

- default ['wordpress']['db']['user'] = "wordpressuser"

- default ['wordpress']['db']['pass'] = nil

If you want to allow the multisite features for your Wordpress site, you can set the corresponding attribute value.

- default ['wordpress']['allow_multisite'] = false

For the purpose of this book, we have set this attribute to 'false'. Now, upload the cookbook to the chef server (see Figure 8-47) by running the following command on your knife workstation, inside the chef repo directory:

```
knife cookbook upload wordpress
```

```
c:\chef-repo>knife cookbook upload wordpress
Uploading wordpress      [2.1.0]
Uploaded 1 cookbook.
```

Figure 8-47. *Uploading the cookbook*

After you have uploaded the cookbook, add the cookbook to the run list (see Figure 8-48) of the node on which Wordpress is to be installed, using knife while inside the chef repo directory.

```
knife node run_list add node_name wordpress
```

```
c:\chef-repo>knife node run_list add chef-testing 'recipe[wordpress]'
chef-testing:
  run_list: recipe[wordpress]
```

Figure 8-48. *Adding the cookbook to the run list*

Client Run

Now, we run the chef client on the node on which we want to install and configure Wordpress (see Figure 8-49). The chef client command can be run from any location on the node file system. (However, it is recommended to run from the user's home folder or the /root location).

```
[root@saltstack ~]# chef-client
[2014-03-11T13:22:26-04:00] INFO: Forking chef instance to converge...
Starting Chef Client, version 11.10.4
[2014-03-11T13:22:26-04:00] INFO: *** Chef 11.10.4 ***
[2014-03-11T13:22:26-04:00] INFO: Chef-client pid: 2098
[2014-03-11T13:22:28-04:00] INFO: Run List is [recipe[wordpress]]
[2014-03-11T13:22:28-04:00] INFO: Run List expands to [wordpress]
[2014-03-11T13:22:28-04:00] INFO: Starting Chef Run for saltstack
[2014-03-11T13:22:28-04:00] INFO: Running start handlers
[2014-03-11T13:22:28-04:00] INFO: Start handlers complete.
[2014-03-11T13:22:28-04:00] INFO: HTTP Request Returned 404 Object Not Found:
resolving cookbooks for run list: ["wordpress"]
[2014-03-11T13:22:29-04:00] INFO: Loading cookbooks [apache2, apt, aws, build-es
sential, chef_handler, database, homebrew, iis, iptables, logrotate, mysql, open
ssl, pacman, php, postgresql, windows, wordpress, xfs, xml, yum, yum-epel]
Synchronizing Cookbooks:
  - xfs
  - aws
  - apt
  - openssl
  - build-essential
  - postgresql
  - mysql
  - database
```

Figure 8-49. *Client run start*

```
Recipe: build-essential::rhel
    * package[autoconf] action install[2014-03-11T13:22:31-04:00] INFO: Processing
 package[autoconf] action install (build-essential::rhel line 35)
[2014-03-11T13:23:46-04:00] INFO: package[autoconf] installing autoconf-2.63-5.1
.el6 from base repository

    - install version 2.63-5.1.el6 of package autoconf

    * package[bison] action install[2014-03-11T13:24:27-04:00] INFO: Processing pa
ckage[bison] action install (build-essential::rhel line 35)
[2014-03-11T13:24:28-04:00] INFO: package[bison] installing bison-2.4.1-5.el6 fr
om base repository

    - install version 2.4.1-5.el6 of package bison
```

Figure 8-50. *Installing support package autoconf*

141

```
   * package[flex] action install[2014-03-11T13:24:37-04:00] INFO: Processing pac
kage[flex] action install (build-essential::rhel line 35)
[2014-03-11T13:24:37-04:00] INFO: package[flex] installing flex-2.5.35-8.el6 fro
m base repository

     - install version 2.5.35-8.el6 of package flex

   * package[gcc] action install[2014-03-11T13:24:45-04:00] INFO: Processing pack
age[gcc] action install (build-essential::rhel line 35)
[2014-03-11T13:24:45-04:00] INFO: package[gcc] installing gcc-4.4.7-4.el6 from b
ase repository

     - install version 4.4.7-4.el6 of package gcc

   * package[gcc-c++] action install[2014-03-11T13:28:57-04:00] INFO: Processing
package[gcc-c++] action install (build-essential::rhel line 35)
[2014-03-11T13:28:57-04:00] INFO: package[gcc-c++] installing gcc-c++-4.4.7-4.el
6 from base repository

     - install version 4.4.7-4.el6 of package gcc-c++
```

Figure 8-51. *Installing support packages*

```
   * package[kernel-devel] action install[2014-03-11T13:29:37-04:00] INFO: Proces
sing package[kernel-devel] action install (build-essential::rhel line 35)
[2014-03-11T13:29:38-04:00] INFO: package[kernel-devel] installing kernel-devel-
2.6.32-431.5.1.el6 from updates repository

     - install version 2.6.32-431.5.1.el6 of package kernel-devel

   * package[make] action install[2014-03-11T13:30:50-04:00] INFO: Processing pac
kage[make] action install (build-essential::rhel line 35)
   (up to date)
   * package[m4] action install[2014-03-11T13:30:50-04:00] INFO: Processing packa
ge[m4] action install (build-essential::rhel line 35)
   (up to date)
Recipe: mysql::client
   * package[mysql] action install[2014-03-11T13:30:50-04:00] INFO: Processing pa
ckage[mysql] action install (mysql::client line 47)
[2014-03-11T13:30:50-04:00] INFO: package[mysql] installing mysql-5.1.73-3.el6_5
 from updates repository

     - install version 5.1.73-3.el6_5 of package mysql
```

Figure 8-52. *Installing MySQL database*

```
[2014-03-11T19:23:15+05:30] INFO: directory[/var/www/wordpress] created director
y /var/www/wordpress

    - create new directory /var/www/wordpress[2014-03-11T19:23:15+05:30] INFO: d
irectory[/var/www/wordpress] owner changed to 0
[2014-03-11T19:23:15+05:30] INFO: directory[/var/www/wordpress] group changed to
 0
[2014-03-11T19:23:15+05:30] INFO: directory[/var/www/wordpress] mode changed to
755

    - change mode from '' to '0755'
    - change owner from '' to 'root'
    - change group from '' to 'root'
    - restore selinux security context

   * execute[extract-wordpress] action run[2014-03-11T19:23:15+05:30] INFO: Proce
ssing execute[extract-wordpress] action run (wordpress::default line 68)
[2014-03-11T19:23:16+05:30] INFO: execute[extract-wordpress] ran successfully

    - execute tar xf /var/chef/cache/wordpress.tar.gz --strip-components 1 -C /v
ar/www/wordpress

   * template[/var/www/wordpress/wp-config.php] action create[2014-03-11T19:23:16
+05:30] INFO: Processing template[/var/www/wordpress/wp-config.php] action creat
```

Figure 8-53. *Installing and configuring Wordpress*

```
   * template[/var/www/wordpress/wp-config.php] action create[2014-03-11T19:23:16
+05:30] INFO: Processing template[/var/www/wordpress/wp-config.php] action creat
e (wordpress::default line 74)
[2014-03-11T19:23:16+05:30] INFO: template[/var/www/wordpress/wp-config.php] cre
ated file /var/www/wordpress/wp-config.php

    - create new file /var/www/wordpress/wp-config.php[2014-03-11T19:23:16+05:30
] INFO: template[/var/www/wordpress/wp-config.php] updated file contents /var/ww
w/wordpress/wp-config.php

    - update content in file /var/www/wordpress/wp-config.php from none to 73262
c
        --- /var/www/wordpress/wp-config.php     2014-03-11 19:23:16.604446301 +0
530
        +++ /tmp/chef-rendered-template20140311-17304-16f3ib4     2014-03-11 19:23
:16.609410017 +0530
        @@ -1 +1,92 @@
        +<?php
        +/**
        + * The base configurations of the WordPress.
        + *
        + * This file has the following configurations: MySQL settings, Table Pr
efix,
        + * Secret Keys, WordPress Language, and ABSPATH. You can find more info
```

Figure 8-54. *Creating wp-config.php file*

ing execute[a2enmod rewrite] action run (apache2::mod_rewrite line 37)
  (skipped due to not_if)
Recipe: apache2::mod_headers
  * file[/etc/httpd/mods-available/headers.load] action create[2014-03-11T19:23:
16+05:30] INFO: Processing file[/etc/httpd/mods-available/headers.load] action c
reate (apache2::mod_headers line 30)
  (up to date)
  * execute[a2enmod headers] action run[2014-03-11T19:23:16+05:30] INFO: Process
ing execute[a2enmod headers] action run (apache2::mod_headers line 37)
  (skipped due to not_if)
Recipe: wordpress::default
  * template[/etc/httpd/sites-available/wordpress.conf] action create[2014-03-11
T19:23:16+05:30] INFO: Processing template[/etc/httpd/sites-available/wordpress.
conf] action create (wordpress::default line 29)
  (up to date)
  * execute[a2ensite wordpress.conf] action run[2014-03-11T19:23:16+05:30] INFO:
Processing execute[a2ensite wordpress.conf] action run (wordpress::default line
24)
  (skipped due to not_if)
[2014-03-11T19:23:17+05:30] INFO: Chef Run complete in 17.801298056 seconds
[2014-03-11T19:23:17+05:30] INFO: Running report handlers
[2014-03-11T19:23:17+05:30] INFO: Report handlers complete
Chef Client finished, 4 resources updated

Figure 8-55. *Chef client run finish*

Now, go to a web browser and open the webadmin ui page for your Wordpress
installation (see Figure 8-56).

http://your_ip_address

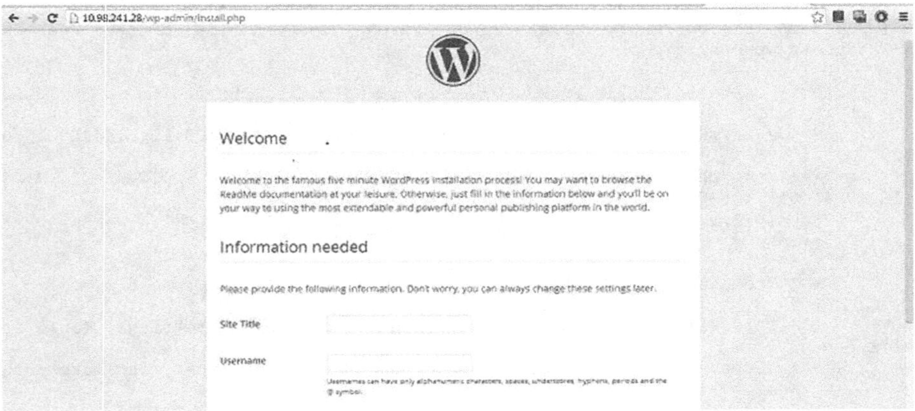

Figure 8-56. *Verifying installation*

Tomcat(0.15.0)

The following platforms support this cookbook:

Platform

- Amazon (> = 0.0.0)
- CentOS 6+
- Debian (> = 0.0.0)
- Fedora (> = 0.0.0)
- Red Hat 7+
- Ubuntu (> = 0.0.0)

Dependencies

- Java, Version (> = 0.0.0)
- OpenSSL, Version (> = 0.0.0)

Cookbook Download

You can download the cookbook (see Figure 8-57) for installing and configuring the Tomcat Server from the Opscode cookbook community site in the cookbooks directory inside your chef repo, on your knife workstation, as follows:

```
Knife cookbook site download tomcat
```

```
c:\chef-repo\cookbooks>knife cookbook site download tomcat
Downloading tomcat from the cookbooks site at version 0.15.4 to c:/chef-repo/coo
kbooks/tomcat-0.15.4.tar.gz
Cookbook saved: c:/chef-repo/cookbooks/tomcat-0.15.4.tar.gz

c:\chef-repo\cookbooks>
```

Figure 8-57. *Downloading the cookbook*

The downloaded cookbook is in 'tar.gz' format. Figure 8-58 shows the extraction of the cookbook

```
tar -xvf squid-0.4.0.tar.gz
```

```
c:\chef-repo>tar -xvf tomcat-0.15.4.tar.gz
x tomcat/
x tomcat/CHANGELOG.md
x tomcat/README.md
x tomcat/attributes
x tomcat/attributes/default.rb
x tomcat/libraries
x tomcat/libraries/chef_tomcat_cookbook.rb
x tomcat/metadata.json
x tomcat/metadata.rb
x tomcat/recipes
x tomcat/recipes/default.rb
x tomcat/recipes/users.rb
x tomcat/templates
x tomcat/templates/default
x tomcat/templates/default/default_tomcat6.erb
x tomcat/templates/default/logging.properties.erb
x tomcat/templates/default/manifest.xml.erb
x tomcat/templates/default/server.xml.erb
x tomcat/templates/default/setenv.sh.erb
x tomcat/templates/default/sysconfig_tomcat6.erb
x tomcat/templates/default/tomcat-users.xml.erb
```

Figure 8-58. *Extracting the cookbook*

Cookbook Upload

In your chef repo directory on your knife workstation, go to the cookbooks folder and open Tomcat cookbook directory and open 'attributes/default.rb' file in the editor of your choice.

Following are some important attributes whose values should be set according to the local setup. We use the values specified for the purpose of this book; they can be changed in the default.rb attribute file accordingly.

- node ["tomcat"]["port"] - 8080

- node ["tomcat"]["proxy_port"] - nil

The rest of the attribute values can be used as mentioned in the cookbook.

Upload the cookbook (see Figure 8-59) using the following command:

```
knife cookbook upload tomcat
```

```
c:\chef-repo>knife cookbook upload tomcat
Uploading tomcat          [0.15.4]
Uploaded 1 cookbook.
```

Figure 8-59. *Uploading the cookbook*

Now, add the recipe to the run list of the node on which Tomcat is to be installed and configured (see Figure 8-60).

```
knife node run_list add node_name 'recipe[tomcat]'
```

```
c:\chef-repo>knife node run_list add chef-testing 'recipe[tomcat]'
chef-testing:
  run_list: recipe[tomcat]
```

Figure 8-60. *Adding recipe to run list*

Client Run

Now, we run the chef client on the node on which we want to install and configure Tomcat (see Figure 8-61). The chef client command can be run from any location on the node file system. (However, it is recommended to run from the user's home folder or the /root location.

```
~]# chef-client
[2014-03-12T14:25:44+05:30] INFO: Forking chef instance to converge...
Starting Chef Client, version 11.8.2
[2014-03-12T14:25:44+05:30] INFO: *** Chef 11.8.2 ***
[2014-03-12T14:25:44+05:30] INFO: Chef-client pid: 21619
[2014-03-12T14:25:46+05:30] INFO: Run List is [recipe[tomcat]]
[2014-03-12T14:25:46+05:30] INFO: Run List expands to [tomcat]
[2014-03-12T14:25:46+05:30] INFO: Starting Chef Run for chef-testing
[2014-03-12T14:25:46+05:30] INFO: Running start handlers
[2014-03-12T14:25:46+05:30] INFO: Start handlers complete.
[2014-03-12T14:25:46+05:30] INFO: HTTP Request Returned 404 Object Not Found:
resolving cookbooks for run list: ["tomcat"]
```

Figure 8-61. *Chef client start*

```
  * package[java-1.6.0-openjdk-devel] action install[2014-03-12T14:29:21+05:30]
INFO: Processing package[java-1.6.0-openjdk-devel] action install (java::openjdk
 line 46)
[2014-03-12T14:29:21+05:30] INFO: package[java-1.6.0-openjdk-devel] installing j
ava-1.6.0-openjdk-devel-1.6.0.0-3.1.13.1.el6_5 from updates repository

    - install version 1.6.0.0-3.1.13.1.el6_5 of package java-1.6.0-openjdk-devel

  * java_alternatives[set-java-alternatives] action set[2014-03-12T14:36:00+05:3
0] INFO: Processing java_alternatives[set-java-alternatives] action set (java::o
penjdk line 50)

    - Add alternative for appletviewer
    - Add alternative for apt
    - Add alternative for extcheck
    - Add alternative for idlj
    - Add alternative for jar
    - Add alternative for jarsigner
    - Add alternative for java
    - Set alternative for java
    - Add alternative for javac
    - Set alternative for javac
    - Add alternative for javadoc
    - Add alternative for javah
```

Figure 8-62. *Installing Java*

```
Recipe: java::set_java_home
  * ruby_block[set-env-java-home] action run[2014-03-12T14:36:06+05:30] INFO: Pr
ocessing ruby_block[set-env-java-home] action run (java::set_java_home line 19)
[2014-03-12T14:36:06+05:30] INFO: ruby_block[set-env-java-home] called

    - execute the ruby block set-env-java-home

  * directory[/etc/profile.d] action create[2014-03-12T14:36:06+05:30] INFO: Pro
cessing directory[/etc/profile.d] action create (java::set_java_home line 26)
 (up to date)
  * file[/etc/profile.d/jdk.sh] action create[2014-03-12T14:36:07+05:30] INFO: P
rocessing file[/etc/profile.d/jdk.sh] action create (java::set_java_home line 30
)
[2014-03-12T14:36:07+05:30] INFO: file[/etc/profile.d/jdk.sh] created file /etc/
profile.d/jdk.sh

    - create new file /etc/profile.d/jdk.sh[2014-03-12T14:36:07+05:30] INFO: fil
e[/etc/profile.d/jdk.sh] updated file contents /etc/profile.d/jdk.sh
```

Figure 8-63. *Setting Java environment variables*

```
        @@ -1 +1,2 @@
        +export JAVA_HOME=/usr/lib/jvm/java-1.6.0[2014-03-12T14:36:07+05:30] INF
O: file[/etc/profile.d/jdk.sh] mode changed to 755

        - change mode from '' to '0755'
        - restore selinux security context

Recipe: tomcat::default
    * package[tomcat6] action install[2014-03-12T14:36:07+05:30] INFO: Processing
package[tomcat6] action install (tomcat::default line 45)
[2014-03-12T14:36:10+05:30] INFO: package[tomcat6] installing tomcat6-6.0.24-62.
el6 from base repository

        - install version 6.0.24-62.el6 of package tomcat6
```

Figure 8-64. *Installing the Tomcat package*

```
    * package[tomcat6-admin-webapps] action install[2014-03-12T14:41:45+05:30] INF
O: Processing package[tomcat6-admin-webapps] action install (tomcat::default lin
e 45)
[2014-03-12T14:41:48+05:30] INFO: package[tomcat6-admin-webapps] installing tomc
at6-admin-webapps-6.0.24-62.el6 from base repository

        - install version 6.0.24-62.el6 of package tomcat6-admin-webapps

    * directory[/usr/share/tomcat6/lib/endorsed] action create[2014-03-12T14:42:07
+05:30] INFO: Processing directory[/usr/share/tomcat6/lib/endorsed] action creat
e (tomcat::default line 51)
[2014-03-12T14:42:07+05:30] INFO: directory[/usr/share/tomcat6/lib/endorsed] cre
ated directory /usr/share/tomcat6/lib/endorsed

        - create new directory /usr/share/tomcat6/lib/endorsed[2014-03-12T14:42:07+0
5:30] INFO: directory[/usr/share/tomcat6/lib/endorsed] mode changed to 755

        - change mode from '' to '0755'
        - restore selinux security context
```

Figure 8-65. *Installing and configuring Tomcat*

```
 * template[/etc/sysconfig/tomcat6] action create[2014-03-12T15:08:34+05:30] IN
FO: Processing template[/etc/sysconfig/tomcat6] action create (tomcat::default l
ine 86)
[2014-03-12T15:08:34+05:30] INFO: template[/etc/sysconfig/tomcat6] created file
/etc/sysconfig/tomcat6

    - create new file /etc/sysconfig/tomcat6[2014-03-12T15:08:34+05:30] INFO: te
mplate[/etc/sysconfig/tomcat6] updated file contents /etc/sysconfig/tomcat6

    - update content in file /etc/sysconfig/tomcat6 from none to e89a49
        --- /etc/sysconfig/tomcat6        2014-03-12 15:08:34.474409800 +0530
        +++ /tmp/chef-rendered-template20140312-10298-fb1acq      2014-03-12 15:08
:34.478411084 +0530
        @@ -1 +1,66 @@
        +#
        +# Dynamically generated by Chef on
        +#
        +# Local modifications will be overwritten by Chef.
        +#
        +
        +# Service-specific configuration file for tomcat6. This will be sourced
by
        +# the SysV init script after the global configuration file
        +# /etc/tomcat6/tomcat6.conf, thus allowing values to be overridden in
```

Figure 8-66. *Creating the Tomcat configuration file*

```
[2014-03-12T15:08:34+05:30] INFO: template[/etc/sysconfig/tomcat6] mode changed
to 644

    - change mode from '' to '0644'
    - change owner from '' to 'root'
    - change group from '' to 'root'
    - restore selinux security context

  * template[/etc/tomcat6/server.xml] action create[2014-03-12T15:08:34+05:30] I
NFO: Processing template[/etc/tomcat6/server.xml] action create (tomcat::default
 line 111)
  (up to date)
   * template[/etc/tomcat6/logging.properties] action create[2014-03-12T15:08:34+
05:30] INFO: Processing template[/etc/tomcat6/logging.properties] action create
(tomcat::default line 119)
  (up to date)
   * execute[Create Tomcat SSL certificate] action run[2014-03-12T15:08:34+05:30]
INFO: Processing execute[Create Tomcat SSL certificate] action run (tomcat::def
ault line 128)
  (up to date)
   * service[tomcat] action start[2014-03-12T15:08:34+05:30] INFO: Processing ser
vice[tomcat] action start (tomcat::default line 178)
  (up to date)
```

Figure 8-67. *Setting read-write permissions on configuration file*

```
   * execute[wait for tomcat] action nothing[2014-03-12T15:08:36+05:30] INFO: Pro
cessing execute[wait for tomcat] action nothing (tomcat::default line 198)
  (skipped due to action :nothing)
[2014-03-12T15:08:36+05:30] INFO: template[/etc/sysconfig/tomcat6] sending resta
rt action to service[tomcat] (delayed)
   * service[tomcat] action restart[2014-03-12T15:08:36+05:30] INFO: Processing s
ervice[tomcat] action restart (tomcat::default line 178)
[2014-03-12T15:08:39+05:30] INFO: service[tomcat] restarted

    - restart service service[tomcat]

[2014-03-12T15:08:39+05:30] INFO: service[tomcat] sending run action to execute[
wait for tomcat] (immediate)
   * execute[wait for tomcat] action run[2014-03-12T15:08:39+05:30] INFO: Process
ing execute[wait for tomcat] action run (tomcat::default line 198)
[2014-03-12T15:08:44+05:30] INFO: execute[wait for tomcat] ran successfully

    - execute sleep 5

[2014-03-12T15:08:44+05:30] INFO: Chef Run complete in 27.630433712 seconds
[2014-03-12T15:08:44+05:30] INFO: Running report handlers
[2014-03-12T15:08:44+05:30] INFO: Report handlers complete
Chef Client finished, 4 resources updated
```

Figure 8-68. *Chef client finish*

Once the client run is finished, we check the port 8080 to check whether the Tomcat service is running (see Figure 8-69).

```
service tomcat6 status
```

```
~]# service tomcat6 status
tomcat6 (pid 31643) is running...                           [  OK  ]
~]# ▓t@chef-testing
```

Figure 8-69. *Verifying service status*

Now, you can go to a web browser and visit the UI using the IP address of the node on port 8080 (see Figure 8-70).

```
http://your_ip_address:8080
```

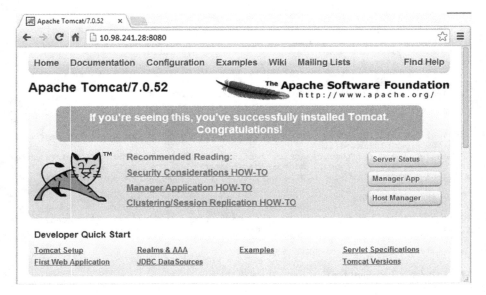

Figure 8-70. *Verifying installation*

We have tried to cover whatever you need in order to use cookbooks. In the next chapter we start with the development of cookbooks.

CHAPTER 9

▓ ▓ ▓

Developing a Cookbook

In this chapter, we walk you through the process of creating a cookbook. The chapter covers all important aspects of developing cookbooks.

Developing Your First Cookbook

Chef uses cookbooks to configure systems the way the administrator wants them to be configured.

We will assume that you have a chef server, a workstation, and a node already configured.

Cookbooks are created on the workstation using knife and are then uploaded to the chef server using knife.

We demonstrate the creation of a basic nginx cookbook that installs the Nginx web server on our node.

Figure 9-1 demonstrates how we will proceed in this chapter.

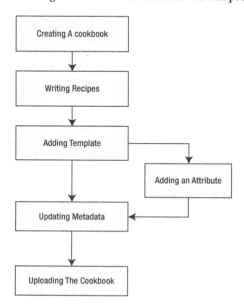

Figure 9-1. *Flow of the chapter*

The general syntax for creating a cookbook is

```
knife cookbook create cookbook_name
```

Since we are creating an nginx cookbook, we will run the following command, as shown in Figure 9-2:

```
knife cookbook create nginx
```

```
~]# knife cookbook create nginx
** Creating cookbook nginx
** Creating README for cookbook: nginx
** Creating CHANGELOG for cookbook: nginx
** Creating metadata for cookbook: nginx
~]# t@chef-testing
```

Figure 9-2. *Creating a cookbook*

Any knife command has to be executed from a workstation only.

The command would create a list of directories that are necessary for a cookbook, as shown in Figure 9-3.

```
cookbooks]# ls -la nginx
total 52
drwxr-xr-x. 10 root root 4096 Apr  2 07:54 .
drwxr-xr-x. 19 root root 4096 Apr  2 07:54 ..
drwxr-xr-x.  2 root root 4096 Apr  2 07:54 attributes
-rw-r--r--.  1 root root  447 Apr  2 07:54 CHANGELOG.md
drwxr-xr-x.  2 root root 4096 Apr  2 07:54 definitions
drwxr-xr-x.  3 root root 4096 Apr  2 07:54 files
drwxr-xr-x.  2 root root 4096 Apr  2 07:54 libraries
-rw-r--r--.  1 root root  274 Apr  2 07:54 metadata.rb
drwxr-xr-x.  2 root root 4096 Apr  2 07:54 providers
-rw-r--r--.  1 root root 1439 Apr  2 07:54 README.md
drwxr-xr-x.  2 root root 4096 Apr  2 07:54 recipes
drwxr-xr-x.  2 root root 4096 Apr  2 07:54 resources
drwxr-xr-x.  3 root root 4096 Apr  2 07:54 templates
cookbooks]# ting
```

Figure 9-3. *Cookbook Directory Structure*

The cookbook will be created in the directory specified in the knife configuration file. By default the directory in Windows is c:/chef/cookbooks and in Linux is /var/chef/cookbooks.

We will start our cookbook with the biggest chunk of configuration (i.e., the recipe).

Writing a Recipe

Go to the recipe subdirectory in the nginx cookbook directory. You will find a file named default.rb. This is the file that references the nginx recipe, and this is where we will add our code, as shown in Figure 9-4.

```
cookbooks]# ls -la nginx/recipes/
total 12
drwxr-xr-x.  2 root root 4096 Apr  2 07:54
drwxr-xr-x. 10 root root 4096 Apr  2 07:54
-rw-r--r--.  1 root root  131 Apr  2 07:54 default.rb
 cookbooks]# kbooks[root@chef-testing
```

Figure 9-4. *Listing the default recipe*

Whenever you create a cookbook with knife it creates a default recipe. This recipe is executed whenever you add the cookbook to the run list of any node. Open the default.rb file in the text editor of your choice. There may be a commented header in the file as shown in Figure 9-5.

```
 recipes]# vi default.rb
#
# Cookbook Name:: nginx
# Recipe:: default
#
# Copyright 2014, YOUR_COMPANY_NAME
#
# All rights reserved - Do Not Redistribute
#
```

Figure 9-5. *Content of a recipe*

The first thing we need to make sure of is that we install the nginx package on the node. We can achieve this using the package resource as shown in Figure 9-6.

```
package 'nginx' do
  action :install
end
```

Figure 9-6. *Adding a resource to our recipe*

The code in Figure 9-6 will use the native functionality based upon the operating system and will install the nginx package on it. If nginx is already installed on the node, then chef agent will do nothing and it will not be reinstalled.

After installing the package, we would like to start the service and enable the service on startup. This can be achieved using the service resource. The piece of code in Figure 9-7 will help us in achieving that goal.

```
service 'nginx' do
  action [ :enable, :start ]
end
```

Figure 9-7. *Adding another resource*

We have included two items in the action. The enable action will enable the nginx service on startup, and the start action will start the nginx service after installing the package.

After making sure that the package is installed and the service is running properly, we need to create a file that will be hosted on our nginx server. We will create a file and will use a cookbook_file resource to distribute the file.

The code shown in Figure 9-8 displays this.

```
cookbook_file "/usr/share/nginx/www/index.html" do
  source "index.html"
  mode "0644"
end
```

Figure 9-8. *Adding the cookbook_file resource*

We are done with the recipe writing. You can save and close your recipe. The final recipe should look like the one shown in Figure 9-9.

```
#
# Cookbook Name:: nginx
# Recipe:: default
#
# Copyright 2014, YOUR_COMPANY_NAME
#
# All rights reserved - Do Not Redistribute
#

package 'nginx' do
  action :install
end

service 'nginx' do
  action [ :enable, :start ]
end

cookbook_file "/usr/share/nginx/www/index.html" do
  source "index.html"
  mode "0644"
end
```

Figure 9-9. *The Recipe*

Creating the Index File

We have used the cookbook_file resource, which will look for the index.html file in the files directory of the cookbook. If the file is not present, then the cookbook will not be compiled properly, so we need to create the index file. Go to the nginx/files/default subdirectory and create the index file as shown in Figure 9-10.

```
<html>
  <head>
    <title>Hello</title>
  </head>
  <body>
    <h1>This is a test cookbook</h1>
    <p>This is an nginx Server</p[>
  </body>
</html>
```

Figure 9-10. *Writing a recipe*

157

Changing the Metadata

This is an optional but recommended step in order to create a cookbook. The metadata file is present in the cookbook subdirectory. By default, it looks like the example shown in Figure 9-11. We can add or change this file as per the requirement. We can change the cookbook version and other things. Also, metadata can be used to provide any dependencies.

```
 nginx]# vi metadata.rb
name               'nginx'
maintainer         'YOUR_COMPANY_NAME'
maintainer_email   'YOUR_EMAIL'
license            'All rights reserved'
description        'Installs/Configures nginx'
long_description   IO.read(File.join(File.dirname(__FILE__), 'README.md'))
version            '0.1.0'
```

Figure 9-11. *Changing the metadata*

Uploading the Cookbook

The next step would be to upload the cookbook to the chef server so that it can be deployed on any client. This can be easily done with the help of knife as shown in Figure 9-12.

```
knife cookbook upload nginx
```

```
 nginx]# knife cookbook upload nginx
Uploading nginx            [0.1.0]
Uploaded 1 cookbook.
 nginx]# f/cookbooks/nginx[root@chef-testing
```

Figure 9-12. *Uploading the cookbook*

Running the Cookbook

After the cookbook has been uploaded to the chef server, we need to add it to the run list of the node on which we want to deploy it. This can be done with the help of knife, as shown in Figure 9-13. These commands are executed from a workstation.

```
knife node run_list add node_name cookbook_name
```

```
nginx]# knife node run_list add chef-testing nginx
chef-testing:
  run_list: recipe[nginx]
```

Figure 9-13. *Adding to run list*

The next step would be to run the chef client on the node to see the cookbook execution (see Figure 9-14). Whenever we install chef client it automatically gets added to the path, and thus it can run from anywhere.

```
nginx]# chef-client
Starting Chef Client, version 11.8.2
resolving cookbooks for run list: ["nginx"]
Synchronizing Cookbooks:
  - nginx
Compiling Cookbooks...
Converging 3 resources
Recipe: nginx::default
  * package[nginx] action install (up to date)
  * service[nginx] action enable (up to date)
  * service[nginx] action start (up to date)
  * cookbook_file[/usr/share/nginx/html/index.html] action create
    - update content in file /usr/share/nginx/html/index.html from 38ffd4 to 210
1e5
```

Figure 9-14. *Running chef client*

```
    -
    -<p>For online documentation and support please refer to
    -<a href="http://nginx.org/">nginx.org</a>.<br/>
    -Commercial support is available at
    -<a href="http://nginx.com/">nginx.com</a>.</p>
    -
    -<p><em>Thank you for using nginx.</em></p>
    -</body>
    +   <head>
    +     <title>Hello</title>
    +   </head>
    +   <body>
    +     <h1>This is a test cookbook</h1>
    +     <p>This is an nginx Server</p[>
    +   </body>
      </html>
  - restore selinux security context
Chef Client finished, 1 resources updated
```

Figure 9-15. *Chef client finished*

To check whether your cookbook has been deployed successfully (see Figure 9-16), open a web browser and enter http://ipaddressofyourserver. You should be able to view the contents of the index page.

This is a test cookbook

This is an nginx Server

Figure 9-16. *Checking whether cookbook is successfully deployed*

Add an Attribute

Now we will add an attribute to our recipe. An attribute can be used to change the default settings on the node. We will change the listen port of nginx. By default, nginx services run on port 80. We will change the port to 82. To change the listen port, add an attribute in the default.rb file present in the attributes subdirectory as shown in Figure 9-17.

```
default['nginx']['listen_port']        = '82'
```

Figure 9-17. *Adding an attribute*

Add a Resource to the Default Recipe

The next step would be to add a template resource to our recipe which will help us in rendering the configuration file. A cookbook template is an Embedded Ruby (ERB) template that is used to generate files based on the variables and logic contained within the template. Templates may contain Ruby expressions and statements and are a great way to manage configuration files across an organization.

Add the template resource as shown in Figure 9-18.

```
template 'default.conf' do
  path    "/etc/nginx/conf.d/default.conf"
  source 'default.conf.erb'
end
```

Figure 9-18. *Adding a template resource*

This would render the default.conf.erb file present in templates/default subdirectory and copy it to /etc/nginx/conf.d/default.conf. We can manage the permissions of the file using the attributes available in the template resource. Refer to Chapter 7 for more on this topic.

Add the Template File

We also need to add the template file that would be rendered. Create a file in the templates/default subdirectory as shown in Figure 9-19.

```
server {
    listen       <%= node['nginx']['listen_port'] %>;
    server_name  localhost;

    #charset koi8-r;
    #access_log  /var/log/nginx/log/host.access.log  main;

    location / {
        root   /usr/share/nginx/html;
        index  index.html index.htm;
    }
```

Figure 9-19. *Adding a template file*

At the time of rendering, the listen port will take from the attribute file by default. The attribute defined earlier is passed on to the template as shown in the code.

The attributes can also be provided in an environment or in roles, and they would be taken according to the precedence level.

Uploading and Running the Cookbook

Upload the cookbook again to the chef server so that the changes are updated. Run chef client again on the node to apply the changes (see Figures 9-20 and 9-21).

```
 nginx]# knife cookbook upload nginx
Uploading nginx              [0.1.0]
Uploaded 1 cookbook.
 nginx]# ▊/cookbooks/nginx[root@chef-testing
```

Figure 9-20. *Testing cookbooks*

```
         --- /etc/nginx/conf.d/default.conf       2014-04-03 08:06:40.785642303 +0
100
         +++ /tmp/chef-rendered-template20140403-21653-133w4ws    2014-04-03 08:10
:26.407633195 +0100
         @@ -1,5 +1,5 @@
          server {
         -     listen     80;
         +     listen     82;
```

Figure 9-21. *Changing the configuration*

Knife commands are executed from a workstation and chef client can run on any node that is under management of chef.

To test whether your changes have been applied, open a web browser and try opening http://ipaddressofyourserver. An error will come up.

Now try opening http://ipaddressofyourserver:82 and it will open the index page as shown in Figure 9-22.

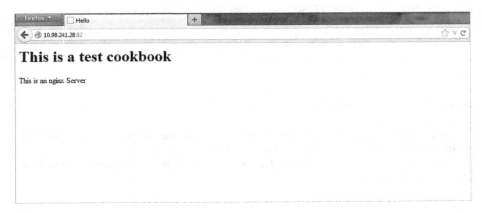

Figure 9-22. *Testing cookbook*

Using Environments

An environment is a way to group our nodes; we can have environment-specific attributes. We can use environments to map the organization's policies.

Chef creates a default environment and puts every node in it by default. We can modify the environment later on by editing the node object. An environment can be created using knife or the management console. This time, we will create the environment using the management console.

After a login to the management console, click the environments tab as shown in Figure 9-23.

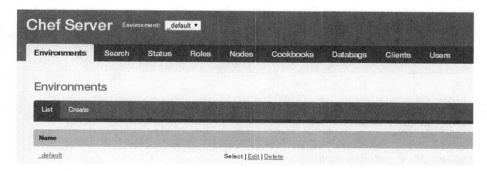

Figure 9-23. *Creating the environment*

Click create to create a new environment. Provide a name for your environment and add some description to it (see Figure 9-24).

Environment

List   Create

Name
test
The name of the Environment

Description
Test enviroment
A description of this Environment

Cookbook Version Constraints

Name	Operator	Version	
▼	~> ▼	0.0.0	Add

Figure 9-24. *Creating an environment*

We can add cookbook version constraints if we want to. We will keep it empty for now. This is used if we want certain configuration on nodes in a particular environment.

The next step is to add some attributes that will be overridden during the next chef run (see Figure 9-25).

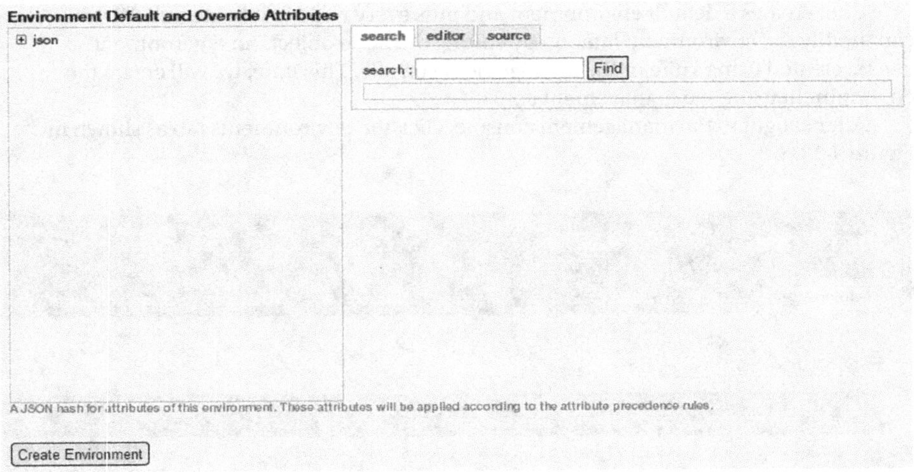

Figure 9-25. *Creating an environment*

Click create environment to create the environment. After the environment has been created, we will edit it using knife and add an override attribute to override the listen port for nginx. This would open up the environment object located on the chef server in the EDITOR environment variable (see Figure 9-26).

```
~]# knife environment edit test
{
  "name": "test",
  "description": "Test enviroment",
  "cookbook_versions": {
  },
  "json_class": "Chef::Environment",
  "chef_type": "environment",
  "default_attributes": {
  },
  "override_attributes": {
    "nginx": {
      "listen_port": [
        "85"
      ]
    }
  }
}
```

Figure 9-26. *Editing an environment*

Save the file and it will be updated on the server. The file gets updated on the chef server database directly. The next step is to change the environment of our node so that the attributes are overridden. Go to the nodes tab in the management console and select the node you want to edit. We can also change a node's environment using knife (see Figure 9-27).

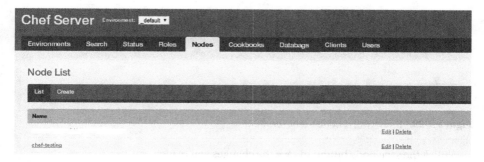

Figure 9-27. *Changing a node's environment(1)*

Click edit and select the environment from the dropdown as shown in Figure 9-28.

Figure 9-28. *Changing a node's environment(2)*

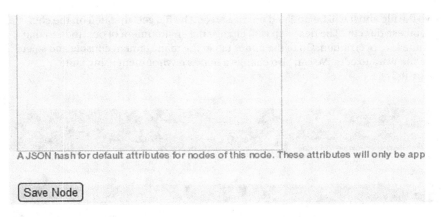

A JSON hash for default attributes for nodes of this node. These attributes will only be app

[Save Node]

Figure 9-29. *Changing a node's environment*

Click the save node button to save the changes you made.

Now run chef client on the node to check whether the attribute is getting overridden. Run chef client on the node where we will deploy the nginx server (Figure 9-30).

```
    - update content in file /etc/nginx/conf.d/default.conf from 441c00 to 3e304
c
        --- /etc/nginx/conf.d/default.conf       2014-04-03 10:42:48.939632666 +0
100
        +++ /tmp/chef-rendered-template20140403-3558-55azq9       2014-04-03 10:43
:16.416631663 +0100
        @@ -1,5 +1,5 @@
          server {
        -     listen       82;
        +     listen       85;
              server_name  localhost;
```

Figure 9-30. *Changing the configuration file*

To test whether your changes have been applied, open a web browser and try opening http://ipaddressofyourserver:85. The index page should come up as shown in figure 9-31.

Figure 9-31. *Testing the changes*

We have demonstrated how environments can be used to manage our nodes. The implementation of environments is specific to an organization's policies and processes. With chef, it becomes simple and easy to manage different environments. As an example, an organization may have Development, Test, QA, and production environments, each with different guidelines and policies. A single chef cookbook can be overridden to provide different attributes for different environments without changing the code in the cookbook. Thus, environments provide an easy mechanism to change or override the configuration based on the environment to which a node belongs.

■ ■ ■

## CHAPTER 10

Lightweight Resource Providers

This chapter discusses lightweight resource providers (LWRPs). They are a way to enhance the functionality of chef to provide new integrations which are not provided for out-of-box in chef.

Lightweight Resource Providers

A resource is something that defines the action that needs to be taken and a provider is something that executes that action.

To implement the functionality of a resource and provider in a recipe which is not an inbuilt resource provider, you can create your own LWRPs. You can use custom Ruby codes and inbuilt chef resources to create an LWRP.

LWRPs help in achieving the core objective of chef which is *idempotence*. One can achieve this state using scripts or recipes by leveraging "if"-type constructs to choose when to run the script; however, this process becomes fairly complex to manage.

LWRPs help us in achieving idempotence for complex and scalable infrastructure to provide reliable configuration management.

LWRPs are loaded from files that are saved in the following cookbook subdirectories:

Directory	Description
providers/	The subdirectory in which lightweight providers are located.
resources/	The subdirectory in which lightweight resources are located.

The name of the cookbook and the name of the files in the resources/ and providers/ subdirectories determine the naming patterns of LWRPs.

For example, if a cookbook named example was downloaded to the chef repository, it would be located under /cookbooks/example/. If that cookbook contained two resources and two providers, the following files would be part of the resources/ directory:

Files	Resource Name	Generated Class
default.rb	Example	Chef::Resource::Example
custom.rb	Custom	Chef::Resource::ExampleCustom

And the following files would be part of the providers/ directory:

Files	Provider Name	Generated Class
default.rb	Example	Chef::Provider::Example
custom.rb	Custom	Chef::Provider::ExampleCustom

Chef-Maintained LWRPs

Chef maintains a number of LWRPs. We will discuss some of the important LWRPs maintained by the Opscode community. These are available in cookbooks. If we need to use them, we need to download the cookbook from the community, upload the cookbook to our chef server, and then use them in our custom recipes.

Cookbook	Description
apt	This cookbook is used to configure APT (Advanced Packaging Tool) for managing APT preferences and repositories.
aws	AWS refers to Amazon Web Services. This cookbook can be used to manage the resources that are running in AWS cloud.
chef_handler	This cookbook is used for exception handling. It distributes and enables the exception and report handlers.
cron	Cron is used to schedule something in Unix. This cookbook is used to install cron and start its service.
daemontools	Daemontools are used to manage Unix services. This cookbook is used to install and configure daemontools.
firewall	This cookbook is used to maintain the firewall rules.
homebrew	Homebrew is a package manager for Mac OS. This cookbook helps us to install and configure Homebrew.
iis	This is a Windows-based cookbook and can be used to install and configure IIS (Internet Information Services) server.

(continued)

(continued)

Cookbook	Description
lvm	This cookbook is used to install the LVM2 package and then manage LVM.
nginx	This cookbook is used to install and configure Nginx from source code or package and then set up configuration handling.
php	This cookbook can be used to install and configure PHP and custom modules for PHP.
postfix	This cookbook can be used to install and configure Postfix.
powershell	This cookbook is used to install the Powershell module on Windows servers.
rabbitmq	This cookbook will install the RabbitMQ-server.
squid	This cookbook is used to install and configure Squid as a caching proxy server.
sudo	This cookbook is used install sudo and then configure the/etc/sudoers file.
windows	This cookbook can be used for the built-in Windows commands.
yum	This cookbook is used for the yum configuration file.

Creating an LWRP

This section will demonstrate how to create an LWRP. We will create an LWRP to download Wordpress setup, extract it to the desired location, and then delete the downloaded file.

1. The first step is to create a cookbook in which we will create the resource and provider. Create a cookbook named wp_setup using the knife. We execute the following command from a workstation:

   ```
   knife cookbook create wp_setup
   ```

2. The command creates the files and directories that are required for developing a cookbook (see Figure 10-1). The cookbook will be created in the local chef repository.

```
attributes
    --default.rb
providers
    --default.rb
resources
    --default.rb
recipes
    --default.rb
```

Figure 10-1. *Directory structure*

3. The resource directory is where we create our resource. Create a default.rb file in the resource directory. In the default.rb, write the following code:

```
actions :extract, :remove
attribute :wp_url, :kind_of=> String, default:
"https://wordpress.org/latest.tar.gz"
attribute :wp_path, :kind_of=> String, default: "/var/www"
```

In this code sample, we are defining the following:

- Actions: this defines the actions that need to be taken in this particular resource. In this case, we are defining two actions: extract and remove.

- Attribute: here we define the attributes that will be passed to the resource. In this example, we are passing an attribute called wp_url, which is kind_of string and is a default parameter. The value of this parameter is the download location of the Wordpress web site tar file.

A default attribute is specified in the resource file so that if an attribute is not specified in the recipe or attribute file, chef client will take the default value from the resource file.

4. The next step after defining the resource is to map the actions that we have defined to actual execution code which is defined in the provider.

When the chef client identifies a custom resource, it will look for the related actions method in the provider.

Create a default.rb file under the folder named providers of wp_setup cookbook. In this file, we define the actions to be performed.

Create methods for the custom actions specified in the resource file.

```
def whyrun_supported?
  true
end
```

We use the whyrun method if we want chef client to tell the changes that would be applied to the node without actually applying them when it is run in whyrun mode. Its value can be true or false. For this example, we will set this value to true. To run the chef client in whyrun mode, run Chef-client -W.

Now we need to define the code that will be executed on calling of actions that we defined in the resources. First we will define the extract action. We will use Ruby and inbuilt chef resources to define the complete set of actions.

In this method we are using the File.exists? method to check if there is an existing Wordpress folder to achieve idempotency.

Chef::Log class is used to log entries in the log file.

A new_resource.updated_by_last_action method notifies the LWRP if the node has successfully updated. True or false is passed as an argument to this method to notify the execution of LWRP.

The converge_by is a wrapper method used when the chef client runs in whyrun mode and displays a message about that block of code.

```
if ::File.exists?("#{new_resource.wp_path}/wordpress")

    Chef::Log.info "#{ @new_resource } already exists - nothing to do."
    new_resource.updated_by_last_action(false)

else

converge_by("Downloading wordpress file") do
```

The remote_file is an inbuilt chef resource that downloads the file from a certain URL (uniform resource locator) to the node.

```
remote_file "#{new_resource.wp_path}/wordpress.tar.gz" do

    source "#{new_resource.wp_url}"
    action :create

end
```

Bash is also an inbuilt chef resource that is used to run bash scripts. We are using the bash resource to extract the downloaded Wordpress file.

```
bash "extracting wordpress" do

    code <<-EOH
    cd /var/www
    mkdir wordpress
    tar -xvf wordpres.tar.gz wordpress
    EOH

end
```

The following snippet shows the whole code clubbed together:

```
action :extract do

 if ::File.exists?("#{new_resource.wp_path}/wordpress")

   Chef::Log.info "#{ @new_resource } already exists - nothing to do."
   new_resource.updated_by_last_action(false)

 else

 converge_by("Downloading wordpress file") do

 remote_file "#{new_resource.wp_path}/wordpress.tar.gz" do

  source "#{new_resource.wp_url}"
  action :create

 end

 bash "extracting wordpress" do

   code <<-EOH
   cd /var/www
   mkdir wordpress
   tar -xvf wordpres.tar.gz wordpress
   EOH

 end

 end

 new_resource.updated_by_last_action(true)

 end

end
```

Action: remove: This method contains the inbuilt file resource which will delete the Wordpress installation file.

Chef::Log class is used to log entries in the log file.

The new_resource.updated_by_last_action method notifies the LWRP if the node has successfully updated. True or false is passed as argument to this method to notify the execution of LWRP.

converge_by is a wrapper method used when chef client runs in whyrun mode and displays a message about that block of code.

File is an inbuilt chef resource that has an action delete, which will delete any file.

```
action :remove do

 unless ::File.exists?("#{new_resource.wp_path}/wordpress.tar.gz")

  Chef::Log.info "#{ @new_resource } file deleted - nothing to do."
  new_resource.updated_by_last_action(false)

 else

 converge_by("removing the compressed wordpress file") do

  file "#{new_resource.wp_path}/wordpress.tar.gz" do
  action :delete

  end

  directory "/root/chefdemo" do

   action :create

  end

 end

 new_resource.updated_by_last_action(true)

 end

end
```

5. You can use the resource name in the recipe once the resource and provider are in place. Since we created the resource and provider in default.rb files, the resource name will be the cookbook's name. If the resource and provider have a name other than default.rb, that name has to be appended to the cookbook name while using it in the recipe.

    ```
    syntax: cookbookname_resourcename
    wp_setup "extracting wordpress" do
    wp_path node[:wordpress][:path]
    wp_url node[:wordpress][:url]
    action :extract
    end
    ```

```
wp_setup "deleting the installation file" do
  wp_path node[:wordpress][:path]
  action :remove
end
```

6. The attributes wp_path and wp_url are passed using the attribute file.

```
default[:wordpress][:url] =
"https://wordpress.org/latest.tar.gz"
default[:wordpress][:path] = "/var/www"
```

7. Upload the cookbook to chef server using knife (see Figure 10-2). Knife commands are executed from a workstation.

```
knife cookbook upload wp_setup
```

```
PS C:\chef-repo\chef> knife cookbook upload wp_setup
Uploading wp_setup        [0.1.0]
Uploaded 1 cookbook.
```

Figure 10-2. *Uploading the cookbook*

8. Run the chef client on the node (see Figure 10-3).

```
root@ip-172-31-39-128:~# chef-client
Starting Chef Client, version 11.10.4
resolving cookbooks for run list: ["wp_setup"]
Synchronizing Cookbooks:
  - wp_setup
Compiling Cookbooks...
Converging 2 resources
Recipe: wp_setup::default
  * wp_setup[download and extract wordpress] action extract
    - Downloading wordpress file
Recipe: <Dynamically Defined Resource>
  * remote_file[/var/www/wordpress.tar.gz] action create
    - create new file /var/www/wordpress.tar.gz
    - update content in file /var/www/wordpress.tar.gz from none to 2c5c56
        (new content is binary, diff output suppressed)
  * bash[extracting wordpress] action run
    - execute "bash" "/tmp/chef-script20140407-4469-4sb7j2"
Recipe: wp_setup::default
  * wp_setup[deleting the installation file] action remove
    - removing the compressed wordpress file
Recipe: <Dynamically Defined Resource>
  * file[/var/www/wordpress.tar.gz] action delete
    - delete file /var/www/wordpress.tar.gz
Running handlers:
Running handlers complete
Chef Client finished, 5/5 resources updated in 5.719641517 seconds
```

Figure 10-3. *Running chef client*

9. Confirm the chef client run (see Figure 10-4) by browsing the
Wordpress directory under the /var/www folder.

```
root@ip-172-31-39-128:/var/www# ls
wordpress
root@ip-172-31-39-128:/var/www# cd wordpress/
root@ip-172-31-39-128:/var/www/wordpress# ls
index.php          wp-blog-header.php     wp-includes        wp-settings.php
license.txt        wp-comments-post.php   wp-links-opml.php  wp-signup.php
readme.html        wp-config-sample.php   wp-load.php        wp-trackback.php
wp-activate.php    wp-content             wp-login.php       xmlrpc.php
wp-admin           wp-cron.php            wp-mail.php
```

Figure 10-4. *Verifying installation*

■ ■ ■

## CHAPTER 11

High Availability

The open source chef server does not offer high availability by default. Therefore, we recommend an enterprise chef production environment, which comes with options for high availability.

In this chapter, we talk about high availability (Database and Application Layer) that can be achieved in the open source version. We set up high availability on AWS (Amazon Web Services) instances.

Prerequisite

It is necessary to have two servers with chef installed. Communication is allowed between the two servers on required ports. An ELB (Elastic Load Balancer) would route the traffic between two instances.

Setting Up HA

The first thing in setting up high availability (HA) is to identify the things we need to replicate for setup.

The following things are required to be replicated in open source chef server:

1. Database replication

2. Bookshelf directory replication (cookbooks replication)

The database used in open source chef is Postgresql, and we will be using native functionality of postgresql (i.e., streaming replication) to set up database replication.

Streaming Replication

Streaming replication continuously ships and applies the WAL XLog to the standby servers. The streaming replication uses continuous archiving to create a cluster configuration with one or more standby servers that can take over if the primary server fails. This is known as a warm standby or log shipping.

In streaming replication, the primary and the standby servers work together. The primary server operates in continuous archiving mode, while each standby server operates in continuous recovery mode, reading the WAL files from the primary server.

No changes to the database tables are required to enable this capability, so it offers low-administration overhead compared to some other replication solutions.

The impact on the primary server performance is low in this configuration.

We will be setting up streaming replication using a third-party tool, repmgr, which automates certain manual steps.

The first thing you have to do is check that chef server is installed on both the servers and is running fine (see Figures 11-1 and 11-2). Run the following command to check:

```
chef-server-ctl status
```

```
[root@chefserver1 ~]# chef-server-ctl status
run: bookshelf: (pid 681) 181s; run: log: (pid 676) 181s
run: chef-expander: (pid 684) 181s; run: log: (pid 678) 181s
run: chef-server-webui: (pid 685) 181s; run: log: (pid 679) 181s
run: chef-solr: (pid 680) 181s; run: log: (pid 674) 181s
run: erchef: (pid 1790) 83s; run: log: (pid 677) 181s
run: nginx: (pid 689) 181s; run: log: (pid 688) 181s
run: postgresql: (pid 686) 181s; run: log: (pid 673) 181s
run: rabbitmq: (pid 682) 181s; run: log: (pid 675) 181s
```

Figure 11-1. *Chef server status on 1ˢᵗ server*

```
[root@chefserver2 ~]# chef-server-ctl status
run: bookshelf: (pid 635) 201s; run: log: (pid 634) 201s
run: chef-expander: (pid 643) 201s; run: log: (pid 637) 201s
run: chef-server-webui: (pid 646) 201s; run: log: (pid 640) 201s
run: chef-solr: (pid 647) 201s; run: log: (pid 644) 201s
run: erchef: (pid 1734) 105s; run: log: (pid 632) 201s
run: nginx: (pid 642) 201s; run: log: (pid 641) 201s
run: postgresql: (pid 638) 201s; run: log: (pid 633) 201s
run: rabbitmq: (pid 645) 201s; run: log: (pid 639) 201s
```

Figure 11-2. *Chef server status on 2ⁿᵈ server*

Setting Up Repmgr

Repmgr requires you to install GCC (GNU Compiler Collection) on the chef server. Install it first before continuing (see Figure 11-3).

```
[root@chefserver2 ~]# yum -y install gcc
Loaded plugins: amazon-id, rhui-lb, security
rhui-REGION-client-config-server-6                          | 2.9 kB     00:00
rhui-REGION-rhel-server-releases                            | 3.7 kB     00:00
rhui-REGION-rhel-server-releases/primary_db                 |  26 MB     00:01
rhui-REGION-rhel-server-releases-optional                   | 3.5 kB     00:00
rhui-REGION-rhel-server-releases-optional/primary_db        | 2.7 MB     00:00
Setting up Install Process
```

Figure 11-3. *Installing GCC*

Download the repmgr package from repmgr's web site (see Figure 11-4). Internet is required to complete this process.

```
[root@chefserver1 ~]# wget http://www.repmgr.org/download/repmgr-1.2.0.tar.gz
--2014-04-09 03:40:21--  http://www.repmgr.org/download/repmgr-1.2.0.tar.gz
Resolving www.repmgr.org... 62.48.53.98
Connecting to www.repmgr.org|62.48.53.98|:80... connected.
HTTP request sent, awaiting response... 200 OK
Length: 51608 (50K) [application/x-gzip]
Saving to: "repmgr-1.2.0.tar.gz"

100%[=======================================>] 51,608         90.6K/s    in 0.6s

2014-04-09 03:40:23 (90.6 KB/s) - "repmgr-1.2.0.tar.gz" saved [51608/51608]
```

Figure 11-4. *Downloading repmgr*

The downloaded file is a tar file. Untar the file (see Figure 11-5).

```
[root@chefserver1 ~]# tar xvzf repmgr-1.2.0.tar.gz
repmgr-1.2.0/
repmgr-1.2.0/.gitignore
repmgr-1.2.0/COPYRIGHT
repmgr-1.2.0/CREDITS
repmgr-1.2.0/HISTORY
repmgr-1.2.0/LICENSE
repmgr-1.2.0/Makefile
repmgr-1.2.0/README.rst
repmgr-1.2.0/TODO
repmgr-1.2.0/check_dir.c
repmgr-1.2.0/check_dir.h
repmgr-1.2.0/config.c
repmgr-1.2.0/config.h
repmgr-1.2.0/dbutils.c
repmgr-1.2.0/dbutils.h
repmgr-1.2.0/debian/
repmgr-1.2.0/debian/DEBIAN/
repmgr-1.2.0/debian/DEBIAN/control
repmgr-1.2.0/errcode.h
repmgr-1.2.0/log.c
repmgr-1.2.0/log.h
repmgr-1.2.0/repmgr.c
```

Figure 11-5. *Extracting repmgr*

The next step is to install repmgr (see Figure 11-6). Go to the repmgr directory.

```
[root@chefserver1 ~]# cd repmgr-1.2.0
[root@chefserver1 repmgr-1.2.0]# █
```

Figure 11-6. *Installing repmgr*

Repmgr requires the postgres directory to be available in the path. To do this, export the path (see Figure 11-7).

```
[root@chefserver1 repmgr-1.2.0]# export PATH=$PATH:/usr/bin:/root/bin:/opt/chef-
server/embedded/bin/
[root@chefserver1 repmgr-1.2.0]# █
```

Figure 11-7. *Exporting the path*

Add the following directory to your path:

/opt/chef-server/embedded/bin/

To install repmgr (see Figure 11-8), use the following command (see Figures 11-8 and 11-9):

make USE_PGXS=1
make USE_PGXS=1 install

```
[root@chefserver1 repmgr-1.2.0]# make USE_PGXS=1
Makefile:34: warning: overriding commands for target `install'
/opt/chef-server/embedded/lib/postgresql/pgxs/src/makefiles/pgxs.mk:120: warning
: ignoring old commands for target `install'
gcc -L/opt/chef-server/embedded/lib -I/opt/chef-server/embedded/include -Wall -W
missing-prototypes -Wpointer-arith -Wdeclaration-after-statement -Wendif-labels
-Wmissing-format-attribute -Wformat-security -fno-strict-aliasing -fwrapv -I/opt
/chef-server/embedded/include -I. -I. -I/opt/chef-server/embedded/include/postgr
esql/server -I/opt/chef-server/embedded/include/postgresql/internal -D_GNU_SOURC
E  -I/opt/chef-server/embedded/include  -c -o dbutils.o dbutils.c
gcc -L/opt/chef-server/embedded/lib -I/opt/chef-server/embedded/include -Wall -W
missing-prototypes -Wpointer-arith -Wdeclaration-after-statement -Wendif-labels
-Wmissing-format-attribute -Wformat-security -fno-strict-aliasing -fwrapv -I/opt
/chef-server/embedded/include -I. -I. -I/opt/chef-server/embedded/include/postgr
esql/server -I/opt/chef-server/embedded/include/postgresql/internal -D_GNU_SOURC
E  -I/opt/chef-server/embedded/include  -c -o config.o config.c
gcc -L/opt/chef-server/embedded/lib -I/opt/chef-server/embedded/include -Wall -W
missing-prototypes -Wpointer-arith -Wdeclaration-after-statement -Wendif-labels
-Wmissing-format-attribute -Wformat-security -fno-strict-aliasing -fwrapv -I/opt
/chef-server/embedded/include -I. -I. -I/opt/chef-server/embedded/include/postgr
esql/server -I/opt/chef-server/embedded/include/postgresql/internal -D_GNU_SOURC
E  -I/opt/chef-server/embedded/include  -c -o repmgrd.o repmgrd.c
gcc -L/opt/chef-server/embedded/lib -I/opt/chef-server/embedded/include -Wall -W
missing-prototypes -Wpointer-arith -Wdeclaration-after-statement -Wendif-labels
```

Figure 11-8. *Installing repmgr*

```
[root@chefserver1 repmgr-1.2.0]# make USE_PGXS=1 install
Makefile:34: warning: overriding commands for target `install'
/opt/chef-server/embedded/lib/postgresql/pgxs/src/makefiles/pgxs.mk:120: warning
: ignoring old commands for target `install'
/bin/mkdir -p '/opt/chef-server/embedded/share/postgresql/contrib'
/bin/sh /opt/chef-server/embedded/lib/postgresql/pgxs/src/makefiles/../../config
/install-sh -c  repmgrd '/opt/chef-server/embedded/bin'
/bin/sh /opt/chef-server/embedded/lib/postgresql/pgxs/src/makefiles/../../config
/install-sh -c  repmgr '/opt/chef-server/embedded/bin'
/bin/sh /opt/chef-server/embedded/lib/postgresql/pgxs/src/makefiles/../../config
/install-sh -c -m 644 ./repmgr.sql '/opt/chef-server/embedded/share/postgresql/c
ontrib'
/bin/sh /opt/chef-server/embedded/lib/postgresql/pgxs/src/makefiles/../../config
/install-sh -c -m 644 ./uninstall_repmgr.sql '/opt/chef-server/embedded/share/po
stgresql/contrib'
[root@chefserver1 repmgr-1.2.0]#
```

Figure 11-9. *Installing repmgr*

Installation is complete. To verify the installation (see Figure 11-10), run the following command:

```
repmgr -V
```

```
[root@chefserver1 repmgr-1.2.0]# repmgr -V
repmgr 1.2.0 (PostgreSQL 9.2.4)
[root@chefserver1 repmgr-1.2.0]#
```

Figure 11-10. *Verifying the installation*

This process needs to be repeated on the slave node as well. Repeat the steps of installing repmgr.

Master Node Settings

On the master node, go to the `postgre` data directory (see Figure 11-11). The default directory created by chef is as follows:

```
/var/opt/chef-server/postgresql/data
```

```
[root@chefserver1 data]# ls
base     pg_hba.conf   pg_notify   pg_stat_tmp  pg_twophase  postgresql.conf
global   pg_ident.conf pg_serial   pg_subtrans  PG_VERSION   postmaster.opts
pg_clog  pg_multixact  pg_snapshots pg_tblspc   pg_xlog      postmaster.pid
[root@chefserver1 data]#
```

Figure 11-11. *Postgre directory*

Open the postgresql.conf file and edit the listen_addresses field so that we are able to connect to the master server from the slave server (see Figure 11-12).

```
# - Connection Settings -

listen_addresses = '*█    # what IP address(es) to listen on;
            # comma-separated list of addresses;
            # defaults to 'localhost', '*' = all
            # (change requires restart)
port = 5432        # (change requires restart)
max_connections = 200   # (change requires restart)
# Note:  Increasing max_connections costs ~400 bytes of shared memory per
# connection slot, plus lock space (see max_locks_per_transaction).
```

Figure 11-12. Changing the configuration file

The next thing to edit in the configuration file is the wal_level (see Figure 11-13). Change it to hot_standby. wal_level determines how much information is written to the WAL. In hot_standby level, the same information is logged as with archive, plus information needed to reconstruct the status of running transactions from the WAL.

```
wal_level = 'hot_standby'
```

```
# - Settings -
wal_level = hot_standby
#wal_level = minimal        # minimal, archive, or hot_standby
            # (change requires restart)
#fsync = on        # turns forced synchronization on or off
#synchronous_commit = on    # synchronization level; on, off, or local
#wal_sync_method = fsync    # the default is the first option
            # supported by the operating system:
            #    open_datasync
            #    fdatasync (default on Linux)
```

Figure 11-13. Changing the configuration file

As streaming replication uses archiving to create logs, we need to enable archiving on the master server (see Figure 11-14). The archive command can be anything which would do nothing. Here we are using cd. You can also use any other command.

```
archive_mode = on
archive_command = 'cd.'
```

```
# - Archiving -

archive_ode =on
archive_command = 'cd .▯

#archive_mode = off    # allows archiving to be done
         # (change requires restart)
#archive_command = ''    # command to use to archive a logfile segment
#archive_timeout = 0     # force a logfile segment switch after this
         # number of seconds; 0 disables
```

Figure 11-14. *Setting up archiving*

After the archiving, change the setting seen in Figure 11-15, which will change the number of sender processes that would ship the log.

```
max_wal_senders = 10
wal_keep_segments = 5000


# - Master Server -

# These settings are ignored on a standby server

max_wal_senders = 10

wal_keep_segments = 5000
#max_wal_senders = 0     # max number of walsender processes
         # (change requires restart)
#wal_sender_delay = 1s    # walsender cycle time, 1-10000 milliseconds
#wal_keep_segments = 0    # in logfile segments, 16MB each; 0 disables
#vacuum_defer_cleanup_age = 0 # number of xacts by which cleanup is delayed
#replication_timeout = 60s  # in milliseconds; 0 disables
#synchronous_standby_names = '' # standby servers that provide sync rep
```

Figure 11-15. *Changing the configuration file*

The configuration changes have been done. Now we need to set up the trust so that the master server will accept connections from the standby server (see Figure 11-16). Edit the pg_hba available in the /var/opt/chef-server/postgresql/data directory and add the ip/subnets from where you want to add trust.

```
# TYPE   DATABASE    USER       CIDR-ADDRESS         METHOD

# "local" is for Unix domain socket connections only
local   all         all                              trust

host    all         all        127.0.0.1/32            trust
host    all         all        ::1/128              trust
host    all         all        10.0.0.0/8           trust
host    replication all        10.0.0.0/8           trust
▮
```

Figure 11-16. *Setting up trust*

Restart the chef server on the master node to apply the changes (see Figure 11-17).

```
[root@chefserver1 data]# chef-server-ctl restart
ok: run: bookshelf: (pid 5570) 0s
ok: run: chef-expander: (pid 5600) 1s
ok: run: chef-server-webui: (pid 5605) 0s
ok: run: chef-solr: (pid 5616) 0s
ok: run: erchef: (pid 5621) 0s
ok: run: nginx: (pid 5633) 1s
ok: run: postgresql: (pid 5673) 0s
ok: run: rabbitmq: (pid 5676) 0s
[root@chefserver1 data]# █
```

Figure 11-17. Restarting the chef server

Run the following command to verify that the configuration on the master server is fine (see Figure 11-18):

```
ps aux | grep postgre
```

```
[root@chefserver1 data]# ps aux | grep postgre
root      2743  0.0  0.0   3936   408 ?        Ss  03:36   0:00 runsv postgresql
root      2744  0.0  0.0   4080   540 ?        S   03:36   0:00 svlogd -tt /var/log/chef-server/postgresql
497       6678  0.4  1.8 493584 32184 ?        Ss  04:01   0:00 /opt/chef-server/embedded/bin/postgres -D /var/opt/chef-s
erver/postgresql/data
497       6704  0.0  0.0 493796  1216 ?        Ss  04:01   0:00 postgres: checkpointer process
497       6705  0.0  0.1 493796  2268 ?        Ss  04:01   0:00 postgres: writer process
497       6706  0.0  0.0 493796  1136 ?        Ss  04:01   0:00 postgres: wal writer process
497       6707  0.0  0.1 494664  2368 ?        Ss  04:01   0:00 postgres: autovacuum launcher process
497       6708  0.0  0.0  26288   924 ?        Ss  04:01   0:00 postgres: archiver process
```

Figure 11-18. Verifying a master configuration

A process should come up with description 'wal writer process.'

Slave Node Settings

For setting up the streaming replication, we need to clone the data directory of the master server on the standby server (see Figure 11-19).

Clear the data directory on the slave node and run the following command:

```
repmgr -D /var/opt/chef-server/postgresql/data/ -d opscode_chef -p 5432 -U
opscode-pgsql -R root --verbose standby clone $masterip
```

Where masterip is the IP (Internet protocol), address of the master node.

- -D – The data directory. (The default directory is /var/opt/chef-server/postgresql/data)

- -d – The database to clone.

- -p – Port on which server is running on the master node.

- -U – The user of the database.

- -R – The user with which keyless SSH is present.

```
[root@chefserver2 data]# repmgr -D /var/opt/chef-server/postgresql/data/ -d opsc
ode_chef -p 5432 -U opscode-pgsql -R root --verbose standby clone 10.0.0.95█
```

Figure 11-19. *Cloning the master server*

```
sent 11 bytes  received 73 bytes  56.00 bytes/sec
total size is 3246  speedup is 38.64
standby clone: master ident file '/var/opt/chef-server/postgresql/data/pg_ident.
conf'
rsync command line: 'rsync --archive --checksum --compress --progress --rsh=ssh
 root@10.0.0.95:/var/opt/chef-server/postgresql/data/pg_ident.conf /var/opt/chef
-server/postgresql/data//.'
receiving incremental file list

sent 11 bytes  received 75 bytes  57.33 bytes/sec
total size is 1636  speedup is 19.02
Finishing backup...
NOTICE:  pg_stop_backup complete, all required WAL segments have been archived
repmgr requires primary to keep WAL files 000000010000000000000003 until at leas
t 000000010000000000000003
repmgr standby clone complete
```

Figure 11-20. *Cloning complete*

```
[root@chefserver2 data]# chown opscode-pgsql.root pg_xlog/
[root@chefserver2 data]# █
```

Figure 11-21. *Cloning complete*

Change the permission of the pg_xlog folder. The folder in present in the data directory. The path to the directory is /var/opt/chef-server/postgresql/data.

Restart the chef server to see the changes (see Figure 11-22).

```
[root@chefserver2 data]# chef-server-ctl restart
ok: run: bookshelf: (pid 3833) 1s
ok: run: chef-expander: (pid 3850) 1s
ok: run: chef-server-webui: (pid 3854) 0s
ok: run: chef-solr: (pid 3861) 0s
ok: run: erchef: (pid 3866) 0s
ok: run: nginx: (pid 3887) 0s
ok: run: postgresql: (pid 3903) 1s
ok: run: rabbitmq: (pid 3911) 0s
[root@chefserver2 data]# ▌
```

Figure 11-22. *Restarting the chef server*

To verify that the slave configuration is complete, run the command shown in Figure 11-23.

```
[root@chefserver2 data]# ps aux | grep postgre
root      2696  0.0  0.0   3936   404 ?        Ss   03:35   0:00 runsv postgresql
root      2697  0.0  0.0   4080   536 ?        S    03:35   0:00 svlogd -tt /var/log/chef-server/postgresql
497       7029  0.6  1.8 493584 32172 ?        Ss   04:21   0:00 /opt/chef-server/embedded/bin/postgres -D /var/opt/chef-s
erver/postgresql/data
497       7042  0.0  0.0 493864  1592 ?        Ss   04:21   0:00 postgres: startup process   waiting for 00000001000000000
0000006
497       7044  0.0  0.0 493796  1216 ?        Ss   04:21   0:00 postgres: checkpointer process
497       7045  0.1  0.0 493796  1616 ?        Ss   04:21   0:00 postgres: writer process
497       7046  0.0  0.0  26288  1088 ?        Ss   04:21   0:00 postgres: stats collector process
497       7047  0.1  0.1 500272  2060 ?        Ss   04:21   0:00 postgres: wal receiver process
```

Figure 11-23. *Verifying the configuration*

A process should come up with the description 'wal receiver process'.

Verifying

To verify that your replication has been set up, create a test database on the master server (see Figure 11-24).

```
opscode_chef=# create database test;
CREATE DATABASE
opscode_chef=# ▌
```

Figure 11-24. *Creating a database*

List the database on the master server (see Figure 11-25).

```
opscode_chef-# \l
                                        List of databases
      Name     |     Owner       | Encoding | Collate | Ctype |          Access privileges
---------------+-----------------+----------+---------+-------+-----------------------------------------
 opscode_chef  | opscode-pgsql   | UTF8     |  C      |  C    | =Tc/"opscode-pgsql"                    +
               |                 |          |         |       | "opscode-pgsql"=CTc/"opscode-pgsql"+
               |                 |          |         |       | opscode_chef=CTc/"opscode-pgsql"      +
               |                 |          |         |       | opscode_chef_ro=CTc/"opscode-pgsql"
 postgres      | opscode-pgsql   | SQL_ASCII |  C      |  C    |
 template0     | opscode-pgsql   | SQL_ASCII |  C      |  C    | =c/"opscode-pgsql"                     +
               |                 |          |         |       | "opscode-pgsql"=CTc/"opscode-pgsql"
 template1     | opscode-pgsql   | SQL_ASCII |  C      |  C    | =c/"opscode-pgsql"                     +
               |                 |          |         |       | "opscode-pgsql"=CTc/"opscode-pgsql"
 test          | opscode-pgsql   | SQL_ASCII |  C      |  C    |
(5 rows)
```

Figure 11-25. *Listing databases on the master server*

List the database on the slave server (see Figure 11-26). The database that was created on the master would be shown in the slave node as well (test).

```
[root@chefserver2 ~]# psql -U opscode-pgsql opscode_chef
psql (9.2.4)
Type "help" for help.

opscode_chef=# \l
                                        List of databases
      Name     |     Owner       | Encoding | Collate | Ctype |          Access privileges
---------------+-----------------+----------+---------+-------+-----------------------------------------
 opscode_chef  | opscode-pgsql   | UTF8     |  C      |  C    | =Tc/"opscode-pgsql"                    +
               |                 |          |         |       | "opscode-pgsql"=CTc/"opscode-pgsql"+
               |                 |          |         |       | opscode_chef=CTc/"opscode-pgsql"      +
               |                 |          |         |       | opscode_chef_ro=CTc/"opscode-pgsql"
 postgres      | opscode-pgsql   | SQL_ASCII |  C      |  C    |
 template0     | opscode-pgsql   | SQL_ASCII |  C      |  C    | =c/"opscode-pgsql"                     +
               |                 |          |         |       | "opscode-pgsql"=CTc/"opscode-pgsql"
 template1     | opscode-pgsql   | SQL_ASCII |  C      |  C    | =c/"opscode-pgsql"                     +
               |                 |          |         |       | "opscode-pgsql"=CTc/"opscode-pgsql"
 test          | opscode-pgsql   | SQL_ASCII |  C      |  C    |
(5 rows)

opscode_chef=# █
```

Figure 11-26. *Listing databases on the slave server*

Cookbook Replication

For the cookbook replication, we can use any shared file system. The directory that needs to be shared among the two servers is

`/var/opt/chef-server/bookshelf/data`

Please make sure that the permissions of the folder are the same on the master and the slave nodes.

As the streaming replication sets up the database replication in a primary-secondary mode, we need to make sure that chef client requests are routed to the primary server or else they will not be completed.

The clients will connect to both the chef servers through a load balancer and will connect to the secondary server in case the primary is down.

What we did is just a workaround for HA. We still need to set up failover/failback, which will be done manually or can be automated using scripts. In case one of the database servers fails, the other one is brought up to take the workload. In case of the failure of the chef server, the other one takes up the load of the application server which is down since all configuration and cookbooks are available to both of the servers.

Enterprise Chef HA

Enterprise chef comes with different types of deployment scenarios. One of them is built-in support for HA. It has a fully automated failover for stateful components. The whole architecture of chef is divided into two tiers.

First would be the web facing tier, which handles the user interface, and the API (application programming interface) requests that come to the chef server.

The second tier is the application tier or the back-end tier, which handles the data storage and retrieval, which consist of

- CouchDB

- PostgreSQL

- Opscode solr

- RabbitMQ

- Redis

- Cookbook data

The failover of the application tier or the back-end tier is achieved using the following:

- DRBD (Distributed Replication Block Device) is used to manage the block-level replication.

- A primary and backup cluster election using VRRP (Virtual Router Redundancy Protocol) over unicast TCP/IP and Keepalived.

- A virtual IP address to the primary server, maintained based on the results of the election done by Keepalived.

The web tier or the front-end tier is a load balancer. Chef recommends a hardware load balancer with SSL offloading and round robin as the load balancing algorithm (see Figure 11-27).

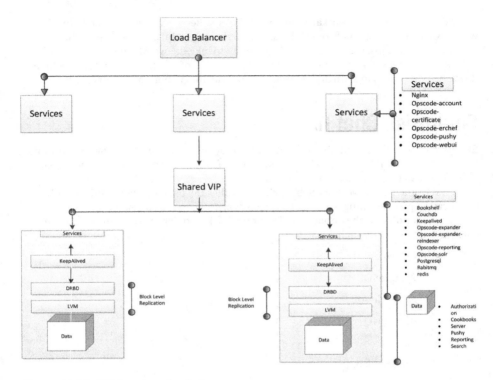

Figure 11-27. *HA in enterprise chef*

■ ■ ■

## CHAPTER 12

Cloud Provisioning Using Chef

Provisioning Using Vagrant and Chef

Until now we have seen how to leverage chef to provision and configure application and database environments. In this chapter we introduce our readers to how Vagrant and chef can work together to bring up complete environments including the virtual infrastructure.

Vagrant is an open source infrastructure provisioning solution that integrates with VMware, AWS, VirtualBox, and other hypervisor and cloud environments to provision virtual and cloud infrastructure.

After provisioning of the cloud or virtual infrastructure through Vagrant, chef can be used to deploy and configure the application servers and databases on the virtual machine.

Thus a combination of Vagrant and chef can provide immense benefits to enterprises looking to automate the infrastructure and environment and build use cases.

Just as chef has a concept of recipe, Vagrant has the concept of a Vagrantfile which provides the configuration details for the virtual machine or cloud infrastructure.

A much used use case of the Vagrant tool is to create disposable infrastructure and environments for developers and testers. As development and test environments need frequent provisioning and deprovisioning, the power of Vagrant to quickly assemble the required infrastructure helps the infrastructure and automation teams in fulfilling the demands of the development and test teams.

With its integrations to various hypervisors and cloud providers the same Vagrant tool can be used to provision the infrastructure in premise virtual infrastructure and the cloud.

Technically, Vagrant is a Ruby-based application. Vagrant can be easily deployed as a virtual machine on VirtualBox or VMware workstation.

Vagrant can quickly deploy the environment using a single command "vagrantup" once the Vagrant tool is up and running and is configured with correct Vagrantfile.

Providers and Provisioners

The development environment can be configured using Vagrant's providers and provisioners.

Providers are the virtual machine solutions such as VirtualBox, VMWare, Amazon AWS, and Digital Ocean.

Provisioners are used to manage the configuration in your development environment. Chef and puppet are few examples of provisioners used by Vagrant. Using provisioners you can automate the application configuration process on a Vagrant box.

Installing Vagrant

Vagrant works on Windows (32 bit and 64 bit), Linux Debian (32 bit and 64 bit), Linux rpm based (32 bit and 64 bit), and MAC OS X (32 bit and 64 bit) environments.

Install Virtual Box

Vagrant works with virtual box in the back end. So, before installing Vagrant, virtual box has to be installed in your system. Virtual box has to be installed on a workstation and not on any virtual machine.

Go to www.virtualbox.org/wiki/Downloads. Download and install the latest virtual box software.

Install Vagrant on Windows

1. Go to www.vagrantup.com/downloads.

2. Download the Vagrant Windows MSI installer package (see Figure 12-1).

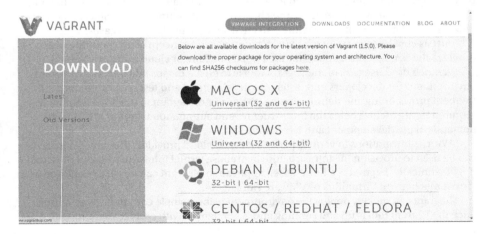

Figure 12-1. *Downloading Vagrant*

3. Run the installer (see Figure 12-2).

Figure 12-2. Running the Vagrant Installer

4. Click next.

Figure 12-3. Installing Vagrant

5.　Accept the license and click next.

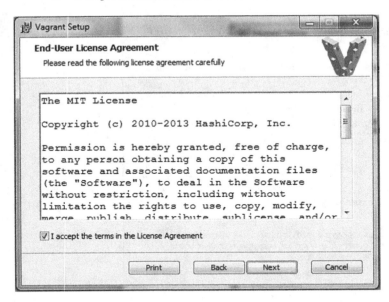

Figure 12-4. Accepting the Terms

6.　Enter the destination folder for Vagrant and click next.

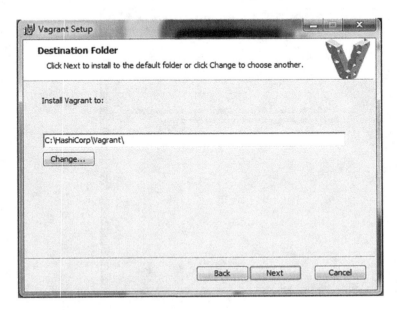

Figure 12-5. Selecting a Installation Directory

7. Click install.

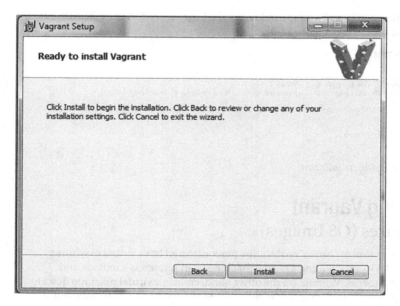

Figure 12-6. Installing Vagrant

8. Click finish.

Figure 12-7. Finishing installation

Verifying Vagrant Installation

Open the windows command prompt and check the Vagrant version to make sure it is installed in your system (see Figure 12-8).

    1.   vagrant –v

```
Microsoft Windows [Version 6.1.7601]
Copyright (c) 2009 Microsoft Corporation.  All rights reserved.

C:\Users\Administrator>vagrant -v
Vagrant 1.3.5

C:\Users\Administrator>
```

Figure 12-8. Verifying installation

Configuring Vagrant
Vagrant Boxes (OS Images)

Vagrant uses the notion of "boxes" to describe preconfigured base virtual machines from which we can work. Creating a virtual machine from scratch is a tedious and time-consuming process. Vagrant, on the other hand, creates a virtual machine quickly by cloning the preconfigured virtual machines. These preconfigured base images are termed as boxes in Vagrant.

You can download Vagrant boxes (Linux based) based on your requirement from here www.vagrantbox.es/.

■ **Note**   Install git bash on your system to work with Vagrant on Windows since Windows command line does not support SSH protocol.

Two Methods to Download Vagrant Box

    1.   Download and add the Vagrant base box (see Figure 12-9) with preconfigured chef using the following command:

```
#syntax vagrant box add {boxname} {box provider url}
vagrant box add ubunt12.04 http://files.vagrantup.com/precise32.box
```

```
ITDtpAdmin@DS-E0CB4EA250EB /c/Users
$ vagrant box add ubunt12.04 http://files.vagrantup.com/precise32.box
Downloading or copying the box...
Progress: 3% (Rate: 102k/s, Estimated time remaining: 0:39:56))
```

Figure 12-9. Adding Vagrant box directly

Vagrant boxes will be downloaded to the users/.vagrant.d/boxes folder.

2. Download the box directly from https://files.vagrantup.com to your file system and you can add that box to Vagrant by specifying the local file system path (see Figure 12-10).

```
vagrant box add vagrant_demo C:\Users\Administrator\centos\CentOS-6.4-i386-v.box
```

```
PS C:\> vagrant box add vagrantdemo C:\Users\Administrator\centos\CentOS-6.4-i386-v20130731.box
Downloading or copying the box...
Extracting box...ate: 1587k/s, Estimated time remaining: --:--:--)
Successfully added box 'vagrantdemo' with provider 'virtualbox'!
PS C:\>
```

Figure 12-10. Adding vagrant box from file system

Vagrantfile

The next step is to configure Vagrant using a Vagrantfile.

1. The first step is to create a root directory. A few configurations related to Vagrant will be relative to this directory

2. Mention the kind of box and provisioners you need to have in your environment in the Vagrantfile.

3. Vagrantfile can be created using vagrant-init command. This command will create a Vagrantfile in your current directory. Adding the existing box title to the vagrant-init command will create a Vagrantfile with the configuration details of the mentioned box.

```
#syntax vagrant init {box-title}
```

```
vagrant init ubunt12.04
```

The foregoing command creates a Vagrantfile (see Figure 12-11) based on the base box titled ubunt12.04.

```
$ mkdir vagrant_demo

ITDtpAdmin@DS-E0CB4EA250EB /c/Users
$ cd vagrant_demo/

ITDtpAdmin@DS-E0CB4EA250EB /c/Users/vagrant_demo
$ vagrant init
A `Vagrantfile` has been placed in this directory. You are now
ready to `vagrant up` your first virtual environment! Please read
the comments in the Vagrantfile as well as documentation on
`vagrantup.com` for more information on using Vagrant.
```

Figure 12-11. Creating a Vagrantfile

Provisioning a New Instance

You can start the virtual machine (see Figure 12-12) using "vagrant up" command. When you use this command, make sure that your present working directory is the directory which contains the Vagrantfile.

```
ITDtpAdmin@DS-E0CB4EA250EB /c/Users/centos
$ vagrant up
Bringing machine 'default' up with 'virtualbox' provider...
[default] Clearing any previously set forwarded ports...
[default] Creating shared folders metadata...
[default] Clearing any previously set network interfaces...
[default] Preparing network interfaces based on configuration...
[default] Forwarding ports...
[default] -- 22 => 2222 (adapter 1)
[default] Booting VM...
[default] Waiting for machine to boot. This may take a few minutes...
[default] Machine booted and ready!
[default] The guest additions on this VM do not match the installed version of
VirtualBox! In most cases this is fine, but in rare cases it can
cause things such as shared folders to not work properly. If you see
shared folder errors, please update the guest additions within the
virtual machine and reload your VM.

Guest Additions Version: 4.2.16
VirtualBox Version: 4.3
[default] Configuring and enabling network interfaces...
[default] Mounting shared folders...
[default] -- /vagrant

ITDtpAdmin@DS-E0CB4EA250EB /c/Users/centos
```

Figure 12-12. *Starting a virtual machine*

Here we are using centos box which has already been downloaded using "vagrant box add" command. The Vagrantfiles relative to centos box are present inside the c:/users/centos folder.

Connecting to a Virtual Machine

The virtual machine (VM) which got spun up by Vagrant can be connected using the "vagrant ssh" command. This command will drop you into a full-fledged SSH session. By default, a Vagrant VM will have username and password "vagrant."

```
ITDtpAdmin@DS-E0CB4EA250EB /c/Users/centos
$ vagrant ssh
Last login: Tue Mar 11 06:49:46 2014 from 10.0.2.2
Welcome to your Vagrant-built virtual machine.
[vagrant@localhost ~]$
```

The network details are fetched from the Vagrantfile. You can have a host-only access static IP or dynamic IP allocated by the public network.

```
# Create a private network, which allows host-only access to the machine
# using a specific IP.
# config.vm.network :private_network, ip: "192.168.33.10"
# Create a public network, which generally matched to bridged network.
# Bridged networks make the machine appear as another physical device on
# your network.
# config.vm.network :public_network
```

Also, you can spin up multiple VMs using one Vagrantfile by defining more than one VM in the Vagrantfile. By default there will be only a box definition inside a Vagrantfile (e.g., config.vm.box = "vagrantdemo"). SSH access can be made to individual VMs using the name given in the definition.

```
config.vm.define "VM1" do |web|
    web.vm.box = "ubuntu"
  end

config.vm.define "VM2" do |db|
    db.vm.box = "centos"
  end
```

When multiple VMs are launched using a single Vagrantfile, the SSH command should include the VM name to connect to it (see Figure 12-13).

```
demo-chef@LP-3C970EE1AB15 /c/demo1
$ vagrant ssh VM1
Last login: Tue Jun  3 09:50:28 2014 from 10.0.2.2
Welcome to your Vagrant-built virtual machine.
[vagrant@localhost ~]$
```

Figure 12-13. *Connecting to a virtual machine*

■ **Note**   All the commands related to the virtual machine have to be run from the root folder of the VM.

Suspending the Virtual Machine

By suspending the VM, you can get a point in time state of the virtual machine (see Figure 12-14). The Vagrant "suspend" command will not shut down the machine completely; you can resume the VM anytime.

```
ITDtpAdmin@DS-E0CB4EA250EB /c/Users/centos
$ vagrant suspend
[default] Saving VM state and suspending execution...

ITDtpAdmin@DS-E0CB4EA250EB /c/Users/centos
```

Figure 12-14. *Suspending a virtual machine*

Halting the Virtual Machine

"Vagrant halt" command shuts down the VM (see Figure 12-15). You can provide –f switch to forcefully shut down the machine. You have to execute this command from the root folder of the VM.

```
ITDtpAdmin@DS-E0CB4EA250EB /c/Users/centos
$ vagrant halt
[default] Attempting graceful shutdown of VM...

ITDtpAdmin@DS-E0CB4EA250EB /c/Users/centos
```

Figure 12-15. *Halting a virtual machine*

Destroying the Virtual Machine

"Vagrant destroy" command will stop the VM and destroys all the resources associated with it (see Figure 12-16). Once you issue the destroy command, it will ask for confirmation to destroy the VM.

```
ITDtpAdmin@DS-E0CB4EA250EB /c/Users/chef
$ vagrant destroy
Are you sure you want to destroy the 'default' VM? [y/N] y
[default] Forcing shutdown of VM...
[default] Destroying VM and associated drives...

ITDtpAdmin@DS-E0CB4EA250EB /c/Users/chef
```

Figure 12-16. *Destroying a virtual machine*

Installing Vagrant Plug-Ins

The following command can be executed from anywhere. Plug-ins are necessary to integrate Vagrant with other services like AWS, Azure, Hyper-V, and so on.

Command: vagrant plugin install <name>

Vagrant plug-ins will be installed from RubyGems and this command also updates the existing gem. The command "vagrant plugin update" is specifically used to update the plug-in. You can also install multiple plug-ins by providing multiple names with the command.

Vagrant Provisioning Using Chef

Provisioners in Vagrant let you automatically install and configure software on the Vagrant machine as part of the "vagrantup" process. If you want to just use Vagrant SSH and install the software by hand, that will work. By using provisioners you can automate the repeatable tasks. To use provisioners, make sure that the particular provisioner is included in the Vagrant box you download. For example, if you want to use chef provisioner, use a box that contains chef client.

The configuration for provisioning by default will be commented out in the Vagrantfile. We have to work on this file and fill in the required details for chef to work with Vagrant. The file will look as shown in Figures 12-17 and 12-18. This file will be present in the root folder you created for the VM.

```
# -*- mode: ruby -*-
# vi: set ft=ruby :

# Vagrantfile API/syntax version. Don't touch unless you know what you're doing!
VAGRANTFILE_API_VERSION = "2"

Vagrant.configure(VAGRANTFILE_API_VERSION) do |config|
  # All Vagrant configuration is done here. The most common configuration
  # options are documented and commented below. For a complete reference,
  # please see the online documentation at vagrantup.com.
  # Every Vagrant virtual environment requires a box to build off of.
  config.vm.box = "base"
  # The url from where the 'config.vm.box' box will be fetched if it
  # doesn't already exist on the user's system.
  # config.vm.box_url = "http://domain.com/path/to/above.box"
  # provisioners
  #   config.vm.provision :chef_solo do |chef|
  #     chef.cookbooks_path = "../my-recipes/cookbooks"
  #     chef.roles_path = "../my-recipes/roles"
  #     chef.data_bags_path = "../my-recipes/data_bags"
  #     chef.add_recipe "mysql"
  #     chef.add_role "web"
  #     # You may also specify custom JSON attributes:
  #     chef.json = { :mysql_password => "foo" }
  # end
```

Figure 12-17. Vagrantfile(1)

```
# Enable provisioning with chef server, specifying the chef server URL,
# and the path to the validation key (relative to this Vagrantfile).
# The Opscode Platform uses HTTPS. Substitute your organization for
# ORGNAME in the URL and validation key.
# If you have your own Chef Server, use the appropriate URL, which may be
# HTTP instead of HTTPS depending on your configuration. Also change the
# validation key to validation.pem.
#
# config.vm.provision :chef_client do |chef|
#    chef.chef_server_url = "https://api.opscode.com/organizations/ORGNAME"
#    chef.validation_key_path = "ORGNAME-validator.pem"
# end
#
# If you're using the Opscode platform, your validator client is
# ORGNAME-validator, replacing ORGNAME with your organization name.
#
# If you have your own Chef Server, the default validation client name is
# chef-validator, unless you changed the configuration.
#
#    chef.validation_client_name = "ORGNAME-validator"
```

Figure 12-18. *Vagrantfile(2)*

Chef Solo Provisioner

Using chef solo provisioner you can provision a guest OS using chef solo. All the configurations needed for chef solo have to be mentioned in the Vagrantfile.

Options

This section lists the complete set of available options for the chef solo provisioner. More detailed examples of how to use the provisioner are available here.

Note that only the chef solo specific options are shown in the following list. There is also a large set of common options available with both the chef solo and chef client provisioners.

cookbooks_path (string or array): A list of paths to where cookbooks are stored. By default this is "cookbooks," expecting a cookbooks folder relative to the Vagrantfile location.

data_bags_path (string): A path where data bags are stored. By default, no data bag path is set.

environments_path (string): A path where environment definitions are located. By default, no environments folder is set.

environment (string): The environment you want the chef run to be a part of. This requires Chef 11.6.0 or later, and it requires the environments_path to be set.

recipe_url (string): URL to an archive of cookbooks that chef will download and use.

roles_path (string or array): A list of paths where roles are defined. By default, it is empty. Multiple role directories are only supported by Chef 11.8.0 and later.

```
# config.vm.provision :chef_solo do |chef|
#    chef.cookbooks_path = "c:/my-recipes/cookbooks"
#    chef.roles_path = "c:/my-recipes/roles"
#    chef.data_bags_path = "c:/my-recipes/data_bags"
#    chef.add_recipe "mysql"
#    chef.add_role "web"
#
#    # You may also specify custom JSON attributes:
#    chef.json = { :mysql_password => "foo" }
# end
```

Specifying a Run List

The run list specified in the Vagrantfile will be configured when the "vagrantup"
command is issued.

```
Vagrant.configure("2") do |config|
  config.vm.provision "chef_solo" do |chef|
    chef.add_recipe "httpd"
  end
end
```

This will make Vagrant run chef solo with the "httpd" cookbook. The cookbook
has to be present in the cookbooks directory of your VM's root directory. The directory
structure should look as shown in Figure 12-19.

```
|-- Vagrantfile
|-- cookbooks
|    |-- apache
|        |-- recipes
|            |-- default.rb
```

Figure 12-19. *Directory structure*

Specifying Roles

You can specify chef roles in a Vagrantfile. By default, Vagrant will look for the roles
directory in the VM's root folder. You can specify the path if the roles folder is in some
other location.

```
Vagrant.configure("2") do |config|
  config.vm.provision "chef_solo" do |chef|
    chef.roles_path = "vagrant_roles"
    chef.add_role("webserver")
  end
end
```

Using Data Bags

You can use data bags with chef solo provisioner. Data bags can be used inside recipes that chef solo uses. By default, Vagrant will search for the data bags folder in the VM root directory.

```
Vagrant.configure("2") do |config|
  config.vm.provision "chef_solo" do |chef|
    chef.data_bags_path = "data_bags"
  end
end
```

Specifying Node Name

You can set a custom node name by mentioning the node_name option.

```
Vagrant.configure("2") do |config|
  config.vm.provision "chef_solo" do |chef|
    chef.node_name = "node_name"
  end
end
```

Custom JSON Data

Additional configuration data for chef attributes can be passed in to chef solo.

You can also pass parameters using JSON (JavaScript Object Notation) in the chef solo provisioner.

```
Vagrant.configure("2") do |config|
  config.vm.provision "chef_solo" do |chef|
      chef.json = {
      "httpd" => {
        "listen_address" => "10.0.1.5"
      }
    }
  end
end
```

Provisioning Chef Client

Using chef client provisioner you can provision a Vagrant guest VM which will be registered to the existing chef server. You have to mention the validation key and chef server URL in the Vagrantfile. By default the chef client will look for the validation key in the VM root directory. If it is not present in the root directory, you have to provide the path of the validation key in the validation_key_path parameter.

```
Vagrant.configure("2") do |config|
  config.vm.provision "chef_client" do |chef|
    chef.chef_server_url = "https://my_chef_server.com:443/"
    chef.validation_key_path = "validation_key.pem"
  end
end
```

Adding Run List

You can override the run list specified by chef server by providing run list in the Vagrantfile. The run lists and recipes added to the Vagrantfile will be pulled from the chef server and applied to the Vagrant VM.

```
Vagrant.configure("2") do |config|
  config.vm.provision "chef_client" do |chef|
    # Adding a recipe
    chef.add_recipe "apache"
    # adding a role
    chef.add_role "web"
  end
end
```

Deleting the Node Details

Once a client is registered with the chef server, two entries are registered in the chef server, a node object and a client entry. These entries have to be deleted for Vagrant VM which is to be destroyed. It can be done by setting the values of two parameters to true.

```
chef.delete_node = true
chef.delete_client = true
```

Verifying Chef Client Registration with Chef Server

1. Run chef client command from the vagrant box by connecting using Vagrant SSH command to ensure that your vagrant box has been successfully registered with the chef server (see Figure 12-20).

```
PS C:\> chef-client
Starting Chef Client, version 11.10.4
resolving cookbooks for run list: []
Synchronizing Cookbooks:
Compiling Cookbooks...
Converging 0 resources

Running handlers:
Running handlers complete
Chef Client finished, 0/0 resources updated in 40.962 seconds
```

Figure 12-20. *Verifying chef client installation*

AWS and Chef Provisioning Using Vagrant

Installing the Plug-ins

The following plug-ins have to be installed in Vagrant for instance and chef client provisioning on AWS (see Figure 12-21):

    1.   vagrant-aws

```
PS C:\> vagrant plugin install vagrant-aws
Installing the 'vagrant-aws' plugin. This can take a few minutes...
Installed the plugin 'vagrant-aws (0.4.1)'!
PS C:\>
```

Figure 12-21. *Installing Vagrant AWS plug-in*

    2.   vagrant-omnibus

This plug-in is used to install chef client on the target AWS instance using the chef omnibus installer (see Figure 12-22).

```
PS C:\> vagrant plugin install vagrant-omnibus
Installing the 'vagrant-omnibus' plugin. This can take a few minutes...
Installed the plugin 'vagrant-omnibus (1.3.0)'!
PS C:\>
```

Figure 12-22. *Installing vagrant-omnibus plug-in*

Adding the AWS Box to Vagrant

Install a Vagrant box set with an AWS provider (see Figure 12-23) using the following URL:

```
https://github.com/mitchellh/vagrant-aws/raw/master/dummy.box
```

```
$ vagrant box add aws-basic https://github.com/mitchellh/vagrant-aws/raw/master/dummy.box

Downloading or copying the box...

Extracting box...e: 0/s, Estimated time remaining: --:--:--)

Successfully added box 'aws-basic' with provider 'aws'!
```

Figure 12-23. *Adding a AWS bos to Vagrant*

Vagrantfile for AWS Provisioner

The Vagrantfile for AWS provisioning should mention the following configurations in the screenshot (see Figure 12-24). By default, it launches instance to EC2-classic, and if EC2-classic is not available in that region, it will be launched in the default VPC (virtual private cloud). For deploying instances in VPC, the following three attributes have to be mentioned in the Vagrantfile:

```
aws.private_ip_address = "10.10.10.10"
aws.security_groups = ["sg-123z212d"]
aws.subnet_id = "subnet-23b9e7h1"
```

```
Vagrant. Configure("2") do |config|
  config.vm.hostname = vagrant-demo"
  config.vm.box = "aws-ec2"
  config.vm.boot_timeout   = 120
  config.omnibus.chef_version = :latest
  config.vm.provider :aws do |aws, override|
    aws.access_key_id = ENV['AWS_ACCESS_KEY_ID']
    aws.secret_access_key = ENV['AWS_SECRET_ACCESS_KEY']
    aws.keypair_name = ENV['AWS_KEYPAIR_NAME']
    aws.security_groups = ['your-security-group-here']
    aws.instance_type = "t1.micro"
    aws.ami = "am-id"
    override.ssh.username = "default user name of the instance"
    override.ssh.private_key_path = ENV['MY_PRIVATE_AWS_SSH_KEY_PATH']
  end
end
```

Figure 12-24. *Vagrantfile for AWS provisioning*

Save the Vagrantfile and use the "vagrantup --provider=aws" command to provision AWS instance with chef client (see Figures 12-25 and 12-26). You have to execute this command from the root folder.

```
$ vagrant up --provider=aws
Bringing machine 'default' up with 'aws' provider...
[default] Warning! The AWS provider doesn't support any of the Vagrant
high-level network configurations (`config.vm.network`). They
will be silently ignored.
[default] Launching an instance with the following settings...
[default]    -- Type: t1.micro
[default]    -- AMI: ami-3c39686e
[default]    -- Region: ap-southeast-1
[default]    -- Keypair: singapore
[default]    -- Security Groups: ["default"]
[default]    -- Block Device Mapping: []
[default]    -- Terminate On Shutdown: false
[default]    -- Monitoring: false
[default]    -- EBS optimized: false
[default] Waiting for instance to become "ready"...
[default] Waiting for SSH to become available...
[default]downloading https://opscode-omnibus-packages.s3.amazonaws.com/ubuntu/12.04/x86_64/chef
  to file /tmp/install.sh.1095/chef_11.10.4-1.ubuntu.12.04_amd64.deb
trying wget...
Comparing checksum with sha256sum...
[default]Installing Chef
[default]installing with dpkg...
Selecting previously unselected package chef.
(Reading database ... 47501 files and directories currently installed.)
Unpacking chef (from .../chef_11.10.4-1.ubuntu.12.04_amd64.deb) ...
Setting up chef (11.10.4-1.ubuntu.12.04) ...
Thank you for installing Chef!
```

Figure 12-25. *Provisioning a machine on AWS(1)*

```
[default]Starting Chef Client, version 11.10.4
resolving cookbooks for run list: ["mysql::server"]
Synchronizing Cookbooks:
 - mysql
Compiling Cookbooks...
Converging 1 resources
Recipe: mysql::server
  * mysql_service[default] action create
    - ubuntu patternRecipe: <Dynamically Defined Resource>
  * package[debconf-utils] action install
 - install version 1.5.42ubuntu1 of package debconf-utils
  * package[mysql-server] action install
 * service[mysql] action restart
    - restart service service[mysql]
Running handlers:
Running handlers complete
Chef Client finished, 14/18 resources updated in 78.336840997 seconds
```

Figure 12-26. *Provisioning a machine on AWS(2)*

You will be able to see the machine being provisioned in the AWS console (see Figure 12-27).

Filter: All instances ▾	All instance types ▾	🔍 java	✕					I< < 1 to 1 of 1 Instances > >I
● Name ▽ ▾	Instance ID ▴	Instance Type ▾	Availability Zone ▾	Instance State ▾	Status Checks ▾	Alarm Status	Public DNS ▾	Public IP
● Java	i-954208bd	t1.micro	ap-southeast-1b	● running	⊘ 2/2 checks ...	None	ec2-54-255-60-209.ap-s...	54.255.60.20

Figure 12-27. *Machine provisioned*

Log in to your instance and run chef client. It should be able to interact with the chef server as shown in Figure 12-28.

```
root@ip-172-31-11-107:~# chef-client
Starting Chef Client, version 11.10.4
resolving cookbooks for run list: []
Synchronizing Cookbooks:
Compiling Cookbooks...
[2014-04-03T06:50:52+00:00] WARN: Node UBUNTU2-AWS has an empty run list.
Converging 0 resources
Running handlers:
Running handlers complete
Chef Client finished, 0/0 resources updated in 3.169865659 seconds
```

Figure 12-28. *Chef client run*

Provisioning Using Knife

Knife EC2 Plug-ins

The knife EC2 plug-in is used to manage or create instances on AWS. In the upcoming section we cover the installation, configuration, use of the plug-in.

Installing the Plug-in

Chef expects the knife plug-in to be located in the /opt/chef/embedded/bin directory. Any plug-in for knife can be installed using the following syntax:

/opt/chef/embedded/bin/gem install plugin_name

To install the knife EC2 plug-in (see Figure 12-29) run the following command:

/opt/chef/embedded/bin/gem install knife-ec2

```
[root@chef-client ~]# /opt/chef/embedded/bin/gem install knife-ec2
Building native extensions.  This could take a while...
Fetching: ffi-1.9.3.gem (100%)
Building native extensions.  This could take a while...
Fetching: gssapi-1.0.3.gem (100%)
Fetching: httpclient-2.3.4.1.gem (100%)
Fetching: rubyntlm-0.1.1.gem (100%)
Fetching: uuidtools-2.1.4.gem (100%)
Fetching: nori-1.1.5.gem (100%)
Fetching: rack-1.5.2.gem (100%)
Fetching: httpi-0.9.7.gem (100%)
Fetching: wasabi-1.0.0.gem (100%)
Fetching: gyoku-1.1.1.gem (100%)
Fetching: akami-1.2.2.gem (100%)
Fetching: savon-0.9.5.gem (100%)
Fetching: little-plugger-1.1.3.gem (100%)
Fetching: logging-1.8.2.gem (100%)
Fetching: winrm-1.1.3.gem (100%)
Fetching: em-winrm-0.5.5.gem (100%)
Fetching: knife-windows-0.5.15.gem (100%)
Fetching: knife-ec2-0.8.0.gem (100%)
Successfully installed eventmachine-1.0.3
Successfully installed ffi-1.9.3
Successfully installed gssapi-1.0.3
```

Figure 12-29. *Installing plug-in*

Configuring

After you complete the installation, the next step is to configure the plug-in so that your plug-in is able to communicate with your AWS account (see Figure 12-30).

211

```
log_level                    :info
log_location                 STDOUT
node_name                    'admin'
client_key                   '/root/.chef/admin.pem'
validation_client_name       'chef-validator'
validation_key               '/root/.chef/chef-validator.pem'
chef_server_url              'https://10.0.0.14'
cache_type                   'BasicFile'
cache_options( :path => '/root/.chef/checksums' )
knife[:aws_access_key_id] = "AKIAJ4RWN4A6DOQC67BQ"
knife[:aws_secret_access_key] =
```

Figure 12-30. *Configuring the EC2 plug-in*

Enter the access key and secret key for your account using the following syntax in the knife configuration file:

```
Knife[:aws_access_key_id] = "Your_Access_Key"
Knife[:aws_secret_access_key] = "Your_Secret_key"
```

Once you complete the configuration, we are ready to use the plug-in. See Figure 12-31 for the available commands in the EC2 plug-in.

```
** EC2 COMMANDS **
knife ec2 flavor list (options)
knife ec2 instance data (options)
knife ec2 server create (options)
knife ec2 server delete SERVER [SERVER] (options)
knife ec2 server list (options)
```

Figure 12-31. *Commands available*

To view the list of instances in your account, run the following command.

```
Knife ec2 server list
```

This command would list out the servers in us-east1 region by default. If we want to list out the servers in any other region, we can do it using the –region option (see Figure 12-32).

```
[root@chef-client ~]# knife ec2 server list
WARNING: No region was specified in knife.rb or as an argument. The default regi
on, us-east-1, will be used:
[fog][WARNING] Unable to load the 'unf' gem. Your AWS strings may not be properl
y encoded.
Instance ID  Name           Public IP  Private IP  Flavor    Image       SSH K
ey           Security Groups     IAM Profile  State
i-8c809be6   AWS Control               10.0.3.25   t1.micro  ami-3d583454  virgi
nia          awscontrol                          stopped
i-c19343ae                             10.0.0.26   t1.micro  ami-df5d31b6  virgi
nia          default                             stopped
i-4b94a524   Hadoop-master             10.0.0.216  t1.micro  ami-a25415cb  hadoo
pvirginia    hadoop-sg, hadoop-sg                stopped
i-4594a52a   Hadoop-slave              10.0.0.215  t1.micro  ami-a25415cb  hadoo
pvirginia    hadoop-sg, hadoop-sg                stopped
i-13191c7c                             10.0.0.12   t1.micro  ami-c95d31a0  virgi
nia          default                             stopped
i-c6d995a3                             10.0.0.101  t1.micro  ami-5f5d3136  virgi
nia          default                             stopped
```

Figure 12-32. *Listing the servers*

To view the type of instances available for our account, run the following command:

Knife ec2 flavor list

This would list out the type of instances available in your account (see Figure 12-33).

```
[root@chef-client ~]# knife ec2 flavor list
ID                          Name
  Architecture              RAM
    Disk                      Cores

c1.medium                   High-CPU Medium
  32-bit                      1740.8
    350 GB                      5

c1.xlarge                   High-CPU Extra Large
  64-bit                      7168
    1690 GB                     20

c3.2xlarge                  C3 Double Extra Large
  64-bit                      15360
    160 GB                      28

c3.4xlarge                  C3 Quadruple Extra Large
  64-bit                      30720
    320 GB                      55

c3.8xlarge                  C3 Eight Extra Large
  64-bit                      61440
    640 GB                      108
```

Figure 12-33. *Type of instances available*

The next step is to provision the server on EC2 (see Figure 12-34). We will use the knife EC2 server to create a command for the same.

```
[root@chef-client ~]# knife ec2 server create --flavor t1.micro --region ap-sou
heast-1 -S singapore -I ami-80bbf3d2 --groups default -x ec2-user
[fog][WARNING] Unable to load the 'unf' gem. Your AWS strings may not be proper
y encoded.
Instance ID: i-667fb74e
Flavor: t1.micro
Image: ami-80bbf3d2
Region: ap-southeast-1
Availability Zone: ap-southeast-1a
Security Groups: default
Tags: Name: i-667fb74e
SSH Key: singapore

Waiting for instance......█
```

Figure 12-34. *Provisioning an instance(1)*

Some of the important options needed in order to provision any instance are

- -f or -flavor: The type of instance to provision.

- -region: The region in which our instance will be provisioned.

- -I or –image: The image to use while provisioning the instance.

- -G or –groups: The name of the security group that would be attached to our instance. If we want to attach more than one security group we can provide them in a command-separated format. These groups should be present in our account.

- -S or –ssh-key - The key that would be used to log in to our instance. This key should be created before running the command.

- -x: This option is used to specify the username that would be used to log in to the instance.

After the instance is provisioned, the details would be displayed on the console (see Figure 12-35).

```
Waiting for instance..............
Public DNS Name: ec2-46-137-232-227.ap-southeast-1.compute.amazonaws.com
Public IP Address: 46.137.232.227
Private DNS Name: ip-10-134-29-161.ap-southeast-1.compute.internal
Private IP Address: 10.134.29.161
```

Figure 12-35. *Provisioning an instance(2)*

To verify that your provisioning has been completed, go to the AWS console (see Figure 12-36).

Instance: ▌ i-667fb74e (i-667fb74e) Public DNS: ec2-46-137-232-227.ap-southeast-1.compute.amazonaws.com	▌

Description	Status Checks	Monitoring	Tags

Instance ID	i-667fb74e	Public DNS	ec2-46-137-232-227.ap-southeast-1.compute.amazonaws.com
Instance state	running	Public IP	46.137.232.227
Instance type	t1.micro	Elastic IP	-
Private DNS	ip-10-134-29-161.ap-southeast-1.compute.internal	Availability zone	ap-southeast-1a
Private IPs	10.134.29.161	Security groups	default . view rules
Secondary private IPs	-	Scheduled events	No scheduled events
VPC ID	-	AMI ID	RHEL-6.4_GA-x86_64-10-Hourly2 (ami-80bbf3d2)
Subnet ID	-	Platform	-
Network interfaces	-	IAM role	-

Figure 12-36. *Verifying*

Knife Azure Plug-ins

Chef expects the knife plug-in to be located in the /opt/chef/embedded/bin directory. Any plug-in for knife can be installed using the following syntax:

```
/opt/chef/embedded/bin/gem install plugin_name
```

To install the knife Azure plug-in (see Figure 12-37), run the following command:

```
/opt/chef/embedded/bin/gem install knife-azure
```

```
[root@chef-client ~]# /opt/chef/embedded/bin/gem install knife-azure
Fetching: rdoc-3.12.2.gem (100%)
Depending on your version of ruby, you may need to install ruby rdoc/ri data:

<= 1.8.6 : unsupported
 = 1.8.7 : gem install rdoc-data; rdoc-data --install
 = 1.9.1 : gem install rdoc-data; rdoc-data --install
>= 1.9.2 : nothing to do! Yay!
Fetching: rubygems-bundler-1.0.7.gem (100%)
Fetching: equivalent-xml-0.2.9.gem (100%)
Fetching: knife-azure-1.2.2.gem (100%)
Successfully installed rdoc-3.12.2
Successfully installed rubygems-bundler-1.0.7
Successfully installed equivalent-xml-0.2.9
Successfully installed knife-azure-1.2.2
4 gems installed
Installing ri documentation for rdoc-3.12.2...
Installing ri documentation for rubygems-bundler-1.0.7...
Installing ri documentation for equivalent-xml-0.2.9...
Installing ri documentation for knife-azure-1.2.2...
Installing RDoc documentation for rdoc-3.12.2...
Installing RDoc documentation for rubygems-bundler-1.0.7...
Installing RDoc documentation for equivalent-xml-0.2.9...
Installing RDoc documentation for knife-azure-1.2.2...
```

Figure 12-37. *Installing plug-in*

Configuring

After you have completed the installation, the next step is to configure the plug-in (see Figure 12-38) so that your plug-in is able to communicate with your Azure account.

```
cache_type                    'BasicFile'
cache_options( :path => '/root/.chef/checksums' )
knife[:azure_publish_settings_file] = '/root/test'
```

Figure 12-38. *Configuring the Azure plug-in*

Enter the access key and secret key for your account using the following syntax in the knife configuration file:

Knife[:azure_publish_setting_file] = "/path_to_file"

Once you have completed the configuration, we are ready to use the plug-in. Figure 12-39 shows the commands available in the Azure plug-in.

```
[root@chef-client ~]# knife azure --help
FATAL: Cannot find sub command for: 'azure --help'
Available azure subcommands: (for details, knife SUB-COMMAND --help)

** AZURE COMMANDS **
knife azure ag create (options)
knife azure ag list (options)
knife azure image list (options)
knife azure server create (options)
knife azure server delete SERVER [SERVER] (options)
knife azure server list (options)
knife azure server show SERVER [SERVER]
knife azure vnet create (options)
knife azure vnet list (options)

[root@chef-client ~]# █
```

Figure 12-39. *List of commands available*

To view the list of images available in your account, run the following command:

Knife azure image list

This command would list out the images available in all the regions (see Figure 12-40).

```
[root@chef-client ~]# knife azure image list

Name

                                        OS          Location

0b11de9248dd4d87b18621318e037d37__RightImage-CentOS-6.2-x64-v5.8.8.1
                                        Linux       East Asia, Southeast Asia, Brazil
  South, North Europe, West Europe, Japan East, Japan West, East US, West US
0b11de9248dd4d87b18621318e037d37__RightImage-CentOS-6.3-x64-v5.8.8
                                        Linux       East Asia, Southeast Asia, Brazil
  South, North Europe, West Europe, Japan East, Japan West, East US, West US
0b11de9248dd4d87b18621318e037d37__RightImage-CentOS-6.3-x64-v5.8.8.5
                                        Linux       East Asia, Southeast Asia, Brazil
  South, North Europe, West Europe, Japan East, Japan West, East US, West US
0b11de9248dd4d87b18621318e037d37__RightImage-CentOS-6.3-x64-v5.8.8.6
                                        Linux       East Asia, Southeast Asia, Brazil
  South, North Europe, West Europe, Japan East, Japan West, East US, West US
0b11de9248dd4d87b18621318e037d37__RightImage-CentOS-6.3-x64-v5.8.8.7
                                        Linux       East Asia, Southeast Asia, Brazil
  South, North Europe, West Europe, Japan East, Japan West, East US, West US
0b11de9248dd4d87b18621318e037d37__RightImage-CentOS-6.3-x64-v5.8.8.8
                                        Linux       East Asia, Southeast Asia, Brazil
  South, North Europe, West Europe, Japan East, Japan West, East US, West US
```

Figure 12-40. *Listing the images*

The next step is to provision the server on Azure. We will use the knife Azure server to create a command for the same.

Some of the important options needed in order to provision any instance (see Figure 12-41) are

- -azure-dns-name: The DNS (Domain Name System)that would be given to our instance

- -azure-source-image: The image that would be used to provision the instance.

- -I or –image: The image to use while provisioning the instance.

- –winrm-password: The password that would be used to log in to the instance.

- -winrm-user: This option is used to specify the username that would be used to log in to the instance.

- -u: This option is used to specify the UDP (User Datagram Protocol) ports that would be opened on the instance.

- -Z: This option is used to specify the size of the VM.

```
..[root@chef-client ~]# knife azure server create --azure-dns-name 'knifeazurede
' --azure-source-image "fb83b3509582419d99629ce476bcb5c8__SQL-Server-2008R2SP2-G
DR-10.50.4021.0-Enterprise-ENU-Win2K8R2-CY13SU12" --winrm-user Manak --winrm-pas
sword 'p@ssw0rd!' --azure-service-location "East Asia"
.........
Waiting for virtual machine to reach status 'provisioning'............vm state '
provisioning' reached after 2.78 minutes.
Waiting for virtual machine to reach status 'ready'....█
```

Figure 12-41. *Provisioning an instance*

After the instance is provisioned, the details would be displayed on the console.

To verify that your provisioning has been completed (see Figure 12-42), go to the Azure console.

Figure 12-42. *Verifying the server provisioned*

■ ■ ■

## CHAPTER 13

Troubleshooting and Debugging

Chef Troubleshooting and Debugging

After having gone through the installation, configuration, and development aspects of chef, let's now look at how we can troubleshoot and debug if something doesn't work in the chef environment. In this chapter, we look at common themes in debugging and troubleshooting a chef environment.

Debugging Chef Client Run

Several approaches can be used to debug a chef client run.

Running Chef Client with an Empty Run List

At times, you may have issues with a chef client run; it may not run a recipe or may not behave as it should for chef runs.

Running the chef client with an empty run list will tell us whether the chef client failed because of recipes in the run list of the node, the chef client configuration of the node, or the issues with connectivity between the chef server and the client.

If chef client fails with an empty run list, it can be for one of the following reasons:

1. Ports required for a chef client are blocked by a firewall or the network connectivity between the server and the client is unavailable. Running an empty run list will indicate whether the connection has become timed out or there is a network down error (see Figure 13-1).

```
root@ip-172-31-39-128:~# chef-client
Starting Chef Client, version 11.10.4

=========================================================================
Chef encountered an error attempting to load the node data for "CHEF-UBUNTU"
=========================================================================

Networking Error:
-----------------
Error connecting to https://api.opscode.com/organizations/comtechies/nodes/CHEF-
UBUNTU - Connection timed out - connect(2)

Your chef_server_url may be misconfigured, or the network could be down.
```

Figure 13-1. *Chef client run*

2. The user does not have permissions to run chef client. When
   users do not have the required permissions on the chef client,
   they get a permission denied error (see Figure 13-2).

```
$ chef-client
[2014-04-02T07:01:37+00:00] ERROR: Permission denied - /var/chef/cache/chef-clie
nt-running.pid
[2014-04-02T07:01:37+00:00] FATAL: Chef::Exceptions::ChildConvergeError: Chef ru
n process exited unsuccessfully (exit code 1)
```

Figure 13-2. *Permissions error*

3. There is an invalid validation key or invalid client.rb file to
   access the chef server. In the case of an invalid client.rb file
   or invalid validation key, you will see the connection refused
   error (see Figure 13-3).

```
root@ip-172-31-39-128:~# chef-client
[2014-04-02T07:13:36+00:00] WARN: *******************************************
[2014-04-02T07:13:36+00:00] WARN: Did not find config file: /etc/chef/client.rb,
using command line options.
[2014-04-02T07:13:36+00:00] WARN: *******************************************
Starting Chef Client, version 11.10.4
[2014-04-02T07:13:37+00:00] ERROR: Connection refused connecting to https://loca
lhost/nodes/ip-172-31-39-128.us-west-2.compute.internal, retry 1/5
```

Figure 13-3. *Configuration file missing*

4. For a hosted chef, if the client node is behind proxy, invalid
   proxy settings can lead to failed chef client runs (see
   Figure 13-4). Due consideration should be given to correct
   proxy configuration to ensure that it allows connection
   between chef client and chef server.

```
PS C:\> chef-client
Starting Chef Client, version 11.10.4

==========================================================================
Chef encountered an error attempting to load the node data for "MYWORKSTATION"
==========================================================================

Networking Error:
-----------------
Error connecting to https://api.opscode.com/organizations/comtechies/nodes/MYWORKSTATION - A connection attempt f
ecause the connected party did not properly respond after a period of time, or established connection failed beca
nected host has failed to respond. - connect(2)

Your chef_server_url may be misconfigured, or the network could be down.
```

Figure 13-4. *Proxy setting error*

Running Chef Client in Debug Mode

Running chef client in debug mode (see Figure 13-5) will give you the verbose output of each and every action executed by the chef client. You can specify the log level in the client.rb file get the output in a client.log file or you can run the debug level command directly from the terminal.

```
root@ip-172-31-39-128:~# chef-client -l debug
[2014-04-02T07:20:35+00:00] INFO: Forking chef instance to converge...
[2014-04-02T07:20:35+00:00] DEBUG: Fork successful. Waiting for new chef pid: 47
49
[2014-04-02T07:20:35+00:00] DEBUG: Forked instance now converging
Starting Chef Client, version 11.10.4
[2014-04-02T07:20:35+00:00] INFO: *** Chef 11.10.4 ***
[2014-04-02T07:20:35+00:00] INFO: Chef-client pid: 4749
[2014-04-02T07:20:35+00:00] DEBUG: Loading plugin os
[2014-04-02T07:20:35+00:00] DEBUG: Loading plugin kernel
[2014-04-02T07:20:35+00:00] DEBUG: Loading plugin ruby
[2014-04-02T07:20:35+00:00] DEBUG: Loading plugin languages
[2014-04-02T07:20:35+00:00] DEBUG: ---- Begin ruby -e "require 'rbconfig'; puts
%Q(platform=#{RUBY_PLATFORM},version=#{RUBY_VERSION},release_date=#{RUBY_RELEASE
_DATE},target=#{::Config::CONFIG['target']},target_cpu=#{::Config::CONFIG['targe
t_cpu']},target_vendor=#{::Config::CONFIG['target_vendor']},target_os=#{::Config
::CONFIG['target_os']},host=#{::Config::CONFIG['host']},host_cpu=#{::Config::CON
FIG['host_cpu']},host_os=#{::Config::CONFIG['host_os']},host_vendor=#{::Config::
CONFIG['host_vendor']},bin_dir=#{::Config::CONFIG['bindir']},ruby_bin=#{::File.j
oin(::Config::CONFIG['bindir'], ::Config::CONFIG['ruby_install_name'])},)" STDOU
T ----
[2014-04-02T07:20:35+00:00] DEBUG: platform=x86_64-linux,version=1.9.3,release_d
```

Figure 13-5. *Debugging chef client*

There are three main levels for debugging chef client runs.

1. Info: To run chef client in this mode run chef-client -l info.

2. Debug: To run chef client in this mode run chef-client -l debug.

3. Warn: To run chef client in this mode run chef-client -l warn.

Using Chef Client Log Files

The log file location has to be mentioned in the client.rb file present inside /etc/chef folder. Use the following parameter in the client.rb file to set the log details.

```
log_location "/var/log/chef/chef-client.log
```

Once the chef client run is finished, you can get insight about the chef client run from the log file (see Figure 13-6).

```
[2014-04-02T07:54:27+00:00] WARN: Node CHEF-UBUNTU has an empty run list.
[2014-04-02T07:59:46+00:00] WARN: Cloning resource attributes for service[apache
2] from prior resource (CHEF-3694)
[2014-04-02T07:59:46+00:00] WARN: Previous service[apache2]: /var/chef/cache/coo
kbooks/apache2/recipes/default.rb:24:in 'from_file'
[2014-04-02T07:59:46+00:00] WARN: Current  service[apache2]: /var/chef/cache/coo
kbooks/apache2/recipes/default.rb:221:in 'from_file'
[2014-04-02T07:59:50+00:00] ERROR: Running exception handlers
[2014-04-02T07:59:50+00:00] ERROR: Exception handlers complete
[2014-04-02T07:59:50+00:00] FATAL: Stacktrace dumped to /var/chef/cache/chef-sta
cktrace.out
[2014-04-02T07:59:50+00:00] ERROR: package[apache2] (apache2::default line 20) h
ad an error: Mixlib::ShellOut::ShellCommandFailed: Expected process to exit with
 [0], but received '100'
---- Begin output of apt-get -q -y install apache2=2.2.22-1ubuntu1.4 ----
STDOUT: Reading package lists...
Building dependency tree...
Reading state information...
The following extra packages will be installed:
  apache2-mpm-worker apache2-utils apache2.2-bin apache2.2-common libapr1
  libaprutil1 libaprutil1-dbd-sqlite3 libaprutil1-ldap libcap2 ssl-cert
Suggested packages:
  apache2-doc apache2-suexec apache2-suexec-custom openssl-blacklist
"client.log" 52L, 4298C                                        1,1        Top
```

Figure 13-6. *Using log files*

Types of Log Errors

A log file starts with the internal chef logs. Following are the types of warning and errors you find in the log file:

> *WARN*: You get a warning when you have situations like an empty run list.

> *FATAL*: This indicates that the chef resource has failed to execute. You can find what failed using the ERROR level in the log file.

> *ERROR*: This indicates that the chef client was unable to load the exception handlers, when it fails to execute a resource, or when a package installation fails.

Using Chef Handler Cookbook

Chef handler is a cookbook that helps in handling exceptions happening during a chef client run. This cookbook can be obtained from the chef community cookbooks. This cookbook has a chef_handler lightweight resource provider. This cookbook can be used to make product specific handlers, so that the chef client will handle the exceptions in the way that you specify in your cookbooks with chef_handler resource.

Put the recipe chef_handler at the start of the node's run list to make sure that custom handlers are loaded early on in the chef run and available for the other recipes.

Download the chef_handler cookbook using knife (see Figure 13-7).

```
Knife cookbook download chef_handler
```

```
PS C:\chef-repo\chef> knife cookbook site download chef_handler
Downloading chef_handler from the cookbooks site at version 1.1.5 to C:/chef-repo/chef/chef_handle
Cookbook saved: C:/chef-repo/chef/chef_handler-1.1.5.tar.gz
```

Figure 13-7. *Downloading chef handler cookbook*

Untar the cookbook and Upload the cookbook to the chef server.

Knife cookbook upload chef_handler

Add the chef_handler recipe to the nodes run list (see Figure 13-8).

```
PS C:\chef-repo\chef> knife node run_list add CHEF-UBUNTU recipe['chef_handler']
CHEF-UBUNTU:
  run_list:
    recipe[mysql::server]
    recipe[chef_handler]
```

Figure 13-8. *Adding the cookbook to the run list*

You can include the chef_handler libraries in your recipes by including the chef_handler recipe to your custom recipe. The chef_handler dependency has to be added to your cookbooks metadata.

include_recipe 'chef_handler'

Debugging Recipes Using Logs

Chef logs can be used to debug recipes. During a chef client run, the logs are written to the log file specified in the client.rb file. For debugging information, chef client has to run in debug mode. This can be set in the client.rb file using log_level parameter value to :debug.

Common Errors
Cookbook Not Found

We get this error if a cookbook is added to the run list of a node but the cookbook is not present on the server. In this case the chef client will fail and "cookbook does not exist on the server" will appear as shown in Figure 13-9.

```
Starting Chef Client, version 11.6.0
resolving cookbooks for run list: ["apache"]

=================================================================================
Error Resolving Cookbooks for Run List:
=================================================================================


Missing Cookbooks:
------------------
The following cookbooks are required by the client but don't exist on the server
:
* apache
```

Figure 13-9. *Cookbook not found*

This error can be resolved by adding the cookbook with a relevant name (see Figures 13-10 and 13-11) to the run list of the node.

```
~]# knife node run_list add chef-testing apache2
chef-testing:
  run list: recipe[apache2]
~]# t@chef-testing
```

Figure 13-10. *Adding the cookbook with the right name*

```
Starting Chef Client, version 11.6.0
resolving cookbooks for run list: ["apache2"]
Synchronizing Cookbooks:
  - pacman
  - logrotate
  - iptables
  - apache2
Compiling Cookbooks...
Converging 74 resources
Recipe: apache2::default
```

Figure 13-11. *Error resolved*

Package Installation Error

If the package installation has any errors (see Figure 13-12), you can find the error in the log file with the package name associated with it.

```
[2014-04-02T07:59:50+00:00] ERROR: package[apache2] (apache2::default line 20) h
ad an error: Mixlib::ShellOut::ShellCommandFailed: Expected process to exit with
[0], but received '100'
---- Begin output of apt-get -q -y install apache2=2.2.22-1ubuntu1.4 ----
STDOUT: Reading package lists...
Building dependency tree...
Reading state information...
```

Figure 13-12. Unable to install package

This error can occur for any of the following reasons:

- Repository not configured.

- Package with that name does not exist in the repository.

This error can be resolved by configuring the repository and ensuring it is reachable. Also, you must provide a valid name for the package.

Using a Log Resource

A log resource can be used inside recipes to write to log files. For example, if you want to log an entry when a particular data bag item is used in your recipe, you can use the log resource in the data bag block to do that. Log resource uses Chef::Provider::Log::ChefLog during the chef client run. The screenshot in Figure 13-13 shows how to use the breakpoints in recipes.

```
data_bag_item = Chef::Cookbook.get_ssl_certificate_data_bag
if data_bag_item[node[:matching_node][:ssl_certificate][:key]]
  log "Used ssl_certificate data bag entry for #{node[:matching_node][:ssl_certificate][:key]}" do
    level :info
  end
  data_bag_item = data_bag_item[node[:matching_node][:ssl_certificate][:key]]
  certificate = Chef::Cookbook.get_ssl_certificate_crt(data_bag_item)
  key = Chef::Cookbook.get_ssl_certificate_key(data_bag_item)
else
  log "Could not find ssl_certificate data bag, default certificate used." do
    level :warn
  end
end
```

Figure 13-13. Using the log resource

Debugging Recipes Using Chef Shell

Chef shell is a recipe debugging tool which runs as an interactive ruby session. Using chef shell, you can run a recipe on debugging mode to trace the errors.

Configuring Chef Shell

The chef shell has three modes:

1. Stand-alone: it is the default mode and no cookbooks will be loaded in this mode. Chef shell stand-alone mode (see Figure 13-14) can be started using chef shell command.

```
root@ip-172-31-39-128:~# chef-shell
loading configuration: none (standalone session)
Session type: standalone
Loading..done.
This is the chef-shell.
 Chef Version: 11.10.4
 http://www.opscode.com/chef
 http://docs.opscode.com/
run `help' for help, `exit' or ^D to quit.
Ohai2u ubuntu@ip-172-31-39-128.us-west-2.compute.internal!
```

Figure 13-14. Stand-alone mode of chef shell

2. Chef solo: in this mode, the chef shell will have the chef solo functionalities (see Figure 13-15). In this mode, chef shell will load the chef solo cookbooks and JSON (Java Script Object Notations) attributes. You can activate the chef solo mode using "chef shell –s" command.

```
root@ip-172-31-39-128:~# chef-shell -s
loading configuration: none (chef-solo session)
Session type: solo
Loading..done.
This is the chef-shell.
 Chef Version: 11.10.4
 http://www.opscode.com/chef
 http://docs.opscode.com/
run `help' for help, `exit' or ^D to quit.
Ohai2u ubuntu@ip-172-31-39-128.us-west-2.compute.internal!
chef >
```

Figure 13-15. Chef solo mode of chef shell

3. Chef client: in this mode, the chef shell will have the chef client functionalities (see Figure 13-16). To use this mode you have to place a chef-shell.rb file with few parameters inside the /etc/chef folder.

```
#this file should be present inside /etc/chef/chef-shel.rb
client_key                File.expand_path('~/etc/chef/client.pem')
chef_server_url           'https://api.opscode.com/organizations/comtechies'
```

Figure 13-16. *Chef client mode of chef shell*

You can run the recipes from the nodes run list in debugging mode and you can trace errors in the recipe (see Figure 13-17). You can activate the chef client mode using "chef shell –z" command.

```
root@ip-172-31-39-128:~# chef-shell -z
loading configuration: /etc/chef/client.rb
Session type: client
Loading...resolving cookbooks for run list: ["mysql"]
.Synchronizing Cookbooks:
  - mysql
done.
This is the chef-shell.
 Chef Version: 11.10.4
 http://www.opscode.com/chef
 http://docs.opscode.com/
run `help' for help, `exit' or ^D to quit.
Ohai2u ubuntu@ip-172-31-39-128.us-west-2.compute.internal!
chef >
```

Figure 13-17. *Running recipes*

Whenever the chef shell is loaded in chef client mode, all the recipes in the nodes run list will be loaded to the cache. You can debug the recipes in the run list using run chef command (see Figure 13-18).

```
chef > run_chef
[2014-04-02T12:57:17+00:00] INFO: Processing directory[/root/demo] action create (mysql::default line 2)
[2014-04-02T12:57:17+00:00] INFO: directory[/root/demo] created directory /root/demo
[2014-04-02T12:57:17+00:00] DEBUG: found current_mode == nil, so we are creating a new file, updating mode
[2014-04-02T12:57:17+00:00] DEBUG: found current_mode == nil, so we are creating a new file, updating mode
[2014-04-02T12:57:17+00:00] DEBUG: found current_uid == nil, so we are creating a new file, updating owner
[2014-04-02T12:57:17+00:00] DEBUG: found current_gid == nil, so we are creating a new file, updating group
[2014-04-02T12:57:17+00:00] DEBUG: found current_uid == nil, so we are creating a new file, updating owner
[2014-04-02T12:57:17+00:00] INFO: directory[/root/demo] owner changed to 0
[2014-04-02T12:57:17+00:00] DEBUG: found current_gid == nil, so we are creating a new file, updating group
[2014-04-02T12:57:17+00:00] INFO: directory[/root/demo] group changed to 0
[2014-04-02T12:57:17+00:00] DEBUG: found current_mode == nil, so we are creating a new file, updating mode
[2014-04-02T12:57:17+00:00] INFO: directory[/root/demo] mode changed to 755
[2014-04-02T12:57:17+00:00] DEBUG: selinux utilities can not be found. Skipping selinux permission fixup.
[2014-04-02T12:57:17+00:00] INFO: Processing log[directory created] action write (mysql::default line 6)
[2014-04-02T12:57:17+00:00] DEBUG: Platform ubuntu version 12.04 found
[2014-04-02T12:57:17+00:00] DEBUG: directory created
 => true
```

Figure 13-18. *Debugging recipes*

Debugging Recipes Using Breakpoint Resource

You can do block level debugging using breakpoint resource (see Figure 13-19). While testing cookbooks include the breakpoint resource after every resource block to have a block level debugging.

```
breakpoint "before yum_key node['yum']['repo_name']['key']" do
  action :break
end
yum_key node['yum']['repo_name']['key'] do
  url  node['yum']['repo_name']['key_url']
  action :add
end
breakpoint "before yum_repository 'repo_name'" do
  action :break
end
yum_repository "repo_name" do
  description "description"
  key node['yum']['repo_name']['key']
  mirrorlist node['yum']['repo_name']['url']
  includepkgs node['yum']['repo_name']['includepkgs']
  exclude node['yum']['repo_name']['exclude']
  action :create
end
```

Figure 13-19. *Debugging recipes using breakpoint resource*

To debug a recipe with breakpoint, change the chef shell mode to recipe mode (see Figure 13-20) using "recipe_mode" command and run the chef client using the "run_chef" command.

```
chef > recipe_mode
chef:recipe > run_chef
[2014-04-02T13:17:11+00:00] INFO: Processing directory[/root/demo] action create (mysql::defa
[2014-04-02T13:17:11+00:00] DEBUG: found target_mode == nil, so no mode was specified on reso
[2014-04-02T13:17:11+00:00] DEBUG: found target_uid == nil, so no owner was specified on reso
[2014-04-02T13:17:11+00:00] DEBUG: found target_gid == nil, so no group was specified on reso
[2014-04-02T13:17:11+00:00] INFO: Processing log[directory created] action write (mysql::defa
[2014-04-02T13:17:11+00:00] DEBUG: Platform ubuntu version 12.04 found
[2014-04-02T13:17:11+00:00] DEBUG: directory created
 => true
chef:recipe >
```

Figure 13-20. *Debugging recipes using breakpoint resource with chef shell*

The "run_chef" command will run the recipe until the breakpoint specified in the recipe. Once you have debugged until the breakpoint, run the "chef_run.resume" command to resume the chef client run from the breakpoint (see Figure 13-21).

```
chef:recipe > chef_run.resume
[2014-04-02T13:21:46+00:00] INFO: Processing log[directory created] action write (mysql::de
 => [<directory[/root/demo] @name: "/root/demo" @noop: nil @before: nil @params:
 {} @provider: Chef::Provider::Directory @allowed_actions: [:nothing, :create, :delete]
 @action: [:create] @updated: false @updated_by_last_action: false @supports: {}
 @ignore_failure: false @retries: 0 @retry_delay: 2
 @source_line: "/var/chef/cache/cookbooks/mysql/recipes/default.rb:2:in `from_file'"
 @elapsed_time: 0.002918764 @resource_name: :directory @path: "/root/demo" mysql" @recipe_
 chef:recipe
```

Figure 13-21. *Resuming the chef client*

Troubleshooting Chef Client

Chef Client Fails to Run a Recipe Successfully at Bootstrapping

Run chef client to set up the connection with the chef server. It will run with an empty run list. After it is connected, log in to http://yourcherver.com:443, add the roles/recipes to the client node, and run the chef client from the client again.

Reregistering a Removed Client

The reregistration process is required if the client is unable to authenticate itself with the chef server. To reregister a removed client from the chef server, remove the client.pem file from /etc/chef folder and run the chef client on the node. Before running the chef client, make sure that the node object of the removed client is also removed from the chef server.

Issues Registering Chef Client with the Server

While registering a node with chef server, the registration might fail for the following reasons:

1. The client name already exists in the chef server (see Figure 13-22): this issue can be fixed by deleting the existing client name from the server.

```
root@ip-172-31-11-107:/etc/chef# chef-client
Starting Chef Client, version 11.10.4
Creating a new client identity for UBUNTU-AWS using the validator key.
================================================================================
Chef encountered an error attempting to create the client "UBUNTU-AWS"
================================================================================
Authorization Error:
--------------------
Your validation client is not authorized to create the client for this node (HTTP 403).

Possible Causes:
----------------
* There may already be a client named "UBUNTU-AWS"
* Your validation client (comtechies-validator) may have misconfigured authorization permission.
```

Figure 13-22. *The client name that exists in error*

2. Invalid chef server URL (uniform resource locator) (see Figure 13-23): check whether the chef server URL is specified correctly in the client.rb file of the node.

```
root@ip-172-31-11-107:/etc/chef# chef-client
Starting Chef Client, version 11.10.4
================================================================================
Chef encountered an error attempting to load the node data for "UBUNTU-AWS"
================================================================================
Resource Not Found:
-------------------
The server returned a HTTP 404. This usually indicates that your chef_server_url is incorrect.
Relevant Config Settings:
-------------------------
chef_server_url "https://api.opscode.com/organizations/chefhcl"
```

Figure 13-23. *The URL not valid error*

3. Invalid validation key (Figure 13-24): check whether the
   validation key specified in the client.rb file and the validation
   key that is present inside the /etc/chef folder are valid.

```
root@ip-172-31-11-107:/etc/chef# chef-client
Starting Chef Client, version 11.10.4
Creating a new client identity for UBUNTU-AWS using the validator key.
================================================================================
Chef encountered an error attempting to create the client "UBUNTU-AWS"
================================================================================
Authentication Error:
---------------------
Failed to authenticate to the chef server (http 401).
Server Response:
----------------
Invalid signature for user or client 'hcl-validator'
Relevant Config Settings:
-------------------------
chef_server_url         "https://api.opscode.com/organizations/hcl"
validation_client_name  "hcl-validator"
validation_key          "/etc/chef/validation.pem"
If these settings are correct, your validation_key may be invalid.
```

Figure 13-24. *The invalid validation key*

401 Unauthorized Errors

401 Unauthorized errors happen (see Figure 13-25) for the following reasons:

1. Incorrect `client.pem` file: this error can be rectified by
    deleting the existing `client.pem` file from the /etc/chef folder
    and reregistering the node with the chef server.

```
root@ip-172-31-11-107:/etc/chef# chef-client
Starting Chef Client, version 11.10.4
================================================================================
Chef encountered an error attempting to load the node data for "UBUNTU-AWS"
================================================================================
Authentication Error:
---------------------
Failed to authenticate to the chef server (http 401).
Server Response:
----------------
Invalid signature for user or client 'UBUNTU-AWS'
Relevant Config Settings:
-------------------------
chef_server_url    "https://api.opscode.com/organizations/comtechies"
node_name          "UBUNTU-AWS"
client_key         "/etc/chef/client.pem"
If these settings are correct, your client_key may be invalid,
```

Figure 13-25. *Authentication error*

Removing chef node from a server:

```
knife client delete NODENAME
knife node delete NODENAME
```

On an affected node, remove the `client.pem` file and run the chef client again.

```
sudo rm /etc/chef/client.pem
sudo chef-client
```

Clock Synchronization Error

This error happens when your client node's clock drifts from the actual time by more than 15 minutes (see Figure 13-26). You can fix this by syncing your clock with an NTP (Network Time Protocol) server. Run the chef client after synching the clock.

```
chef]# chef-client
Starting Chef Client, version 11.8.2

===============================================================================
Chef encountered an error attempting to load the node data for "chef-testing"
===============================================================================


Authentication Error:
--------------------
Failed to authenticate to the chef server (http 401).
The request failed because your clock has drifted by more than 15 minutes.
Syncing your clock to an NTP Time source should resolve the issue.
```

Figure 13-26. *A clock sync error*

No Such File or Directory: /etc/chef/validation.pem

This error happens when the validation key is not present in the default /etc/chef folder. This can be rectified by copying the validator key from the chef server to the nodes /etc/ chef folder.

Cannot Find Config File

This error happens when the client.rb file is not present in the default chef directory on the node (see Figure 13-27). You can work around this issue by adding the path to of client.rb file using –c switch.

```
chef-client -c C:\chef\client.rb
```

```
PS D:\> chef-client
[2014-03-21T17:41:35+05:30] WARN: *****************************************
[2014-03-21T17:41:35+05:30] WARN: Did not find config file: C:\chef\client.rb, using command line optio
[2014-03-21T17:41:35+05:30] WARN: *****************************************
```

Figure 13-27. *Not able to find the client configuration file*

Index

■ W, X, Y, Z

Get the eBook for only $10!

Now you can take the weightless companion with you anywhere, anytime. Your purchase of this book entitles you to 3 electronic versions for only $10.

This Apress title will prove so indispensible that you'll want to carry it with you everywhere, which is why we are offering the eBook in 3 formats for only $10 if you have already purchased the print book.

Convenient and fully searchable, the PDF version enables you to easily find and copy code—or perform examples by quickly toggling between instructions and   applications. The MOBI format is ideal for your Kindle, while the ePUB can be utilized on a variety of mobile devices.

Go to www.apress.com/promo/tendollars to purchase your companion eBook.